The

HANK WILLIAMS

Popular Culture Bio-Bibliographies: A Reference Series
Series Editor: M. Thomas Inge

Crockett: A Bio-Bibliography
Richard Boyd Hauck

Knute Rockne: A Bio-Bibliography
Michael R. Steele

John Henry: A Bio-Bibliography
Brett Williams

Charlie Chaplin: A Bio-Bibliography
Wes D. Gehring

HANK WILLIAMS
A Bio-Bibliography

George William Koon

Popular Culture Bio-Bibliographies

Greenwood Press
Westport, Connecticut • London, England

Library of Congress Cataloging in Publication Data

Koon, George William.
    Hank Williams : a bio-bibliography in popular culture.

(Popular culture bio-bibliographies, ISSN 0198-9871)
    Includes index.
    Bibliography: p.
    Discography: p.
    1. Williams, Hank, 1923-1953.   2. Country musicians—
United States—Biography.   I. Title.   II. Series.
ML420.W55K7   1983   784.5'2'00924   82-24162
ISBN 0-313-22982-1 (lib. bdg.)

Library of Congress Catalog Card Number: 82-24162
ISBN: 0-313-22982-1
ISSN: 0198-9871

First published in 1983

Greenwood Press
A division of Congressional Information Service, Inc.
88 Post Road West
Westport, Connecticut 06881

Printed in the United States of America

10   9   8   7   6   5   4   3   2   1

for
My Parents
and for
Barbara, Holly, and Mary

CONTENTS

ILLUSTRATIONS

PREFACE

A little over thirty years ago, my father took our family from Columbia, South Carolina, to Nashville for The Grand Ole Opry. My memory of the show is vague; I recall mainly the things of childhood—the R. C. Cola's the square dancers drank on stage, a master of ceremonies who actually solicited applause from the audience, and my souvenir Ernest Tubb songbook. Now, looking back over the history of the Opry, I realize that Hank Williams might have performed that night. I knew his songs, but I did not really know who Hank was. I may have seen him, though. In another ten years, I expect to claim that I did see Hank Williams.

The small town near where I live now features a large feed and seed store. It is built like a Quonset, its roof curving nearly to the ground. Before the feed and seed, before television, it was a movie house. Several of my friends in the area have told me that once when Hank was traveling throughout South Carolina he spotted a crowd there and stopped to give a free performance. Another rumor among them is that Hank actually died in that Carolina town and not in West Virginia as history has it. Such is the way myth works, especially in the South. We tend to appropriate for ourselves the stories we like, giving them our own settings along with the other particulars that we prefer.

Few American lives lend themselves better to myth than that of Hank Williams. He went, quite literally, from rags to riches, from a tough depression Alabama to a Nashville so affluent for him that he could order tailored California suits, from shining shoes to leaving hundred-dollar tips for shine boys. His passions for whiskey and women pulled against a natural inclination to religion, just as though he might have sensed that Americans wanted some wholesomeness in their heroes—but with a good portion of mischief stirred in. He bucked the system, resisting the domesticity of marriage and at the same time irritating The Grand Ole Opry until its officials finally fired him. He died on New Year's Day before he was thirty, and his life and death were as dramatic and important as any in the history of American music.

We should, it seems, be able to chronicle the times and influences of such an important figure, especially because he lived until recently and was known by so many. But myth cuts across the trail of biography constantly; and country music has taken so many paths since his death that, in spite of Hank's obvious presence in Nashville, it is not easy to identify all of his accomplishments and legacies.

Hank's story, though, is so striking and so bound up in the history of country music itself that it will always call for telling. The following pages tell the story. The first section is biographical. It makes use of the many volumes that have gone before it; but I believe that, without replacing them, it supersedes them with new research, careful documentation, and a straightforward approach. The evaluation that follows the biography is, I think, the first extended essay on the subject. Then, by way of acknowledging that Hank's story still needs more research and thought, I offer some resource materials. First are three interviews: one is with Hank Williams and his first wife, Audrey; one is with Bob Pinson of The Country Music Foundation Library and Media Center, who is one of the most meticulous scholars of Hank's music; and one is with Jerry Rivers and Don Helms, the members of Hank's band who probably knew him best. These are followed by a bibliographical essay and bibliography that identifies, locates, and evaluates the documents used in this project. A chronology and an extensive discography follow the bibliography. I hope that this work will satisfy those people who want more information about Hank Williams and that it will encourage and guide those who want to do further research and evaluation.

More people than I can name here have helped me. But at the risk of omitting the names of some of those who have meant much to this project, I must thank J. J. St. Vincent, Ronnie Pugh, Bob Pinson, Bob Oermann, Kyle Young, Chuck Perry, Bruce Gidoll, Ernie Denny, Jerry Rivers, Don Helms, Bob McKinnon, Taft and Erleen Skipper, Mr. and Mrs. J. C. McNeil, Mr. and Mrs. Walt McNeil, Mr. and Mrs. Braxton Schuffert, Leila Williams Griffin, Mark Steadman, Pearl Parker, Judy Payne, Byron Harder, George Merritt, Wally Bowen, John Rumble, Marian Withington, Nancy Keffler, "Hadacol" Hal Smith, Bill Strong, and Mike Moyle, not to mention the many who have written well on Hank already. The Country Music Foundation has been generous with its help, as has my home institution, Clemson University.

George William Koon
Clemson, South Carolina

HANK WILLIAMS

1

THE SINGER:
A BIOGRAPHY

"If the good Lord's willing, and the creek don't rise. . . ."

THE ORIGINS

Nobody bothered to chronicle the childhood of a scruffy, dirt-poor kid growing up in rural Alabama. History got interested in him only as that child came to be famous; and even then it did not rush to his door, for few guessed that Hank Williams might be dead well before his thirtieth birthday. Time seemed abundant. Hank himself would not have told much, anyway. His interviews are few, and they are consistently terse. Childhood was not an especially fond memory for him, and he seemed willing to let it lie. The result is that his early years are difficult to pin down. The information is sketchy, and therefore it has been particularly susceptible to the mythologizing of friends and relatives.

If everyone who claims to have given him his first guitar had really done so, Hank might have opened a music store instead of going into the band business. And if he really became so excited when he got his guitar that he ran out through the yard, jumped on a calf and twisted its tail, getting thrown and breaking his arm—an injury that kept him from picking any music for a while—I would be surprised. I also find it a little hard to believe that Hank squandered thirty cents on fireworks only to get home to a spanking that set off his purchase in his back pocket. And if all who claimed to be at Mt. Olive Baptist Church while a three-year-old Hank Williams sat by his mother as she played the organ, learning there his first rhythm and religion, then Mt. Olive Community would have more Baptists than citizens.

A few facts survive, however. The parents of Hank Williams were married on 12 November 1916, by Reverend J. C. Dunlap, in Butler County, Alabama.[1] Elonzo H. Williams was almost twenty-five, and his bride, Jessie Lillie Belle Skipper, was eighteen. Lon, the youngest of eleven children, was from Lowndes County, the county adjacent to and just south of Montgomery. He had quit school after the sixth grade and left home to begin his working life as a water boy in the logging camps in an area of pine, oak, poplar, beech, and sweet gum. He worked his way up in the logging business, eventually becoming a locomotive driver for the W. T. Smith Lumber Company, an outfit that employed as many as twelve hundred hands, sawing timber and building fruit and produce crates.

His bride, Lillie, was from the next county, Butler, just down the road (one would travel I-65 today) from Lon's haunts. She grew up near Georgiana, a small town about sixty miles south of Montgomery. She was living with her family on a farm and in a house owned by the Mixon family when Lon came to propose. According to a story reported by Chet Flippo, Lon hitched a ride to his intended's house, proposed, and then hitched a ride to the church for the wedding, all in one day.[2] That the wedding license was taken out the day before indicates a little more planning than this tale allows.

The scene here is fairly bleak. Times had never been easy in this part of the world, not since the Civil War, and a depression loomed ahead. Lowndes County—part of a region known as the "Black Belt," not for its black population, which is considerable, but for its dark soil—was basically agricultural. Its population of twenty-three thousand in 1930 is about half that today. Thirty thousand people lived in Butler County in 1930, and I am sure that officials then would have been quick to report that 51 percent of them were white. The following is a promotional description, more or less a Junior Chamber of Commerce job, on Butler's largest towns, Greenville and Georgiana, both of which figure in the early years of Hank Williams:

> Greenville, with a population of about 5,000, remains the largest and most important town. It has paved streets, electricity, white way posts and sanitary sewerage, with a number of modern business buildings and homes adjoining the venerable ones of historic construction. Cotton gins, grist mills, a lumber mill, a pants factory, a machine shop, a fertilizer mixing plant and ice factory contribute to an industrial inventory whose overwhelmingly largest item is a 10,000 spindle cotton mill for which the citizens of Greenville made a notable subscription. This is one of the two cities in the United States to have a plant for the preservation of magnolia, beach and oak leaves for decorative purposes. Georgiana, the second ranking community, is a shipping and timber manufacturing center with paved streets, electric lights, a large casket factory, and a municipally owned water system.[3]

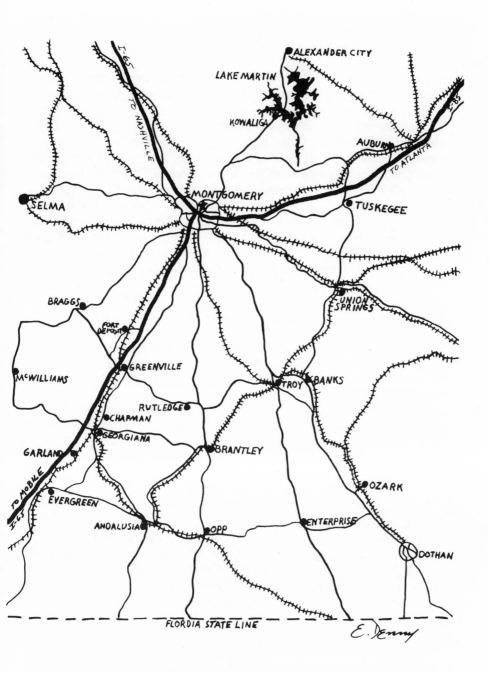

1. Hank's territory.

It could not have been easy to be so enthusiastic about such details of small-town South trying to get from agriculture to industry. And we have to keep in mind that, in its beginnings, the Williams family did not exactly live in the city.

The newlyweds spent their first six months with Lillie's family, on the Mixon farm outside Georgiana. The first place they were to have to themselves was a leased home near Mt. Olive Community in Butler County. The "double pen" house was in two three-room sections joined by a wide hall, sometimes called a "dog run." The couple, already searching for a steady means of support, opened a store in one side of the house. At the same time, they bought a small patch and started a strawberry business.

Lon's life was tough. The time and place had little to offer, especially to an uneducated man; and his wife, who was capable of surviving on her own, offered no sympathy. His way was complicated when he was drafted into the military, where he served from 9 July 1918 through 26 June 1919, part of that time in France. Just what happened to him overseas is not entirely clear. Jay Caress reports that he was shell-shocked and gassed,[4] while Chet Flippo, apparently working with a fairly obscure interview with Lon, says that he was injured in a fight with another GI over a French girl.[5] Leila Williams Griffin, Lon's daughter by a later marriage and thus Hank's half-sister, told me that her father fell from a truck, breaking his collarbone and suffering a blow to the head that was to cause him problems for years to come. Lon Williams came home from Europe a nervous and unsteady man who was no match for either a large and aggressive wife or a mean economy.

Lon's difficulties increased as his children were born. One infant died. Then Irene was born on 8 August 1922; and just over a year later, on 17 September 1923, Lillie gave birth to Hank Williams.[6] One rumor is that Lon wanted to name the boy "King" but that Lillie held out for "Hiram," the name Hank was to live with until he broke with the outback of Alabama in 1937, when the family moved to Montgomery.

The picture is this: an already poor Alabama getting set for a depression; a husband/father weak because of his injury; a dominant wife/mother; and two children. The best facsimile of their life as a young family is probably in the photographs that Walker Evans took for James Agee's text in the classic *Let Us Now Praise Famous Men.*[7] The pictures of Alabama in the early 1930s include an excellent one of a "double pen" house that could have been Hank's; and the families depicted could have been his as well. "Poor but proud" will do as a general description, though poverty may dominate as it did throughout the time and region.

Life of this sort leads one to pursue every possible means of making a little money. A small farm may help feed a family, but hard cash—and what it will buy—looks all the better for its absence. Lon worked off and on at the lumber yards; he and Lillie opened another store; they tried the strawberry business on land burned out with cotton; Lillie worked as a nurse, worked at the cannery, took in sewing, and gardened. Hank and Irene sold peanuts and seeds, picked cotton and strawberries; Hank delivered groceries and shined shoes. Pursuit of a better life meant a good many moves—to places like Chapman, Garland, McWilliams, and Georgiana—all before 1935, when the family moved to Greenville, two years before they moved to Montgomery.

Lon had trouble keeping up, and sometime near the end of 1929—probably in November—he left home. He was not in Garland when Hank's cousin, Taft Skipper, and his bride, Erleen, moved in with Lillie, Irene, Hank, and Grandma Skipper in December of 1929. He apparently had begun a long series of stays in Veterans Administration (VA) hospitals. Leila Williams Griffin explains that the blow Lon suffered in France produced an aneurysm close to his brain, paralyzing his face and destroying his ability to speak. The VA diagnosed dementia praecox, and in the early 1930s, Lon began receiving total disability benefits. Because of this particular diagnosis, the money was sent directly to his family, who probably got a retroactive, lump-sum payment and then a regular monthly installment. The new income was fine, but it was a constant reminder that Hank was practically fatherless.

Lillie managed fairly well without her husband. When their place in Georgiana burned down, she was quick to find another house, this one on Rose Street and large enough for her to inaugurate her career as manager of boardinghouses. Her resourcefulness and her instinct for money identified her as the basic stock of a rising mercantile class in the South. Had she not had a famous son to manage, she might have turned her various houses into a motel chain. Interviews with neighbors and family reveal different opinions of Lillie. Some people found her honest and hardworking, if given to the dollar. Others who came to know her after Hank had established his career found her pushy and greedy. The point seems to be that early in her marriage, her energies, dedicated to survival, were attractive. Later, as her son became better known, those same energies became less appealing as they went toward making certain that she realized every dollar possible from his life and death.

Her son, as child and as adult, was frail and withdrawn. Roger Williams's interviews with various relatives tell us as much:

> From the start, Hank was a thin and none too healthy boy. His sister, Irene, describes him as "pretty frail. He was no athlete. Every time he tried sports, it seemed, he broke something." One such effort, perhaps at ice skating, resulted in a ruptured disk, contributing to back problems that were to plague him most of his adult life.

> Another cousin, J. C. McNeil, who spent a great deal of time with young Hank, remembers him as "a real loner. He never was a happy boy, in a way. He didn't laugh and carry on like other children. It seemed like somethin' was always on his mind."[8]

A really hard life and a dominant mother explain much of this. But an additional factor was involved: Hank Williams always had chronic back problems. The narcotics that he came to depend on, which probably were at least partially responsible for his death, were allowed at first because of his ailment. The origin of this problem cannot be certified, though it is unlikely that Hank started it with an ice-skating accident. The skates would have been as scarce as the ice in Hank's world. Another story, reported both by Roger Williams[9] and by Jay Caress,[10] is that Hank ran away West at the age of seventeen, got drunk, entered a rodeo, and was thrown from a horse. Documenting this episode seems to be impossible. This is not to dismiss the rodeo story entirely, but a better explanation of Hank's problem lies in Chet Flippo's identification of the symptoms of *Spina Bifida Occulta* (SBO) in Hank's medical reports and in his autopsy.[11] SBO is a birth defect; the vertebral arches fail to unite and thus allow the spinal cord to herniate, to extend outward from the spine. The most serious version of this problem, known as *Spina Bifida,* creates a large protrusion or tumor on the back and can cause partial or complete paralysis as well as the loss of sensation and sphincter control. Hank's type was not so severe. There evidently was no external growth, but even the lesser version (the *Occulta*) can leave a mark on the back and cause problems with the lower extremities. That this ailment is progressive may explain some of Hank's problems, especially his occasional paralysis, along with his trouble with sports as a child. Alcohol and drugs certainly complicated his adult problems, but only the SBO seems to explain Hank's lifelong difficulties.

This kind of spinal herniation makes nerves particularly vulnerable to injury. The most ordinary fall could cause a real problem, not to mention a fall from ice skates or from a rodeo horse. That a variety of falls, which only aggravated his problem, got credit for the problem itself is not surprising. We might like to think that an early diagnosis and appropriate surgery could have corrected his problem and perhaps changed his life entirely. But such a situation was rare during Hank's childhood; an open spinal column in the days before the regular use of antibiotics would have been disastrous. For Hank Williams, fate designed a time and place that admitted no relief from a serious and painful ailment.

Not everything in Hank's early years was gloomy. His mother provided for him well enough, and though he may not have been a good athlete, he was an active child. And he seems to have had a particularly good year in 1934-1935 when he lived with his cousins, J. C. and Walt McNeil, near Fountain in Monroe County. He had swapped situations with their sister, who had moved into Georgiana to live with Lillie and finish high school. The McNeils lived in the Pool lumber camp, where Mr. McNeil worked, in a boxcar that had been converted into living quarters—nothing unfamiliar or embarrasing because many of the company's employees lived in the cars, which could be moved easily as the camp followed timber. The benefits for Hank were several. He and the McNeil boys were good pals, and this meant much to the loner, Hank Williams. The McNeils had more of a family life than Hank was used to, and by all reports they were very kind to their guest. Certainly Hank did not have to hit the streets to hawk whatever goods Lillie had come up with for him to sell. Buy maybe the most attractive thing here was that Hank was not socially inferior among the McNeils and their friends. Their neighbors were alike; all worked for the same company, and the neighborhood moved as one. Here Hank was not the fatherless kid from the next town, shining shoes in the barbershop.

Hank took to the basic item on the McNeil social calendar—the Saturday night dances that the lumber camps loved. He liked the live country music and the frolicking that went with it. He was not ignorant of music at this point; his mother had been the church organist, and she had had Hank on the organ bench beside her for services. But the Pool camp may have been the place where he first saw music played in the context of so much fun. The people in the logging camps knew how to have a good time. And part of their method, of course, involved a little strong drink. The gentle irony involved in drinking in many rural areas, especially in the South, is that most know that it goes on, but few see it happen. Drink is not so much a social matter as a preparation for social matters. It happens, and those who are courteous pretend that it does not happen.

All of this means hiding the booze, drinking it in the woods or in a car, and then stashing it away to return to the party. Kids, then, have easy access to it, much easier than if the drinking were public. All that a child has to do is observe and then partake of the elixir. The eleven-year-old Hank apparently caught on to the code quickly. It is not easy to identify a particular point where Hank's alcoholism started; the problems were probably built into him, for he seems to have been highly susceptible to drink. Had he not gotten into it at the McNeils', he would have gotten into it elsewhere. But he did come home from their house with some new knowledge. He must have been aware of the deficiencies in his own family life, perhaps even aware that Lillie was a little exploitative. He knew how much fun the music could be, and he may have associated the whiskey with that.

THE FAME

One of the best things hard times can produce is music. Hard times produced the blues for the poor black, and they produced country for the poor white. In fact, singers establishing themselves in either genre even today when the socioeconomic implications have faded had still better be able to convince audiences that authentic suffering stands behind their work. Hank Williams had no trouble providing that history. He took up his profession with full and legitimate credentials. Alabama in the 1930s could produce as much music as the dust bowl, a West Virginia coal mine, a cotton field, or a New Orleans slum.

Finding the precise point where Hank started his music is impossible. Much of his ability must have been innate; maybe he inherited it from his grandfather Skipper, a blacksmith who supposedly composed some rhythmic songs for his hammering. Maybe he got some of it from his mother who pumped away at those good four-square hymns at the Baptist Church. And, of course, he heard plenty of music at the McNeils' in 1934-1935, both at the lumber yard parties and at home where Mrs. McNeil played the guitar. Wherever his inclination was born, Hank seems to have come out of that particular year ready to make his own music.

Roger Williams, in some of his interviews in Georgiana, tried to find out just who presented Hank Williams with an instrument; he received enough answers to confuse the issue for good. Lillie claimed credit, saying she bought Hank a three-dollar-and-fifty-cent guitar, at fifty cents a month, in order to encourage him to do better work in school. Hank confirmed his mother's part later, although he mentioned nothing about school. Fred Thigpen, who ran the Ford place in Georgiana, says that he bought Hank his first guitar, a two-fifty number, from Warren's store. Others report that Jim Warren himself gave Hank the guitar.[12] The only consistency in any of this is the chronology: It was about 1935 when Hank, twelve years old, started picking. Should there be continuing argument about who was really responsible, we should note that Hank was not destined to become any great picker, anyway. Basic rhythm was about all he ever mastered; and even at that he was sometimes encouraged to leave his guitar at home when he came to recording sessions. Among his numerous recordings, he has only one brief guitar solo, that on "My Bucket's Got A Hole In It."

He did get a little instruction from an old-time fiddler, Cade Durham, who ran Georgiana's shoe shop and had a string band fairly well known in those parts. And no doubt he picked up some help from the street singers who were so common in that time and place. After all, Hank certainly moved among them on his various missions for Lillie. He probably came across a singer named Dove Hazelip and another, Connie "Big Day" McKee. But the biggest influence in this part of Hank's life was black street singer, Rufe Payne, known generally as "Tee Tot." He was from Greenville, just up the L&N railroad line, but he drifted down to hustle Georgiana occasionally.

Rufe Payne was a beggar with talent, the kind who continued well through my own childhood in the 1940s and 1950s, especially in the South. Food stamps and ordinances against begging finally took care of these beggars in the 1960s and 1970s. Many of them were handicapped—blind men, amputees, or winos—who tried to stop passersby long enough to perform and to collect a few coins, usually in a tin cup tied to the neck of a guitar. The problem, of course, came in stopping people long enough for the whole show. That called for more than simple songs; it called for the showmanship that Rufe had mastered—some jokes, some shuffling, some music, and no small amount of flattery of the crowd that might well mean sustenance. Hank learned some music from Rufe, but maybe even better than that, he learned considerable showmanship from him.

The fate that had played some mean tricks on Hank suddenly served him well: Hank, Lillie, and Irene moved up to Greenville, Rufe's hometown, in 1935. Hank had almost constant access to his mentor now; he was much on the streets. Lillie was a demanding mother, and his stay with the McNeils probably had led him to realize that life with her was not exactly cozy. Hank was twelve, into his adolescence, hard to keep up with, streetwise, and tall enough to pass for an adult. He was to spend more time with Rufe Payne.

They had much in common: music, of course, and a sense of the urgency of survival. Neither one of them ever really belonged to a normal social order, and neither one of them took much to ordinary, day-to-day work. If Lillie was giving Hank a bad time, he could stay with Rufe and enjoy the commiseration. Unfortunately, Rufe solaced himself with whiskey as well as with music. Thus Hank had his second major encounter with alcohol. Rufe taught him plenty of music, and in the bargain he gave him access to booze, a place to drink it, and a place to sleep it off well out of the way of Lillie Williams.

Such was Hank's apprenticeship. When he left Rufe, Hank was almost full grown; he had an adult profession and an adult habit. He was ready to travel. And once again, one of his family's many moves was to serve him well. On 10 July 1937, Lillie, Irene, and the fourteen-year-old Hank Williams headed for Montgomery—a hot, flat town of seventy-five thousand people who knew plenty about country music, and the home of a really good country radio station, WSFA.

Lillie went straight into the boardinghouse business at 114 South Perry Street. Irene made lunches to peddle around town, and Hank was supposed to be back shining shoes and selling peanuts. Actually, he spent most of his time looking for a way to pick up where he had left off with Rufe Payne. He was ready to get off the streets and onto the stage, ready to be discovered. He met a young cowboy singer, Braxton Schuffert, who had his own radio show and who performed with Smith "Hezzy" Adair. Schuffert, who was to become one of Hank's most dependable friends, made Hank Williams all the more anxious to be a professional performer.

He found his chance late in the fall of that year. The Empire Theatre ran a sort of "Bijou" operation: full entertainment for the kids—movies of the Bomba and Tex Ritter type, serials, cartoons—and a talent show, usually

2. Hank Williams at thirteen. *Photo courtesy of Bruce Gidoll.*

dominated by spoon players, pantomimists, and yo-yo artists. Hank entered a talent show, singing his own composition, a tune called "The WPA Blues," which was obviously based on Riley Puckett's "Dissatisfied" (1930) and which went like this:

> I got a home in Montgomery
> A place I like to stay
> But I have to work for the WPA,
> And I'm dissatisfied—I'm dissatisfied.

That tune never made it onto any of his records, nor does it turn up in the Hank Williams catalog. But it is a good place to start Hank's career since it identified what Hank was to come to do so well—sing about a tough life that he shared with his audiences. It is also a good place to mark the start of his career because he won first prize in the talent show; Hank left the Empire Theatre that night with fifteen bucks. He must have been trying to calculate how many pairs of shoes he would have to shine to get that kind of loot. And there was more good news: Lillie, with her eagle eye for either talent or money, gave her son a new Gibson guitar as an advance on his Christmas present.

None of this was doing Hank much good at Baldwin Junior High School, on South McDonough Street, where he was struggling with the seventh grade. But it helped get him on WSFA, where he became "The Singing Kid" with Dad Crysel's band. He was a big success and soon had his own fifteen-minute program that came on twice a week.

This arrangement established a pattern that was to become a part of Hank Williams's life. WSFA had a fairly large broadcast area. The result was a good constituency for live appearances around the countryside. The Louisiana Hayride and The Grand Ole Opry work in the same way. A performer is promoted over the air, and then he hits the road, showing up at every schoolhouse and barn dance he can book. Then he heads back to the radio station for more promotion and then back on the road.

Going on the road, of course, meant that Hank needed a band; not even a Hank Williams could carry an entire road show by himself. Hank had already lured Hezzy Adair away from Brack Schuffert; Hezzy, an orphan who had been living with Schuffert's family, had moved into Lillie's boardinghouse, where the supervision was not quite so constant. He could crack the usual jokes expected of a country bass player; and Brack, who booked the first dates for Hank and the band, filled in occasionally on lead guitar. Irene served as vocalist and ticket-taker, and Freddy Beech joined up as fiddler. Chet Flippo, who includes a good photograph of the band in his book, notes that Beech, married and the father of two children, was, at nineteen, the oldest member of the group.[13] Such was the prototype for Hank's "Drifting Cowboys." They played, Hezzy told his jokes, the band members chattered with Hank, and then there was a moment of sacred music (at least until they started getting into the honky-tonks). This was to be Hank's most basic pattern. It survives today in the highly visible "Wagonmasters" of Porter Waggoner and less visibly, but probably more authentically, in Snuffy Jenkins and the "Hired Hands." The idea is to entertain any way possible. Rufe Payne would have understood it well.

Hank was obviously the drawing card, and band personnel was not a crucial issue at this point. It shifted regularly. Don Helms, the first of the permanent Drifting Cowboys, did not join the group until 1943. The WSFA studio photograph of the Cowboys, in fact, shows an outfit entirely different from the one just described. This group had Mexican Charlie Mays on fiddle, Shorty Seals on bass, Indian Joe Hatcher playing lead guitar, and Boots Harris on steel guitar, an instrument which came to identify Hank's sound best.

Hank had good control of his band. After all, they were not too big a draw without him, and besides, Lillie's boardinghouse, recently moved to 236 Catoma Street, was a good place to hole up. And they must have had a fairly good time—men their age, most of them used to precious little money—on the road with a man who was to become the best ever in country music. One catch, though. If Hank had control of the band, Lillie had control of Hank. Maybe she sensed his lack of direction, maybe she was interested in his well-being, maybe she sensed the money to be made. Whatever, she went at Hank's new business with dedication—feeding and sleeping the crew, arranging engagements, collecting admission (usually twenty-five cents), and trying to keep Hank (already deep into drink long before he was old enough to buy whiskey) sober enough to perform.

According to Flippo, Lillie made one other contribution: She had a pretty good right cross.[14] And every punch helped in the spots Hank and the Drifting Cowboys came to play. They did the schoolhouses and other respectable places, but they also did the roadhouses, the gutbuckets—in places like Rutledge, Evergreen, Andalusia, Fort Deposit, and, of course, Montgomery—where the major pastimes were drinking, dancing, picking up women—and then fighting over the women just picked up. The saying, standard in all of these places, is that the owner has to sweep out the eyeballs every morning. Those who have been in such joints know that something about them creates trouble. Maybe it is the loose women to be fought over, or maybe something about tossing down a fast drink in the parking lot makes a good old boy a little surly when he roars in as if he were a cowhand come to town after a long cattle drive. Or maybe it is all just part of a night's entertainment, something to talk about next week.

The band was not exempt from the fighting. And places like these have actually strung chicken wire between the customers and the performers. Hank supposedly equipped his band with blackjacks on one occasion; he himself often carried a pistol, and evidently he broke more than one guitar

3. Thigpen's Log Cabin near Georgiana, Alabama, one of the honky-tonks that Hank played regularly. *Photo by E. Denny.*

on a jealous boyfriend. The leg off a steel guitar was not a bad weapon; neither was the steel bar used to chord the instrument. According to a Roger Williams interview of Sammy Pruett, a longtime Drifting Cowboy from Alabama, Hank was using the bar on a customer "when another local guy coming to Hank's assistance, almost cut the first guy in two. He had to hold his guts in. They took Hank into court the next day, but the judge let him off. Hell, it wasn't his fault." In another tale, a customer bit out a chunk of Hank's eyebrow.[15] Stories like this wind through Hank's history. Not all of them could be true, but they certainly are accurate in capturing the texture of many years of Hank Williams's environment.

Things come to a strange and quick pause here, though. Hank left Montgomery. One might suppose that the honky-tonk circuit had gotten to him, that the drinking and fighting had accumulated and taken their toll. But the likelihood is that Hank was restless, and Lillie was a continuing problem. He was a successful performer, a man able to make his own way, and yet one who had to report to his mother, letting her count his change and hand out his assignments. Many of his acquaintances had gone into the service by now; Irene had left to work at Gunter Field. School was not going well; his vision was bad, and staying awake after playing half the night was hard. He was nineteen and only in the ninth grade when he decided to give up formal education for good. Lillie did not try to stop him and later, in her book on Hank, justified the parental indulgence by saying that "too much book learning might have spoiled the wonderful, natural flow of his song-words."[16] The army rejected him because of his back, so Hank, maybe a little embarrassed by this rejection and certainly hounded by the other problems mentioned, headed for Mobile, the next real city down the way. It was the fall of 1942.

In Mobile, he lived with his uncle, Bob Skipper, and worked for the Alabama Drydock and Shipbuilding Company as a shipfitter's helper (at sixty-six cents per hour) and later as a welding trainee. He was to be there until August of 1944. Just what went on in Mobile is not recorded. We might want to see the stint as meditative, a period during which Hank Williams got himself together to charge the music scene once more. Such may have been the indirect effect, but Hank's life was never so highly designed. Besides, the break was not quite so clean. Hank's record in the shipyards was short of being exemplary, for even while he was in Mobile, he kept up with his band and played dates out of Montgomery. Don Helms, in fact, is certain that he first joined the Drifting Cowboys in 1943, right in the middle of Hank's term with the Alabama Drydock and Shipbuilding Company. Hank kept the road from Mobile to Montgomery well traveled.

The deal seemed to be a pretty good one for Hank, as if it took the miles down to Mobile to separate him from Lillie's dominance. And why he came home is hazy still. Lillie, in her book, claims she went to get him. She says she traveled to Montgomery, booking shows for Hank for sixty days

4. Hank and Lillie Williams. *Photo courtesy of Bruce Gidoll.*

straight, drove to Mobile and brought Hank home. She quotes Hank, upon his seeing his mother and the schedule of shows: "Thank God, mother. You have made me the happiest boy in the world."[17] Imagining any such conversation between Hank and Lillie Williams is difficult. Hank had been around quite a bit by this time; and though he could be the contrite son, I find it hard to believe that he was so thrilled by the rescue. Besides, Lillie botches her romantic tale by saying that Hank was gone for only three weeks; Hank was gone for nearly two years. But Lillie always loved the idea that Hank was so affectionate and that he could not get along without her.

A better reason for Hank's return was the extra woman now on the scene. Audrey Mae Sheppard Guy, about half a year older than Hank, was from a community known as Enon, just outside a little town called Banks. The place is about fifty miles southeast of Montgomery. She was the oldest of three daughters who were, stories have it, closely guarded by their father, Charley Sheldon Sheppard. Charley was not especially prosperous as a peanut and cotton grower. Audrey, a high school dropout, was as restless as Hank Williams, and his life must have looked pretty good to her. Besides that, she wanted to be a singer. That she was married to Erskine Guy did not dampen her interest in Hank. Guy was overseas; Audrey and their daughter, Lycrecia Ann, born 13 August 1941, had been living with the Sheppards. But sometime in 1942, the tall blonde and her daughter moved into Lillie's boardinghouse in Montgomery. No one in the family seems certain of the motive. Some think Audrey had seen Hank in a show down in Banks and had come to Montgomery specifically to get him. Others think she had come to Montgomery looking for work and that her sharing a roof with Hank was coincidence. Regardless of Audrey's motives, this romance seems to have been inevitable.

Hank had a reputation for pursuing women, but nothing indicates that he had any enduring romance before he met Audrey. This woman really took his fancy, and the courtship must have been one of the reasons he kept the road from Mobile hot. Ed Linn, one of Hank's early biographers, says that the fights started almost immediately, usually over Hank's drinking.[18] And more than a few friends of the couple have confirmed Linn's point. But the bad times of the relationship seemed to make the good times all the better. And Hank and Audrey were to be lovers, if not friends, for a good many years to come.

When Hank got back from Mobile in the fall of 1944, he was ready to get serious about his music and his romance. The two charms merged as Audrey, ambitious would-be singer, came to be vocalist with the Drifting Cowboys. She could hardly carry a tune,[19] and she proved to be no songwriter; but the business of being able to perform with his true love really overwhelmed Hank Williams. Besides, she was aggressive enough to take over when Hank was drunk.

Audrey finally ditched Erskine Guy on 5 December 1944, a few months after Hank had moved back to Montgomery from Mobile. The divorce decree, issued in Pike County, Alabama, cited Guy for "Voluntary Abandonment" and made him responsible for financing the "support of his dependent child . . . Lycrecia Ann Guy, age nearly four years." He was to pay a monthly sum equal to whatever the War Department allowed military personnel for support of a dependent child.[20] In short, he was to continue the check that Audrey was already getting for Lycrecia. One of the harder rumors has it that Hank and Audrey were living on Lycrecia's check when the divorce came through. But such seems unlikely because room and board were free for Hank at home.

Audrey's divorce decree includes the statement standard in Alabama that, "It is further ordered, adjudged and decreed that neither party to this suit shall again marry except to each other until sixty days after the rendition of this decree." Ten days later, on 15 December 1944, she and Hank were applying for a marriage license in Andalusia, Alabama. Hank filled out the form, listing himself as a "Band Leader," white, and age twenty-one. He passed the venereal disease test, not required of Audrey, given by Dr. L. L. Parker. Audrey indicates clearly on the form that she had been divorced on 5 December. The notary, Annie R. Broxson, evidently unaware of Alabama's sixty-day reconciliation period, approved the license. The pair married that same day, in a Texaco station outside Andalusia. The Drifting Cowboys, who supposedly had to chip in to pay Justice of the Peace M. A. Boyett, were witnesses.[21] Hank and Audrey went home to Lillie's boardinghouse. They did not file their license and certificate for nearly two months; but they did not need to rush because, due to the violation of Audrey's period of reconciliation, their marriage was to be one of common law, anyway.

Life must have looked pretty good to Hank now. He had Audrey, apparently for keeps, and his band was really getting solid. Don Helms and Sammy Pruett, who were to be a part of the most famous version of the Drifting Cowboys, both rejoined as World War II wound down. The money was better now: Hank could pay a man ten dollars for a performance, and they were out three or four nights a week. Lillie had a decent place for them to stay, though it did not come free of charge. Audrey was taking on some of her mother-in-law's chores with the band—handling bookings, keeping up with the money, taking tickets, performing, and especially keeping the show rolling when Hank did not quite make it.

Hank was having more and more success, but his domestic life was getting messier by the day. He had two women to take care of him now, or two women to fight over the benefits of his success. He seemed to be getting famous for them, and that took the edge off his progress. Chet Flippo puts it well:

The better Hank became, the less he seemed to care about his career. Lilly and Audrey both tried lecturing him and they both received hostile stares for their trouble. They resolved that it was their duty to stroke the career along, since Hank wasn't responsible enough to do so. Audrey, too, still had designs of making it big as a singer herself.[22]

The scene was tense: Audrey and Lillie were not really getting along but were banding together to push Hank. Hank apparently resented them for their trouble; he was drinking far too much; his back was hurting; the drink and the back together may have even caused him some impotence; his wife was a nag, trying to become the star of his band. All of this went on in Lillie's boardinghouse, with a handful of strangers and some of the Drifting Cowboys to witness. Lycrecia was there, too. Though Hank seemed to like the child, she must have complicated this particular situation. And Lillie's domestic life was not exactly even. She had run off a Mr. Bozzard, whipping him out the door with a belt, not too long before she took on her next husband, W. W. Stone.

In the midst of all this, Hank was still trying to carry on his career with a daily radio show at one o'clock for WSFA, usually followed by a stand in a joint somewhere in the outback full of drunks perfectly willing to bit off an eyebrow or slice you in half with a jackknife. No one who knows much about Hank Williams would be surprised to find him entering the hospital in Prattville, Alabama, for his first treatment for alcoholism. He was twenty-two years old.

In spite of his many problems, though, Hank had been writing a good bit of music. "The WPA Blues" had encouraged him. He had had some time for writing in Mobile, and he had had some time while lying around Lillie's boardinghouse, listening to the women scrap with each other or complain about his drinking. His songs were not bad. And by the time the war ended, Hank had a pretty good stash of music, enough to put out *Songs of Hank Williams "The Drifting Cowboy,"* his first WSFA songbook. It included ten uncopyrighted songs and sold for thirty-five cents. The book was a matter of trying out Hank's commercial value, and apparently it proved to be good enough. For within a year, the *Hank Williams and His Drifting Cowboys, Stars of WSFA, Deluxe Song Book* was out. This second book offered thirty uncopyrighted songs, including nine from the first book, and three photos. Hank wrote a brief preface, thanking his fans and saying that "many of the ideas for these songs have come from their cards and letters." A second preface, by WSFA Program Director Caldwell Stewart, describes Hank as being six feet tall and weighing one hundred and eighty pounds. "He has brown eyes and black hair and a lazy good-natured air about him. . . . He is happily married and he and 'Miss Audrey' are already famous as a team."[23]

Most of the songs are forgettable ditties like "I Bid You Free To Go" or "Grandad's Musket," which includes a sharpshooting old man, a grandma who knits socks, and a sister who buys savings stamps. Audrey had gotten her hand into one, a sentimental piece called "My Darling Baby Girl," obviously for Lycrecia. Nothing here yet to get one into the Hall of Fame. But "Honkey-Tonkey" turned up; much later known as "Honky-Tonkin'," it practically became the trademark of Hank Williams. And another song should be noted: "Back Ache Blues" may indicate something of Hank's physical ailment, and certainly it forecast a lot of good comic tunes—like "Move It On Over" and "Kaw-Liga"—as it tells of being squeezed so hard by a lover that he gets a backache. The more serious love songs in the collection are the weakest. "I Don't Care [If Tomorrow Never Comes]" offers little to remember as its speaker gives up on life because his girl has left him. "Never Again [Will I knock On Your Door]" works hard on the theme of lovers who have tried to patch it up too many times. "My Love For You [Has Turned To Hate]" is another song of betrayal; the faithful lover who thought his beloved was true is left behind. And "Six More Miles" is a terse bit about seeing a true love to her grave. The two religious songs are startlingly simple. "When God Comes And Gathers His Jewels" depicts a boy, alone and crying, at a graveside. A minister appears to take his hand and predicts a reunion in heaven. "Wealth Won't Save Your Soul" says simply that a search for material goods will not bring salvation.

I do not think that anyone wants to get eloquent about the greatness of these songs. But I do think they indicate something important about Hank Williams. The love songs are apparently autobiographical as they speak of lovers like Hank and Audrey who do not seem to be able to get it together and also because they hint at unfaithfulness. The religious songs suggest a pattern in Hank's work. The adult Hank Williams rarely darkened church doors, but he never escaped the religiosity of his childhood. And singing about loose living always seemed to call for a little of the gospel. The other point to make concerns the remarkable directness of Hank's work. If most songwriters are busy trying to find unique ways to state the familiar, Hank seemed to be content to go straight at it. The threat of a cliché never bothered him; and though this may well be counted a weakness, it seemed to contribute to the basic honesty that makes his music appealing.

This stash of songs, especially the last six, were going to help Hank make the change of scene that he needed. Montgomery had no music publisher, and it certainly had no recording studios. The big recording outfits occasionally sent out talent scouts, on a kind of Lewis and Clark expedition. Victor had found both the Carter family and Jimmie Rodgers on such a trek, but no one had spotted Hank Williams yet. So it seemed time to head for Nashville and Acuff-Rose, the publisher who dealt primarily with country music.

If Hank was a provincial, emerging from Alabama for nearly the first time, Fred Rose had been around. Born in 1897 in Evansville, Illinois, Rose had grown up in St. Louis. Before he drifted south, he had become an accomplished songwriter, author of songs like "Red Hot Mama" and "Deed I Do." The Rose song best known today is probably "Blue Eyes Crying In The Rain." He had worked for Fibber McGee and Molly and Paul Whiteman, and he had had his own radio show, "Fred Rose's Song Shop," during which he composed songs on the spot. He had even been to Hollywood, to do some writing for Gene Autry. That he settled in Nashville, about the time of World War II, was to be a blessing for Hank Williams and the city as well.

The war was to bring considerable popularity to country music because it spread the good old boys who liked it so much across the world. What country music needed desperately at the time was an agency to collect its royalties and a publishing house. The American Society of Composers, Authors, and Publishers (ASCAP), the outfit that collected royalties for public use of any song by its members, paid little attention to country music. The result, as Bill Malone notes in his history of country music, was that "the performance of hillbilly songs was, on the whole, unprotected."[24] ASCAP's contract with the radio networks had expired on 31 December 1940, and the agency wanted to double the price for the next five-year period. The National Association of Broadcasters had seen all this coming and had established a new licensing outfit, Broadcast Music, Inc. (BMI), on 14 October 1939. And at the beginning of 1941, the broadcasters banned all ASCAP material. BMI, then, was in business, and what it needed was a stable of writers and songs. The effect was some democracy for the music world; country music, and what is sometimes called "race music," started getting the standard protection through BMI.

Roy Acuff and Fred Rose came to the rescue on the publishing house problem. Acuff, one of the best songwriters of the day and nearly always a gubernatorial candidate, had been having trouble copyrighting his music. So many of his songs had been pirated that he even tried protecting them by writing them on postcards and mailing them to himself in the hope that the postmarks would somehow help demonstrate ownership. Acuff had made a small fortune in 1941 when he sold nearly a million copies of a twenty-five-cent, foldout songbook, *Roy Acuff's Folio of Original Songs Featured over WSM Grand Ole Opry,* that could be mailed to fans as a postcard. Music publishing, then, was much on his mind when he met Fred Rose. In October 1942, Acuff gave Rose $25,000 to start Acuff-Rose. Elizabeth Schlappi describes the company:

> Though the years Acuff-Rose has expanded from a tiny firm founded on "a handshake and a promise" to a mammoth corporation which is one of the largest music business complexes in the world and which

has played a large part in the growth of country music. From the beginning, Roy Acuff and Fred Rose agreed that the firm would be scrupulously honest and also that it would go out of its way to help deserving talent. Acuff-Rose has done just that—the prime example is Hank Williams.[25]

Hank and Audrey had picked a pretty good time to step off the bus into Nashville. It was 1946, country music was practically everywhere, BMI was on its feet, and good new talent was welcome. What is more, Hank's longtime idol, Roy Acuff, was in the publishing business now; and Hank's stuff needed nothing more than the really professional hand of Acuff's partner, Fred Rose, a reformed alcoholic, now a Christian Scientist.

Nashville is nearly as full of the mythology of "being discovered" as Hollywood, and the suicide rate is equally high. Half the writers in the former group can perform a full show of their own compositions; people do walk into town with guitars on their backs; and "writers' night," an occasion when anyone is welcome to perform, goes on somewhere every night. One just hopes that the right person will stumble onto his act. Audrey Williams was not so patient; she was not going to wait for her husband's discovery. She took him straight to the best talent promoters in Nashville.

She and Hank showed up at the WSM building at lunchtime on 14 September 1946. Fred Rose, who was looking for some country songs for Molly O'Day, was finishing off the hour with a game of Ping-Pong with his son, Wesley. Audrey announced that her husband had songs to sing; Fred invited them to a studio, where Hank did several numbers including "My Love For You [Has Turned To Hate]," "Six More Miles," and "When God Comes And Gathers His Jewels." One of the myths that intervenes here is that Fred Rose was impressed with the music but was not convinced that Hank had written it. To make Hank prove his claim to the music, Fred gave him a boy-girl plot and asked him to write a song about it then and there. Hank supposedly turned out one of his well-known numbers, "Mansion On The Hill," in thirty minutes. MGM liked the idea, and one can see George Hamilton, as Hank, write the song in the film *Your Cheatin' Heart*. The source of the myth seems to be Lillie's book, *Our Hank Williams*. And Chet Flippo speculates, accurately I think, that the tale, long since proven false, was Lillie's attempt to deemphasize Audrey's part in the discovery of Hank Williams.[26]

Fred Rose, though, was impressed enough to discuss a standard song-writing contract that would give Hank three cents for each copy of sheet music sold and 50 percent of record royalties. Supposedly they came to the three-cent figure when Hank claimed that he did not understand how much 3 percent would be. At any rate, Hank and Audrey headed back to Montgomery. And there, on 31 October, Hank took a sheet of Audrey's printed stationery and wrote Mr. Rose: "Here is the two (2) songs you asked for, and the recordings of them left yesterday. If you can use more at any time, let me know and what type."[27] The manuscripts of "Six More Miles" and "When God Comes And Gathers His Jewels" accompanied the letter. On 21 November, Hank wrote Rose to say that he had received his contract and to "offer 3 or 4 more numbers." Rose responded on 23 November to the effect that the contracts were in order and that Molly O'Day had seen the songs. Rose also noted: "I must change the lyrics around in order to make them consistent. These will be minor changes, and will not interfere with what you have already written." Actually he cut the third stanza of "Six More Miles" and changed a phrase that improved the rhyme of the refrain. The changes in "When God Comes And Gathers His Jewels" were negligible. Molly O'Day was soon to record both songs. So Hank Williams was in the songwriting business.

Before the end of the year, he was back in Nashville and into the recording business. The Roses, who at first saw Hank as only a writer, had gone to Montgomery to see him perform and had come home to look for the chance to record him. In December of 1946, Sterling Records called from New York to see if Acuff-Rose could recommend a western band and a country singer for some recording sessions. The Roses thought immediately of a band—the Oklahoma Wranglers, sometimes known as the Willis Brothers, a band consisting of Guy, Vic, and Skeeter Willis. The country singer was going to be Hank Williams.

Hank's first session was done by the Castle Recording Company in studio D of WSM. As if to forecast part of Hank's destiny, WSM resided in the building of National Life and Accident Insurance Company, the primary sponsor of The Grand Ole Opry. Hank cut his first record there on 11 December 1946; the backup music was by the Oklahoma Wranglers, with a character known as Chuck "The Indian" on bass. Hank recorded four of his own songs: "Wealth Won't Save Your Soul," "When God Comes And Gathers His Jewels," "Never Again [Will I knock On Your Door]," and "Calling You"—good songs, but all of them pretty sad as they take up lost souls or lost love.

Sterling liked the cuts, paid Hank a flat $82.50, and invited him back for a second session. On 13 February 1947, a slightly bolder Hank Williams recorded four more songs: "I Don't Care [If Tomorrow Never Comes]," "My Love For You [Has Turned To Hate]," "Honky Tonkin'," and "Pan American." The first two songs carried the same dreariness of the first records. But "Honky Tonkin' " and "Pan American" were a sharp departure from Hank's mournful tone. "Pan American" is an upbeat number about the L&N train that Hank heard whip through Greenville and Georgiana on its way to New Orleans. "Honky Tonkin'," of course, is that rowdy number in which the singer invites somebody else's baby to grab some money and join him in the city.

5.   Hank early in his career as a member of The Louisiana Hayride. *Photo courtesy of Bruce Gidoll.*

Hank made another $82.50 and proved that he was not just a one-beat performer. Fred Rose liked "Honky Tonkin' " especially and called Frank Walker, a music promoter who had been involved with the careers of singers from Caruso to Al Jolson to Gene Autry. Walker was setting up a recording division of MGM, and he could use Hank Williams. He commissioned Hank's first MGM recording. Hank signed on and pulled out four more of his compositions for the 21 April 1947 session. In "Last Night I Heard You Crying In Your Sleep," "Six More Miles," and "I Saw The Light," Hank was as serious as ever. But the fourth number, "Move It On Over," was a lively novelty about coming home late, being locked out by an angry wife, and sleeping with the dog. The session was certainly remarkable for a new artist. In fact, John W. Rumble, in his doctoral dissertation on Fred Rose, claims that "Move It On Over" was important in setting MGM Records on "a firm basis."[28] And Hank was to be recording in the Castle studios again in August and again in November when he did "Mansion On The Hill" and another cut of "Honky Tonkin'."

All Hank needed now was a good promotional base. He had been doing a six o'clock show every morning in Montgomery, but he was too big for WSFA; and he was not yet big enough for The Grand Ole Opry. Fred Rose had a good contact in Henry Clay, an entrepreneur who cranked up the Louisiana Hayride in April of 1948. The Hayride convened at Shreveport's Municipal Auditorium, from eight until eleven-thirty every Saturday night. The fifty thousand watts of KWKH carried it over western Louisiana and into Texas. It became a kind of training ground, sometimes known as "the cradle of the stars," for quite a few famous performers, among them George Jones, Webb Pierce, Jim Reeves, Slim Whitman, Kitty Wells, and Faron Young. Hank would be a regular there before fall.

But Hank had a domestic crisis to get through first. He and Audrey had been fighting hard. And this was not just a matter of love's not running smoothly. They could get down to blows quickly; and the tales of their fights are many. The situation was one of those that emphasized the wild extremes in Hank Williams. Women dominated him fairly easily, and he seemed to resent it. The result was that he was either giving them a terrible time or doing everything he could to please them. In the interview with disc jockey Bob McKinnon, which is printed further on in this book, Hank calls Audrey his "War Department"—not a bad description, even if intended as a joke. In the same interview, he turns the conversation quickly to her recent recording contract. Hank knew she could not sing. But his bad behavior seemed to leave him feeling in her debt; he tried to appease her by promoting the singing career she wanted so badly. This passage from his 19 August 1947 letter to Fred Rose is nearly pathetic in this regard:

I sent you the recordings of Audrey and myself yesterday. We didn't do much on that "I Saw The Light" we never had tried it until we

went to make the records. Maybe you can get an idea of it. The others
are good I think. I also sent that thing—entitled "Every things O. K."

Here's hoping you can use the Duet.

The problem, no doubt, was Audrey's voice and not the lack of rehearsal
that Hank mentions. And sadly ironic is Hank's final line, the recommen-
dation of the duet that he had just identified as the weakest piece. He had
gotten along with Lillie the same way; Hank was either the hell raiser who
was breaking her heart or the loving son come home.

Audrey got her fill of all this after about four years of marriage. She left
in February 1948 and filed for a divorce, which was granted on 26 May of
that year. Hank paid the court costs and went back to his drinking.[29] Had it
not been for the offer to appear on The Louisiana Hayride, most of us
would never have heard of him. He was, in fact, on a binge and unavailable
when the offer came. But he straightened up quickly and accepted. The
other good news was that his divorce turned out to be nominal only. He and
Audrey were traveling together in Norfolk less than a month after the court
proceedings, when, on 23 June they wrote Fred Rose a postcard: "Having
Big Time, Hank & Audrey." And before the fall, the couple had conceived
Hank Williams, Jr. Thus began what may have been the most clearheaded
part of the career of Hank Williams. He was soon to be a major figure on
the Hayride, and though he was still divorced, his domestic situation was
shaping up a little.

Hank and Audrey moved to Shreveport. He appeared on the Hayride on
Saturday nights and did a daily radio show, sponsored by Johnny Fair
Syrup, as the "Old Syrup Sopper." His jingle—"When I die, bury me
deep/ In a bucket of Johnny Fair,/ From my head to my feet"—is not
especially original, but supposedly it saved a company that was near
bankruptcy until Hank Williams showed up. When he was not on the
Hayride or at the radio station, he toured the countryside, hitting places like
Lake Charles, Texarkana, and Baton Rouge. The towns were just a little
bigger than Hank had known in the WSFA days. He had bought a blue,
1949 touring Packard, one big enough to hold his band and pull a trailer.
Hank actually drove very little—perhaps because of his weak vision,
perhaps because of his back problems, or perhaps because he liked to slouch
in the back seat and try to compose a song or two. He had already gotten at
least one good song that way, back in Montgomery when, after a long road
trip, he had seen the first light of the city and had written "I Saw The
Light"—or so the story goes.

The Louisiana branch of the Drifting Cowboys was minus Don Helms
and Sammy Pruett. Neither of them wanted to move to Shreveport. But
Hank gathered a pretty good band, the best known being bass player Lum
York and lead guitarist Bob McNett. McNett had been working the Hayride

with Patsy Montana. The basic Hank Williams show involved a few numbers by the band to warm up the crowd, the introduction and entrance of Hank, a number by Hank, and then his own personalized and rambling introductions of the individual band members, followed by more music, concluding with maybe a recitation or with a sincerely put gospel number, something everyone knew. Hank had done this act out of Montgomery; he would do it again out of Nashville.

He was getting even better with audiences. He was handsome, well decked out in a stage uniform that always included a hat to cover his balding head. He seemed unselfconsciously provocative as he hunched over a microphone or gathered himself around a guitar. The Hayride audiences were to see nothing like that again until Elvis showed up. That Hank seemed both aggressive and vulnerable really appealed to the Hayride fans. Maybe it was just Hank Williams, a man whose successes and disasters went hand in hand, coming straight through. Maybe audiences just sensed that he knew whereof he spoke, that he had lived a good many of his songs. Whatever the formula, Hank Williams came to life when he hit the stage. In a Roger Williams interview, Frank Page, then producer of the Hayride, says that Hank "was just electrifying on stage. . . .He had the people in the palm of his hands from the moment he walked out there. They were with him, whatever he wanted to do."[30]

Things were rolling. He was still drinking some—enough to get himself in trouble for pulling the stage curtain in the middle of a Bailes Brothers act in Lake Charles, enough to keep Audrey, who was slowly fading from the professional part of his life, stirred up. And he had to live with the reputation of being a dangerous property, one who might not show or one who might not be entirely in charge of himself when he did show. But Hank was just too good to be ignored, whatever the complications of his personal life.

Things soon came together for him. He recorded a song called "The Lovesick Blues" in Cincinnati, at the Herzog studio, on 22 December 1948. The record was released in February of 1949. The song was not his; Irving Mills and Cliff Friend had copyrighted it in 1922. It had been recorded by Emmett Miller and Rex Griffin and probably sung by Rufe Payne. Hank had been playing it for some time, making the song more or less his own with a kind of jaunty yodeling despair that he could do better than anyone. Besides that, the content of the song could easily be taken as the hallmark of a Hank Williams number. The song was a wild hit. *Billboard* was to list it as the number one country and western record of 1949, and *Cash Box* voted it the "Best Hillbilly Record" of the year. Songs like George Morgan's "Candy Kisses," Red Foley's "Tennessee Border," and Eddie Arnold's "Bouquet of Roses" provided "Lovesick Blues" with some good competition that year. And Hank picked up the nickname of his success; he became "the lovesick blues boy," or just "Lovesick," among his friends who were joshing him about both his personal and his professional lives. This song, along with "Wedding Bells," which was number five that year, had made him the number two man in *Billboard*'s top selling folk artist category.

The problem now belonged to The Grand Ole Opry and its officials, Harry Stone and Jim Denny. The Opry has always successfully cultivated a family image. Country music lovers come from everywhere to see the show, and they behave marvelously well. Those good southern rules of drink that Hank knew in his childhood certainly applied here. Stone and Denny knew about Hank's affection for whiskey, and they knew there might be something a little lascivious about the way he went at a love song. They were frightened of him, yet his "Lovesick Blues" was one of the best records in the country. Their solution was to offer Hank a guest appearance.

Hank Williams, introduced by Red Foley, appeared for the first time on The Grand Ole Opry on 11 June 1949. The audience's response to his coming on stage was slight; not everyone knew exactly who Hank Williams was. But everybody knew "Lovesick Blues," and before the twenty-five-year-old singer could get through a few lines, the crowd of more than thirty-five hundred was up off the hard oak pews that served as seats in Ryman Auditorium. They called him back six times.

All he had to do was accept the Opry contract that was inevitable and put together a good band so he could get on the road, just as he had done in Shreveport, except now it was for much more money. Before coming to Nashville, he had dismissed his Hayride band, an act that many see as Hank's confidence in being through with the minor leagues. He caught up with Don Helms, one of the employees who had not been willing to move to Shreveport. Don was certainly interested in Nashville and The Grand Ole Opry, and he rejoined the Cowboys. Bob McNett came up from Shreveport. Jerry Rivers, who had declined at least one earlier offer to be a Drifting Cowboy, agreed now to be fiddler. Hillous Butrum, a twenty-one-year-old who had been an Opry sideman for five years, signed on as bass player. Hank was set. They went on the road so fast that several of them had to borrow the appropriate western clothing.

Meanwhile, of course, Hank had to deal with his domestic situation. And it was a little more complicated than it had been. His son, Randall Hank Williams, had been born just sixteen days before Hank had opened on the Opry. The child's birthday, 26 May 1949, fell exactly on the anniversary of the divorce of his parents. Nonetheless, Hank was the proud father. At about 3:45 A.M., he wired Mr. and Mrs. Fred Rose in Nashville: "10 LB BOY BORNED THIS MORNING AT 145 BOTH DOEING FINE." Hank had treated Lycrecia, Audrey's daughter by Erskine Guy, well enough— though he never legally adopted her. But he was especially proud of

Hank Jr., whom he called "Bocephus" after a puppet used by Opry comedian Rod Brasfield. And Hank took to closing his radio shows with his usual "If the good Lord's willing and the creek don't rise, we'll be back for another visit" but now with the addition of "See you in a little while, Bocephus," or "I'm coming, Bocephus," He was good about gifts for his children, horses for Lycrecia and cowboy suits and boots for Hank Jr. He must have been remembering his own more or less fatherless childhood, and he must have imagined that he could give his boy much more than he himself had had. Whatever he was thinking, he had a good son and a successful Opry appearance, all in just a little over two weeks; and he was moving to Nashville. Hank must have felt that his world was in pretty good order.

Either the birth of the child or the move up to Nashville got Hank and Audrey busy taking care of the 1948 divorce. They had it amended *Nunc pro tunc* on 9 August 1949. The "back to the beginning" emendation left the original decree meaningless as it eliminated all three of its points, particularly the one stating that "Audrey Mae Williams is forever divorced from the said Hank Williams." The document states that such seems to be "in the best interest of both petitioners and of their minor son, Randall Hank Williams."[31]

Audrey was pleased enough about the document and about moving to Nashville. She wanted Hank to be successful, but she did crave a larger part in that success. Even if no one else noticed, she was certainly aware of her absence at the 11 June Opry performance. She was probably changing a diaper in Louisiana while Hank was taking his six encores. And little Hank was going to continue to keep her out of action for a while. When she was finally ready to return to the stage, back to her singing career, her husband was not especially eager to have her. Love might have conquered Hank's reservations about her singing in an Alabama honky-tonk five years before; but Hank was not thrilled about tampering with his success on the Opry, about tampering with something as good as Hank Williams and the Drifting Cowboys.

Besides, he was on the road, away from Audrey quite a bit. The Opry worked like the Hayride; WSM served the same function as KWKH and, for that matter WSFA. But the Opry was the central point for country music. The stars performed there on Saturday night, for union scale, and then hit the road for the real money in the places where they had been heard courtesy of WSM. Then they returned to Ryman Auditorium for the Saturday shows, or at least for the twenty-six shows called for in the standard contract. Hank knew the cycle well; it was making him famous and killing him all at once.

In his recounting of his days as a Drifting Cowboy, Jerry Rivers is especially nostalgic about the first part of Hank's stay in Nashville:

The days from 1949 till 1951 were some of the best times of my life. . . . This was the period when Hank Williams made the fastest rise in popularity, wrote his best songs, and probably helped advance country music further than in any previous decade. During this time Hank's health was good, his attitude and enthusiasm were at an all-time high and no one ever gained the professional respect and acceptance of the industry so rapidly.[32]

Rivers is probably a little too kind here. But this was by far the best part of the career of Hank Williams. The *Billboard* summary of recordings with the best retail sales for 1950 included three of his numbers: "Why Don't You Love Me" (4), "Long Gone Lonesome Blues" (5), and "Moanin' The Blues" (30). And in 1951 there would be "Cold, Cold Heart" (1), "Hey Good Lookin' " (8), and "Crazy Heart" (29).

Hank and the Cowboys took advantage of their currency. They played in every kind of setting, from civic auditoriums to the rooftops of drive-in movie snack bars. And they worked hard on stage. If the traveling music show of today usually carries several acts, performers, or groups working for twenty or thirty minutes each, Hank and the Drifting Cowboys often had to do an entire show. Sometimes a comedian was thrown in, and occasionally another unit joined; but basically it was Hank and the band carrying the load.

The group, then, had to be versatile. A bass player like Hillous Butrum, called "Buel" on stage, had to play, sing, and tell jokes. All were counted on for the stage chatter that may be responsible for a good bit of the corniness associated with country music. Hank carried on a standard set of jokes with the band. Jerry Rivers was known as "Burrhead" because of his closely cut blond hair, and he was the object of newlywed jokes for many months after his 1949 marriage. Bob McNett had to go by his full name, Rupert Robert McNett, in Hank's introductions. And because he was a native of Pennsylvania, he had to put up with Hank's long string of North-South jokes. Don Helms performed as "Shag," and Hank had to go by the name "Harm," a countrified version of Hiram.

They still traveled in Hank's big blue 1949 Packard—band, instruments, and all. The small aluminum trailor they had pulled was hard on the car's brakes and had to be abandoned. The car had no power equipment, no air conditioning. Driving the car from Nashville on a Sunday morning after an Opry show, up into the outback of West Virginia or Ohio or down through Carolina for a one-shot performance at a drive-in movie, was a tough assignment. The crew, though, was young and resilient, and their travels produced many good on-the-road stories. Jerry Rivers's book, *Hank Williams: From Life To Legend* is the best source of these tales. Cigarette loads were popular, especially because Hank was so bad about bumming smokes and was brazen enough to simply fish them out of someone else's pocket. A newfangled window air conditioner, which was desperately needed down through Louisiana, voluntarily dumped its several gallons of water on Hank, who then smashed it on the roadside. They hit a buzzard, which came through the windshield, and spread itself through the car. Shag Helms supposedly helped Hank with "I Can't Help It [If I'm Still In Love With You]," which concerns passing an old lover on the street by supplying the line, "And I smelled your rotten feet." Hank kept writing, at least when he was not trying to keep up with two or three baseball games on the Packard's radio.

Hank Williams was big enough then to be included in the first Grand Ole Opry/R. J. Reynolds Tobacco Company Tour of U.S. military bases abroad, which began 13 November 1949. Stars like Roy Acuff, Red Foley, Minnie Pearl, and Jimmy Dickens were his colleagues. And though the company was fast, Hank held his own easily with "Lovesick Blues," which was as popular with the soldiers in Germany as it was stateside. The Drifting Cowboys did not make the trip, but Audrey did. And both Jimmy Dickens and Minnie Pearl recalled for Roger Williams that the trip went well for the couple.[33]

Whatever the status of the Williams romance, the cash and the attention were booming. Hank was doing a Saturday afternoon show for Duckhead Work Clothes, and he was touring constantly, even into Canada. In 1949, he was getting $250 a show; the price went to $1,000 for 1950. He could afford the $40,000 home back in Nashville at 4916 Franklin Road, near the governor's mansion. Eventually the house was to have a wrought iron fence with the notes of "Lovesick Blues" cast in it. And soon Hank was buying a five-hundred acre farm on Carter's Creek in Franklin, just outside of Nashville. He was going to hunt and ride there, maybe restore the old house, and generally lead the life of a country music success. He bought himself a new, green 1950 Cadillac. And to keep things more or less even on Franklin Road, he bought Audrey a yellow 1949 Caddy convertible, with a platinum watch and a diamond ring thrown in for good measure. Some still swear that Hank Williams would take both cars on his visits to Montgomery.

He was well enough off that, although the band drove, he could fly to the west coast for several shows in 1950. Henry Cannon, Minnie Pearl's husband, was usually his private pilot. In Sacramento, Fresno, San Jose, and Long Beach, Hank and the Cowboys played before the large crowds that were turning out to hear the eight- to twelve-piece western swing bands that were popular in the huge ballrooms, in places like Tex Williams's Riverside Rancho, Spade Cooley's Santa Monica Ballroom, and Smokey Rogers's Bostonia Ballroom. That a five-piece, hard country band could carry a show for two thousand patrons who were accustomed to the swing

6. The Drifting Cowboys and their families at Hank's home on Franklin Road in Nashville. (From left to right) Bob McNett, Hank Williams, Audrey Williams, Hank Williams, Jr., Lycrecia Guy, Hazel Helms, Frankie Helms, June Rivers, Don Helms, Betty Butrum, Hillous Butrum (standing), and Jerry Rivers. *Photo courtesy of Bruce Gidoll.*

orchestras is remarkable testimony to the skill and popularity of Hank and the band.

He was well enough known that he took an alias, Herman P. Willis, when he went to Dallas to work for Jack Ruby in July of 1950. The band thought he had ducked out on them until they spotted him in a hotel lobby. Hank appointed Jerry Rivers head of the group for the rest of the trip. And he had the following statement notarized on 5 July: "This is to certify that Jerry M. Rivers is the General Manager of Hank Williams & Band. Including Hank Williams. During my stay in State of Texas. Hank Williams."[34] Whether he was getting ready for some serious drinking or was in need of anonymity for other reasons, the celebrity was lying low.

His record sales went over a million in 1950; for that year and the next, his releases averaged half-a-million sales each. He got Sam Hunt, a vice-president of Nashville's Third National Bank, to help with his money. But Hank bothered little with the sophisticated investments that we associate with superstars today. He was a cash man who supposedly came off the road and into the bank lugging bills and checks that he had not even counted, telling the cashiers that if he could make it, they could count it. Supposedly, he once took $5,000 in small bills to toss around and roll in at home.

Hank did have a few small schemes to turn some extra cash. He started marketing his rather depressing and dogmatic recitations under the name of "Luke the Drifter." Hank seemed to enjoy the melodrama of Luke's pronouncements about life in numbers like "Pictures From Life's Other Side," which shows the tragedy of fallen lives, "Too Many Parties And Too Many Pals," which does the same, "The Funeral," which uses the burial of a black child to get to a point about God's loving all, and "Be Careful Of Stones That You Throw," which is about the obvious. And if Roy Acuff had written "Advice to Joe," a number warning Stalin about his soul, Luke and Fred Rose were ready to follow up with a bouncy recitation called "No, No, Joe," which identified a place in hell for the dictator. Hank, basically known as a honky-tonker, could have a second image through Luke. Moreover, the pseudonym helped let those who ran the juke box concessions know when to buy Hank's work. They would take everything by Hank but skip anything by Luke because the latter was more suitable for radio and retail sales than for the juke joints. Hank cut his first four "Luke" sides on 10 January 1950. He was to do at least ten more.

In 1951, Hank and Jimmy Rule, a math teacher in a private Nashville school who moonlighted as a songwriter, put out a small book called *How To Write Folk And Western Music To Sell*. The book could be ordered from Nashville for one dollar, postage paid. The advice was good, if ordinary: get a good title; remember the basic types of songs—those about love, the novelties (like "Rag Mop"), and the "Chamber of Commerce" songs (like "Tennessee Waltz"); keep a notebook; work with 4/4 time; keep it clean; and watch out for song sharks (that is, never pay to have a song published).

Hank's other gesture toward the financial world came in 1951 when he and Audrey opened a western wear store in downtown Nashville, on Commerce Street; but the impression is that this was less investment and more Audrey's keeping the pace of fame in a town where stars are involved in selling everything from records and cowboy boots to fried chicken. Chet Flippo says that the place was "decorated in true Audrey style. The outside was fake-log cabin, there was a big wagon wheel lamp hanging over the entrance, and there was a big neon sign with pictures of Hank and Audrey on it."[35] WSM broadcast the opening; Hank, Audrey, Big Bill Lister, and the Drifting Cowboys performed; and the crowds must have been impressed both by the hoopla and by the Hank and Audrey dolls that were for sale.

Music, though, was the main business of Hank Williams, and it was the source of his money. He had had to revise his band somewhat. Bob McNett, much against Hank's wishes, had left the drifting Cowboys in May 1950 to open a country music park in his native Pennsylvania. Sammy Pruett, who had been playing in Birmingham as one of Happy Wilson's Golden River Boys, rejoined the group as McNett's replacement. In July, Hillous Butrum left to join Hank Snow's band. Howard Watts, the bass player well known as "Cedric Rainwater," left Lester Flatt and Earl Scruggs to become Butrum's replacement. The band was as good as ever, and so was business.

Hank's songs were even spreading into pop, a rare accomplishment for country music at that time. Polly Bergen recorded "Honky Tonkin'." And then, in 1951, Mitch Miller assigned "Cold, Cold Heart," which Hank had recorded in December 1950, to Tony Bennett. The Bennett version was the number one song of the year, a million seller that stayed on the charts for forty-six weeks. Supposedly, Hank could hardly get past a juke box without stopping to hear Bennett do his number. Jerry Rivers explains Hank's fascination with the Bennett recording: "Hank Williams usually recorded with five musicians and played his own open rhythm guitar, used no drums and only occasional light piano for rhythm. . . . You can imagine the thrill it was to Hank when Tony Bennett recorded 'Cold, Cold Heart' with the full Hollywood treatment."[36] Hank might also have been thrilled at the thought of the fees BMI was collecting for him each time the record played. And he must have been just as pleased to find that Joni James, Frankie Laine, Jo Stafford, and Rosemary Clooney were quick to get in on his music.

Late in the summer of 1951, Hank got involved in a show put on by a wild-eyed Cajun, Dudley "Couzain Dud" LeBlanc. Dudley, described by one historian as a "mercurio-politico," had run for governor of Louisiana in 1932. His campaign statement, that "the state needs an honest man and I must make the sacrifice," did not carry him into office.[37] And he had to be content with a smaller life as president pro tempore of the state senate and as quack inventor. He had come up with "Happy Day Headache Powders" and "Dixie Dew Cough Remedy." But his greatest accomplishment was "Hadacol," a murky patent medicine that was certainly 12 percent alcohol and probably 88 percent swamp water. Hadacol was a big hit, especially across a fairly dry American South, where the belt of a good cocktail, delivered in the guise of medicine, was more than welcome. Dudley promoted it as being especially good for one's sex life, and Hadacol jokes flourished: One joke concerned a thin, exhausted man who goes to the doctor and says that his problem might be the Hadacol. When the doctor tells him to quit taking it, he responds, "It ain't me that's taking it, it's my wife." Another concerned a woman who could not sleep because of her husband's snoring and started drinking a bottle every night. She wrote to thank "Couzain Dud," saying that now she could sleep with anyone.

Dudley's great marketing trick involved the Hadacol Caravan, a traveling show of well-known performers. Dudley would schedule the show in an area that was not blessed with his medicine and announce that admission would be the box top from his product—the box top, of course, completely refundable if the show did not please. The citizenry would besiege the drugstores that had no Hadacol, and then Dudley's salesmen would arrive to supply the stuff in the nick of time.

Dudley had pulled this off very well in 1950. But he had the bad habit of overextending himself and of getting into tax trouble. By the middle of 1951, he had serious problems and was ready to sell the company. In order to give it the air of prosperity, he organized another caravan. This tour was to start in New Iberia, Louisiana, and travel several southern states and then move on to Ohio, Indiana, Kansas, and Texas. The show traveled by private train, seventeen cars' worth, and was to make forty-nine one-night stops. Dudley assembled a corps of acts including some circus groups as well as performers like Tony Martin, Candy Candido, Carmen Miranda, Dick Haymes, Jack Dempsey, and Hank Williams and the Drifting Cowboys. Stars like Bob Hope and Milton Berle had contracts for a few of the shows and flew in to perform. Dudley, of course, showed up to campaign the Louisiana stops.

The tour got started on 15 August 1951, and the fun was on for Hank and the boys. The circumstances were plush—no driving, good food, free cleaning, and no end of pretty girls. The lovelies included a troup of dancing girls from Chicago's Chez Paree and ten "Hadacol Queens," who had won the tour in regional beauty contests. The main thing, though, was the association with so many major stars and the discovery that the Cowboys were more popular with many fans than the better known figures. As Jerry Rivers points out in an interview printed in another section of this book, it was finally becoming clear that Hank and the Cowboys were a

7. Hank (top left corner) on the Hadacol Caravan in 1951. Candy Candido is second from Hank's left. *Photo courtesy of Marie Harvell.*

major attraction. The story that illustrates that point best concerns one of the two performances in Louisville. Bob Hope arrived to close out the show. Hank, who had been closing for Hadacol, preceded Hope. Hank did "Lovesick Blues" that night; and even after three encores, the crowd was still so wild over him that Hope could not get recognized on stage. Finally Hope put on a cowboy hat and went out to introduce himself as "Hank Hope"; after the show, he made it plain that he did not intend to follow Hank Williams again.

In another incident, this one in Kansas City, Hank stood his ground with Milton Berle. Supposedly, Berle had been trying to run off a photographer backstage until Hank intervened on behalf of the photographer. And during the show, Berle was being a ham and upstaging Dick Haymes's performance of "Old Man River." Hank, the story goes, sent word to Berle that he would crack his skull with a guitar if he did not behave. Berle withdrew, and Hank took his place at the end of the show.

The point here is not so much to argue that Hank Williams was more talented than comedian Bob Hope or tougher than Milton Berle, or that any one of them was a bigger attraction than the other. The comparisons do not get very far in any case because the Hadacol crowd might have been much more the audience of Hank Williams than that of the others. But what we do see here is Hank Williams holding his own with some really major stars, just as he had done on the tour of Germany two years before. Both tours, the one for R. J. Reynolds and the other for Hadacol, indicated the growing status of country music as well as that of Hank Williams.

Hank was pleased with all of it; he had proved his appeal, and he had behaved fairly well. He did not seem especially upset when the Hadacol Caravan disbanded in Dallas after only thirty-four shows. Dudley had claimed that he was selling the company for $8 million, but the sale and the company went down the drain when the government put a tax lien of $665,000 on the company and the Federal Trade Commission filed a complaint of "false, misleading, and deceptive advertising" against Hadacol. There has been some question about whether or not the performers even got paid. Hank was supposed to be getting $1,000 a week plus his expenses, but one story is that only Bob Hope ever got paid. In a letter to me, on 25 March 1982, Jerry Rivers discounts that story:

> Hank and Minnie [Pearl] had a "wedge" not available to all the artists. Most every Saturday they would fly in to the Opry in Nashville, and they would leave word that they would not return unless they were paid in full to date. Don [Helms] seems to recall that Hank may have been out a thousand or two for some of the last dates before the collapse of the tour. Furthermore, I would question that superstars such as Milton Berle, Jimmy Durante, Jack Benny, Bob

Hope, etc. would perform without advance deposit and likely full pay prior to performance time. More than likely, those artists who were "hungry" for the work were the ones who got shafted.

Paid in full or not, a confident Hank Williams was on his way back to Nashville in Henry Cannon's Beechcraft Bonanza on 18 September.

The point that comes out of this part of Hank's career is that he was potentially one of America's best-known performers and writers. He had reached practically everyone with "Cold, Cold Heart," through either his own recording or Tony Bennett's, and he had shared stages equally with the best from two realms of entertainment, Roy Acuff and Bob Hope. One can only speculate about what the television age would have done for Hank Williams; we can only imagine what a series of appearances on "The Ed Sullivan Show" would have made of his name. Another thirty years, from 1953 to 1983, which would have doubled his life span, would surely have made him as familiar as Acuff and Hope. Or, at least, he would have become so familiar if he could have lived those thirty years in good health and with a clear head.

Hank was not quite finished; he just was not able to seize the opportunities that were coming at him so fast. He missed a chance with Hollywood. Joe Pasternak offered him a bit part, as sheriff, with Jane Powell and Farley Granger in *Small Town Girl*. When Hank turned it down, MGM came through with a better offer. Jerry Rivers says it was worth about $5,000 a week.[38] Hank and Frank Walker signed the contract. The next step was to go to Hollywood to meet Dore Schary. No one says much about what happened there. Apparently, Hank was surly and, according to one source, put his feet on Schary's desk and refused to take off his hat. But I suspect that Schary could contend with such minor problems. Wesley Rose says that in addition to the above discourtesies, Hank had "otherwise acted disrespectful."[39] My suspicion is that Hank misbehaved so broadly that even Hollywood was to mark him as an undependable property. But whatever happened, Hank came home empty-handed; and MGM was later to deny that a contract had ever been issued.

Hank was in better form for a couple of TV appearances, one on "The Perry Como Show" and another on "The Kate Smith Evening Hour." A kinescope of the latter is available at The Country Music Foundation Library and Media Center in Nashville. Hank sang "Hey, Good Lookin' " on this 1952 program, and he did a decent job—although he looked especially gaunt and hollow-eyed. He did not do as well on his trip to Las Vegas. The place had seen the likes of Rex Allen and Judy Canova, but it was unfamiliar with really hard country music. Hank did not further Nashville's cause any. He was drinking heavily; at the insistence of Jim Denny, Jerry Rivers and Don Helms had driven him to Nevada, thus giving him time to dry out some. Even so, Hank was not in very good shape when he hit the stage of the Last Frontier Casino. Hard country was going to be awhile getting back to Vegas, partly because of Hank and partly because its fans were not much interested in the blackjack tables. Hank was never going back. And the episode testified once more that his opportunities were sliding away.

THE END

A neat chronology of the rise and fall of Hank Williams is impossible, just as impossible as giving a firm explanation of what did him in. We might like to see him thriving through 1951 and then declining as fame got to be too much for the country boy or as his back problem and marriage grew worse. All of these were factors; but Hank was a committed drinker on his own, and the various problems of his life only intensified a long-time bad habit.

He had grown up in a hard-drinking world. J. C. McNeil, who now lives in Mobile, explains that drink was a matter of course with Hank and several of his cousins. J. C. is now a teetotaler, but for many years he matched Hank drink for drink. He says that they were binge drinkers who did not go at it "just for a day or two but until it was gone." And he says that his own survival resulted from an understanding family who took care of him when he was drinking. Hank had no such benefit. Lillie almost always gave him a bad time when he was on a binge, and she was quick to put him in St. Jude's Hospital in Montgomery, with a "No Visitors" sign. Audrey almost always went home to her family when Hank mentioned whiskey. Occasionally Hank would turn up at his father's place in McWilliams, and sometimes one of the McNeil brothers would help take care of him. But he was usually on his own when he was hitting the bottle.

Nashville was not much help; something can be said for the idea that Hank was really a country boy fallen into that town's fast living. He never overcame his rural ways, and, to his credit probably, he never intended to. He was comfortable only around the people he knew very well, most of them relatives or members of the band. These people almost never said a hard word about him. He visited cousins like Taft and Erleen Skipper faithfully and, according to J. C. McNeil, had no trouble returning to his rural origins even after fame had set in. He became especially fond of Lon and was faithful to friends like Braxton and Ola Schuffert.

But he had trouble with the city and the success it represented to him. As already indicated, he built none of the financial empires expected of stars; he made his cash, as he had done shining shoes and delivering groceries, and he and Audrey spent it. He was not smooth socially. The dinner party circuit was not for him, either because he drank too much or because he put ketchup on practically everything he ate. His grammar was bad, as witnessed by the letters already cited. His pronunciations were sometimes off: "picture" was "pitcher," 'hired" was "hard," and "Canada" was "Canader," for example.

He read little except comic books, which he called "goof" books, and the *Billboard* charts that he could produce from his wallet in a flash. He clung to his hunting and fishing but did not go into the big-time versions of the sports. He liked to ride his horse "Highlife" out on the Franklin farm. Tennis and golf must have struck him as a little strange and fraudulent, if they struck him at all; bowling was sophisticated enough for Hank. He collected guns and sometimes carried one, a habit that startled quite a few, particularly when he was taking his drinking seriously.

Nashville is not inept at accommodating this kind of man. Good old boys can still flourish there in spite of the more or less cosmopolitan urges of the city and its music business. But being a little rough around the edges created a problem for Hank at home. Audrey, actually just as homespun as Hank, had social ambitions. She wanted the house on Franklin Road, and she was responsible for eventually expanding the three-bedroom, two-bath place to some fourteen thousand square feet including seven bedrooms and six-and-one-half baths, a ballroom and a Polynesian garden with pool. She was to design an all white "angel" room for herself, along with a bar covered with hearts. She wanted the store on Commerce Street, the clothes, and the social life that came with the success she had helped accumulate for her husband.

The conflict of styles was not their only problem. Hank did not help the marriage by singing "Cold, Cold Heart" and "Your Cheatin' Heart" with so much sincerity. Fans had a good idea who he was singing about. And Hank and Audrey fought over who was responsibile for his success. The talent was obviously his, but she had sold him to the Roses. Women were also a problem; they flocked to Hank, and he found them hard to refuse. Taft Skipper, Hank's cousin, claims that the men in the family were always bad about that. Hereditary or not, Hank's womanizing certainly brought down the wrath of Miss Audrey; and Hank seemed to have a little trouble handling the guilt that came with his affairs. Audrey was quick to get even with him, and she returned the unfaithfulness. Her carryings-on in Hank's absence became notorious. They tortured Hank, especially on the road, where he seemed to do his hardest drinking. Sometimes he would phone her over and over, usually finding her out. Then he would drink harder until he returned to Nashville for either a stint at Madison Sanitarium or a major fight there on Franklin Road. At least one of those fights included some gunfire, another found Hank breaking out a storm door with his guitar, and another involved his throwing her new wardrobe into the yard.

A basic element of Hank's personality is probably confirmed in his domestic mess, in his infidelities, and in the effect of her infidelities. Hank, practically from beginning to end, was insecure. His case is classic, a

Nashville version of what happened to people like Marilyn Monroe, perhaps even John Belushi, in Hollywood. He came out of a shaky family; his father was gone for most of his childhood, and moving was nearly an annual matter; he moved from a domineering mother to a domineering wife; and he won fame and success that he did not altogether understand, that he was not sure he really deserved.

His matriarchal background seems to have kept him from making good friendships with men, and his tough upbringing made him suspicious of all strangers. His lack of pretense was attractive, but practically everyone who knew Hank found him difficult at times. Lum York, one of his bass players, says in a Roger Williams interview that "a lot of people didn't like Hank as a person. . . . You had to be around him to understand him."[40] Bob McNett found Hank "abrupt." On the Good Vibrations recording of Jim Owen's *Hank Williams . . . The Man, The Legend,* McNett describes the way he was hired. Bob, who had never met Hank Williams, was working for Patsy Montana when Hank came up to him backstage at the Louisiana Hayride and said, "Can you take the introduction to 'Lovesick Blues'?" That was it; Bob played that same night and became a Drifting Cowboy. In Jay Caress's book, McNett describes the way he was fired when Hank disbanded the Hayride crew: "Hank came offstage quickly after a Louisiana Hayride appearance and said, 'I'm going to Texas tomorrow. If I call you, you have a job. If I don't you don't.' "[41] Ed Linn refers to Hank's "hard core of bitterness" and then quotes Jim Denny:

> I never knew anybody I liked better than Hank, but I don't think I ever really got close to him. I don't know if anyone really could. He was so bitter. He thought everybody, in the final analysis, had some sort of angle on him. I suppose that's why everybody has misinterpreted him. Because despite it all, he was very kind and generous and very determined to be the top man in his profession.[42]

Sol Handwerger, publicity director of MGM Records, says that Hank "was a most friendly person—provided he believed in your sincerity; if he did not, he could be cold and blunt." Handwerger saw Hank through a publicity tour of New York and found him "cynical and suspicious of big cities."[43] Roger Williams sums it up well when he says that the paradox of Hank was that the "insecurity and depth of feeling that nurtured his creative genius also drove him to self-ruin."[44]

Hank's personality and his physical situation seemed to nurture his bad habits. He was taking painkillers for his back problem. And he overdid the medication. In addition, Hank's binge drinking meant that he was either not drinking at all or he was completely ruined. His binges grew closer and closer together until they practically started merging just before his death.

He had a low tolerance for alcohol and got drunk so quickly that it was almost impossible to catch him at it. Even when he was being watched carefully, adoring fans or hangers-on had a bad way of getting some whiskey to Hank. He could even get it from the attendants at the sanitarium. He hid airline bottles in his boots; supposedly he once tried to bribe Hillous Butrum for drinks, promising Hillous a recording contract, swearing he could get it for him because he had gotten one for Audrey. That he almost never ate when he was drinking helped wreck his health. Sammy Pruett says, "I've seen him drunk to where he couldn't hold water on his stomach. He'd be foaming at the mouth like a goddamned mad dog."[45] Hank was about six-one and probably never weighed much over one hundred and forty pounds; usually he weighed much less. His suits had to be specially altered; the band called him "gimly-ass," "Bones," or "lovesick"; Chet Flippo says Hank could change clothes in a shotgun barrel.[46]

Obviously, the whiskey was not a problem that sprang up with fame. He had been at it a long time, practically since childhood. He had been in the Prattville, Alabama, hospital in 1945. He had been to Madison Sanitarium, "the Hut," as early as the fall of 1949. In the fall of 1950, he had been drunk at the Hippodrome in Baltimore and had introduced Don Helms four times. He was drunk at that Last Frontier performance in Las Vegas. He fell off the stage in Peterborough, Ontario. The crowd was angry, and the Mounties had to see Hank safely out of town. Chet Flippo has discovered that Hank went into North Louisiana Sanitarium on 21 May 1951, taken there by ambulance and treated by Dr. G. H. Cassity with Demerol, vitamin B, and Vitadex. He was complaining of severe back pain; x-rays revealed the *Spina Bifida Occulta,* and Dr. Cassity fitted him with a lumbosacral brace. He was discharged on 24 May.[47]

The various treatments could not rescue Hank. He would still go on sprees, hole up at the Hermitage Hotel, and shoot up the room a little; or he would check into the Tulane Hotel, get drunk, and supposedly run naked down the hall after a lady wrestler similarly out of her clothes. One report has it that he tried to shoot a maid in Chattanooga and that he shot the portraits off the wall in a Birmingham hotel. His worst hotel episode occurred in 1952, at the New York Savoy, where in a drunken fit he pushed Frank Walker down against a radiator; he left Walker unconscious and apparently never realized exactly what happened. When in trouble, Hank often passed himself off as "Herman P. Willis" or as George Morgan, whom he disliked because his hit "Candy Kisses' competed with Hank's songs. In addition, police indulged him because of his fame.

Hank was becoming less and less dependable, and bookings were harder and harder to come by. His back problem had been aggravated by a fall he took trying to jump a gully while squirrel hunting with Jerry Rivers. Jerry had had to carry him back to the car. Not long thereafter, on 13 December 1951, Hank was admitted to the Vanderbilt Hospital for back surgery. He came out on Christmas Eve, wearing a back brace and taking more of the painkillers that were to aggravate his miserably rundown health. And, according to Rivers, he was never quite himself again:

> Hank began to indicate periods of mental depression and personal conflict in addition to the discomfort and pain from his injury, from which he never fully recovered. After his operation and subsequent convalescence Hank never seemed to regain the close personal relationship with the band and his friends that he had once enjoyed, and all of us had shared.[48]

The band was already playing with Ray Price during the time that was left by Hank's cancellations and by his stay in the hospital.

Hank's surgery, and the fact that he had to use a walking cane briefly, did not soften Audrey. They fought on; and one believable story has it that Hank shot at her on New Year's Eve 1951. He moved out a few days later, on 3 January 1952. Audrey filed for separate maintenance on 10 January. Hank could do little in response to her charge of cruel and inhuman treatment. She wanted nearly everything he had, including Bocephus, and half of everything he was going to get. He was not to go near her under any circumstances. Hank was just too broken down to fight it all; he felt that he had to accept the terms and that he had to drink more.

His worst performance was close at hand. He was scheduled to appear on January 29 and 30 in a Richmond, Virginia, show promoted by B. C. Gates. The fans there were voting a "Hillbilly of the Month," and Gates was bringing in the winners. Hank was really roaring drunk by matinee time on the twenty-ninth, and Ray Price had to stall the crowd by singing, by apologizing for Hank, and then by declaring a thirty-minute intermission. Hank finally came on to stumble through a couple of songs; he was so bad that many fans started demanding refunds. Price sang again. Then Hank gave it a second try, first explaining that he had had back surgery and then threatening to show the crowd his scars or to have a doctor come and verify his problem. The show was a disaster, and a second show was still to come that night. Some food, coffee, and a long walk in the cold straightened him out enough to get him through the next performance. But he was no hit. Howard Watts was so disgusted that he pulled out for Nashville.

The *Richmond Times-Dispatch* ran a scathing review the following day (30 January 1952). The author of the review, Edith Lindeman, noted that Hank's spine "most certainly was not holding him erect. He sang 'Cold, Cold Heart,' but did not get some of the words in the right places. Then he sang 'Lonesome Blues,' with a good deal of off-key yodeling." The balance of the review was not much kinder.

Edith Lindeman, though, produced a good effect. Jim Denny had sent Charlie Sanders to Richmond to keep Hank straight for the shows. Charlie did not earn his keep in the first instance, but the review produced new zeal, and he got rid of Hank's booze and got the singer some medical attention, which probably involved some Demerol, which allowed Hank to sleep off much of his problem of the moment. Hank was on his feet for the 30 January show. After Ray Price's introduction, he came on to do "Mind Your Own Business," dedicated to Edith Lindeman. The crowd loved it; and for one of the last few times, Hank was really in charge of his audience.

Nashville, though, held little for him. He had to face up to the divorce, which became final on 29 May 1952. Audrey got what she wanted including half of all royalties still to come. She would avoid scrupulously the remarriage that would have meant forfeiture of her claims on Hank. He got his cars, the farm at Franklin with its considerable mortgage, the clothing store, visitation rights, and a bill for $4,000 from Audrey's lawyer, Carmack Cochran. Hank signed over power of attorney to Sam Hunt and then disappeared briefly; he told Ray Price later that he had been hospitalized in Lexington, Kentucky; the indication may be that he was in the federal narcotics hospital there.

The scene was pretty wild out on Natchez Trace in Nashville, where Hank was living with Price. Hank was often drunk and/or hauling women in and out of the place. His guns, cigarettes, whiskey, and drugs made him a constant menace. Price finally had to move out on him. Hank did a bad tour of California, where he stumbled through shows in Bakersfield, San Diego, Long Beach, and Oakland. Minnie Pearl was just coming off stage in San Diego when she saw Hank enter the auditorium:

> I got off just in time to see this pathetic, emaciated, haunted-looking, tragic figure of a man being assisted through the stage door—not too gently—by a male nurse. The male nurse had undoubtedly had enough problems with Hank to warrant being impatient with him, but it upset me to see my friend handled that way. . . . I ran to him and hugged him. He threw his arms around me and clung to me, crying. I tried to comfort him, to tell him that everything was going to be all right, just as you would try to comfort a child crying in the dark. No one will ever know what tortured dreams he had. Perhaps all of life was a bad dream to Hank. By this time he was killing himself with drugs and alcohol, and his mind had undoubtedly been affected.[49]

Minnie spent much of that evening trying to sober Hank up.

Trips to the sanitarium were almost routine by this time. Nothing seemed to make any difference; he was on his last legs. He did manage to record "Jambalaya" in June, and in July he was able to cut "You Win Again." But he had trouble making his Opry performances; and finally, after he missed a Friday night WSM show, The Grand Ole Opry fired Hank Williams. Jim Denny, who had done as much as anyone to keep Hank going, phoned the word on 11 August. Hank had been on the Opry a little over three years. Apparently, he was not startled when Denny called. He was not expecting much, and he began to get ready to head back to Montgomery. From there he would go on to Shreveport, where he would return to the Hayride, for $250 a week. Johnny Wright, husband of Kitty Wells and partner of Jack Anglin, drove Hank out of Nashville; he stopped only long enough for Hank to get his last check and a bottle.

The next several weeks were really crowded. By 15 August, Hank was recovering in a fishing camp on Lake Martin, northeast of Montgomery and near the Creek Indian town called "Kowaliga." The name, of course, stimulated one of his most famous songs, "Kaw-Liga." Two days later he was in trouble in a small town nearby. Police Chief Winfred Patterson says that he arrested Hank in the Alexander City Hotel on 17 August 1952. According to Patterson, in an *Alabama Journal* interview of 20 February 1971, Hank "more or less was having DTs (delirium tremens). He was running up and down the hall, yelling that somebody was whipping old ladies and he was going to stop them."

The episode must have slowed Hank a bit, for he turned up at his mother's in Montgomery next. She put him in St. Jude's Hospital, where he continued a relationship with Father Harold Purcell, whom he had met during an earlier stay in the hospital, probably in 1950. Father Purcell worked with spastic children there. Lillie had practically eliminated Hank's visitors; and Purcell, who died in the fall of 1952, came to be of much consolation to Hank. Purcell's dream was to have a hospital for spastic children, and Hank contributed $1,000 to the fund for a fifty-bed addition to St. Jude's for that purpose. Several people have claimed that Hank pledged $400 a month additionally; I cannot document that, but it is well known that Fred Rose encouraged Hank and other performers to make such contributions.

Purcell and St. Jude's must have helped Hank a little, for on 20 September he was back on the Hayride, and on the twenty-third he was in Nashville, at the Castle Studios for his last recording session. He cut four sides: "I Could Never Be Ashamed Of You," "Your Cheatin' Heart," "Kaw-Liga," and "Take These Chains From My Heart." Adversity was still producing some pretty good music.

A few days later, Hank was back at Lillie's. Allen Rankin, the *Montgomery Advertiser* columnist who followed Hank so closely, reported on 28 September 1952 that Hank's two Cadillacs were parked at 318 North McDonough, that neither of them was being driven. Rankin went on, "Inside, Hank, too, lay still for a while. He had slipped on the pavement, hit his head and developed blood poison." A little over a week later, on 8

October, Hank wired Fred Rose: "FRED PLEASE SEND MY CHECKS TO ME IN CARE OF MY MOTHER MRS WILLIAMS 318 NORTH MCDONOUGH MONTGOMERY ALA."

One can imagine that things were tough at Lillie's. She was always hard to deal with, but an additional problem turned up. Lillie had taken in a woman, identified as "Bobbie Jett" in a *Montgomery Advertiser* story of 31 January 1968, who claimed to be carrying Hank's child. In one of her more generous acts, Lillie saw the woman through confinement and childbirth, and she saw to the child's proper adoption. But regardless of her helpfulness, things could not have been too easy for Hank. And they must have been especially difficult when he brought home his new girl friend, Billie Jean Jones Eshliman, to meet Lillie.

Billie Jean was a strikingly beautiful and naive telephone operator, the daughter of a Bossier City policeman. She had quit school in the twelfth grade and had married an airman, Harrison Eshliman, on 4 June 1949. Their child, Jerry Lynn, was born on 11 March the following year; but the marriage was fading fast, and Billie Jean had shown up in Nashville with Faron Young, who had been performing on the Louisiana Hayride. Hank met Billie Jean backstage at the Opry and, as the story goes, immediately pledged to marry her. He and Faron double-dated that night; and before the evening was out, they had switched girl friends. Faron claims that Hank got about "half stoned" that evening, called him into a bedroom of the Natchez Trace house, pointed a pistol at him, and said: "I don't want no hard feelings out of you, but I'm in love with Billie Jean." Faron conceded quickly. Hank took Billie Jean, and she must have brought him solace as he exited Nashville. But she must have been angry when she got to the Montgomery boardinghouse to meet her future mother-in-law. What happened when Billie Jean, Lillie, and Bobbie Jett were all on the same premises remains another mystery in the life of Hank Williams. Billie Jean left North McDonough Street for Shreveport, without her boyfriend.

Hank, though, patched up the romance as he began his work on the Hayride. The couple were married by Justice of the Peace P. E. Burton in Minden, Louisiana, on 18 October 1952.[50] The story of their wedding night is the traditional one of complications; the couple's car supposedly ran out of gas after the wedding and they had to hitch a ride home. Hank reportedly invited their benefactor to come along for the celebration; the gentleman declined discreetly. However, the events of that night were all preliminary. Hank and Billie Jean were going to marry again the next day, twice as a matter of fact, at a three o'clock matinee and at a seven o'clock evening performance at the New Orleans Civic Auditorium. Oscar Davis, probably best known for bringing Elvis and Colonel Parker together, promoted the show, sold out the fourteen thousand seats twice at prices ranging from seventy-five cents to a dollar and a half, and solicited wedding gifts for the newlyweds from local merchants. One minister refused to perform the ceremony, either because the marriage had been pronounced once already or because Hank had gotten into the champagne too soon. But L. R. Shelton, pastor of the First Baptist Church of Algiers, Louisiana, was there to marry the couple before the admiring throngs who got to hear a Hank Williams concert as well as see the wedding. Hank, though, was in bad shape when it was all over, and he had to cancel the planned honeymoon to Cuba. He just could not travel, and he and Billie Jean honeymooned at the Jung Hotel in New Orleans.

The new husband worked the Hayride and toured the area for concerts. Billie Jean traveled with him some; and in a Shreveport interview with Wesley Pruden, she discussed her naiveté:

> I was awful young and didn't know much. I hadn't ever been anywhere, or done anything. When I married Hank, I hadn't ever stayed in a hotel. I didn't even have a suitcase. We stayed in the good hotels, but I still carried my shoes in one hand and all my things in a big Kotex box. I didn't even know enough to get another kind of box; it didn't embarrass me, and I guess Hank thought I was kind of cute. He never said anything. He carried my iron. I didn't even know they made travel irons, and I'd never heard of valets in hotels.[51]

She was naive about more than Kotex boxes: Her divorce from Harrison Eshliman, filed on 25 September 1952, was not final until 28 October 1952.[52] Hank had married Audrey fifty days before the end of the sixty-day reconciliation period prescribed in her divorce decree; he had married Billie Jean ten days before she was divorced from her first husband. The rush to marry was to cause Billie Jean a lot of grief in her claims on Hank's estate.

Billie Jean worked hard at straightening Hank out; she tried to see that he ate and that he did not drink. But Hank was so deeply into booze and pills that he could not be stopped, not even by a new bride. Chet Flippo had discovered that she sent him to the North Louisiana Sanitarium on 31 October, again on 27 November, and still again on 11 December.[53] The trips did not help much, and Hank's career was slipping badly. He was so undependable that local promoters would not handle him. He had to make all of his own arrangements. The star who had been getting fifteen hundred for a show now had to take whatever he could hustle. He botched a good many of those shows: he was nearly mobbed in Lafayette, Louisiana, for refusing to sing "Lovesick Blues," and Lillie had pulled him off the stage in Biloxi, Mississippi, to be flown home to her care in Montgomery.

As if his problems were not intense enough, Hank got involved with a fake doctor, Horace Raphol "Toby" Marshall, whom he had met in Oklahoma City. Born in Michigan in 1901, Toby had moved west to do time in San Quentin for forgery and armed robbery. He had gone into Oklahoma

8.   Hank and Billie Jean at their New Orleans wedding in 1952. *Photo courtesy of Bruce Gidoll.*

State Penitentiary on 15 October 1950 on a three-year sentence for forgery but was paroled on 9 October 1951. He was a high school dropout who claimed a B.S. degree, an M.A., and a "D.S.C." He had bought the latter for $35 from the Chicago School of Applied Science. According to Jay Caress, he had had the diploma printed "D.S.C." to stand for "Doctor of Science and Psychology."[54] Toby was a reformed alcoholic who claimed that he could help Hank. Actually, though, he was little more than a drug contact who, with a series of fraudulent prescriptions, some of them written in the name of a Dr. C. W. Lemon, kept Hank in amphetamines, Seconal, chloral hydrate, and morphine. His last prescription for Hank, probably written when the singer was in Oklahoma in December 1952, was for twenty-four grains of chloral hydrate, a sedative that depresses the central nervous system. Hank filled and then refilled the prescription in Montgomery. Within much less than a month he would be dead and his family would receive a bill for $736.39 from Dr. Marshall.

The frantic activity of the last few months slowed somewhat just before Christmas. Hank and Billie Jean went to Georgiana to see Hank's cousin, Taft Skipper, and his wife Erleen who still talk about how lovely and courteous Billie Jean was. They arrived late on Sunday the twenty-first and went to church with the Skippers. Hank turned down requests to sing that night, but the next morning he did a few songs at Taft's store; one of them was "The Log Train," a fine number that Hank had written for his father and one that was not issued until 1982. Hank and Billie Jean then went on to Lillie's in Montgomery. On Christmas Day, they drove over to McWilliams to see Lon, who had gone to Selma for the holiday. Hank wanted to show "The Log Train" to his father, but he had to be content to leave some gifts and return to Lillie's. On Saturday the twenty-seventh, Taft and his niece Mary Skipper drove up to Montgomery and went with Hank and Billie Jean to the Blue-Gray football game. Taft and Mary had good seats down close to the field; but Hank and Billie Jean were in the upper stands, and the cold sent them home at halftime. The Gray team, led by Ray Graves, went on to beat Ted Marchibroda and the Blue squad in Hank's absence.

The next night, Sunday the twenty-eighth, Hank performed for the Montgomery chapter of the American Federation of Musicians (AFM). The group was raising money for Charlie Davis, a radio announcer and drummer, who was recovering from polio. In his column in the *Montgomery Advertiser* the next day, Allen Rankin described Hank as "a thin, tired-looking ex-country boy with a guitar. He got up and sang (or howled) a number of his tunes that started out to be hillbilly but ended up as 'pop' numbers played and sung by every band in the land." Like a good many writers then and now, Rankin did not seem sure of how seriously he should take Hank Williams. But his tone would change in a few days, and very shortly he would be ghostwriting Lillie's book on Hank.

Hank was well received by the AFM group that night, and he was thinking almost certainly of a possible return to The Grand Ole Opry. Some believe that he attached a possible reconciliation with Audrey to those thoughts of Nashville, but no real evidence of that has surfaced. At any rate, he had accepted a chance to play a New Year's Day show in Canton, Ohio. A. V. Bamford of Nashville had booked it for him. It would be Hank's first date out of the South since he left the Opry, and, of course, it would be a step back to the stage of Ryman Auditorium. Moreover, Hank had a good feeling about Canton; he had played well there on 27 April 1951, at the height of his success. The Drifting Cowboys were already booked into Cleveland with Ray Price, but Don Helms agreed to come to Canton and to bring with him guitarist Autry Inman.

The thirtieth of December brought snow to Montgomery and that meant no flying for Hank. He hired Charles Harold Carr, an eighteen-year-old Auburn freshman who sometimes worked for his father at the Lee Street Taxi Company, to drive the baby-blue Cadillac convertible for the twenty hours it would take to get to Canton. Hank was in rough shape. He had been in a fight sometime during the visit home. His habit was to return to old haunts while in Montgomery, and he was usually eager to display his success. The bragging had gotten him into more than one brawl. He was to leave Montgomery this time with his left arm, either sprained or broken, in a bandage.

He and Carr took Highway 31 to Birmingham, where they spent the first night. Then it was up Highway 11 to Chattanooga and on into Knoxville. Hank was drinking beer and taking chloral hydrate while Carr drove. In Knoxville Hank and Carr caught a 3:30 P.M. plane for Ohio. But bad weather forced the flight back to Knoxville, where it landed at 5:57 P.M. The two travelers then headed for the Andrew Johnson Hotel, where Carr checked them in at 7:08 P.M. Assistant hotel manager Dan McCrary talked to a nervous Charles Carr but did not see Hank, who was carried up to a room by porters.

Carr ordered two steaks, but Hank was unable to eat. Dr. P. H. Cardwell arrived and noted that Hank was extremely drunk and that he was carrying several capsules. Cardwell gave Hank two B12 shots; each contained one-quarter grain of morphine. The B12 was probably for the vitamin deficiency standard in alcoholics. The morphine could have been for Hank's back pain, but it is also a recognized treatment for pulmonary edema—excess fluid in the lungs. Hank's fight might have caused the edema, but the condition is symptomatic of drug overdose as well. It seems that Hank was subject to the problem on both counts. Why didn't Carr and Cardwell get Hank to a hospital? Perhaps they were frightened or perhaps they were disgusted with their obviously inebriated patient. Besides, Carr still seemed intent on getting Hank to Canton in time to rest before the show; he was well aware that Hank's contract carried a one-thousand-dollar default penalty. He got the porters to help dress Hank and then carry the singer back out to the Cadillac convertible. Hank showed no sign of life except for a slight cough when he was picked up. Carr checked them out of the Andrew Johnson at 10:45 P.M.

At 11:45 P.M. Carr was stopped for reckless driving near Blaine, Tennessee. He had been trying to pass a car and had nearly run head on into Patrol Corporal Swann H. Kitts. The patrolman questioned Carr about the lifeless-looking man on the back seat. Carr explained that Hank had been drinking and had taken a sedative. Kitts seemed to accept the explanation and led the travelers into Rutledge, Tennessee, where Carr paid his $25 fine to Magistrate Olin H. Marshall. Carr then drove on toward Canton until about dawn on New Year's Day when, in Oak Hill, West Virginia, he decided to stop and check on Hank. He pulled into Glen Burdette's Pure Oil, now a Union '76 station, and reached back to find his passenger cold. Patrolman Howard Jamey came to the scene and arranged for Hank to be taken to the Oak Hill Hospital, where he was pronounced dead on arrival. The body was taken to the Tyree Funeral Home and embalmed.

The show went on in Canton. The master of ceremonies, Cliff Rodgers, a local disc jockey, arranged a single spotlight on an empty stage. Rodgers stepped into the light and made the startling announcement that the twenty-nine-year-old singer was dead. The audience, aware of Hank's habit of missing shows, laughed at what they took to be the ultimate in bad excuses. But Rodgers assured them of the truth and then stepped out of the spot. The cast, gathered behind the curtain, sang "I Saw The Light," with more than a few of the four thousand fans joining in. The regular show then went on with performances by Hawkshaw Hawkins, Homer and Jethro, and June Webb.

Such was the day of Hank Williams's death. The details of the events in and around Knoxville are fortuitously available to us for one reason: When Captain John Davis of the Tennessee Highway Patrol heard of the death and of the involvement of Patrolman Kitts, he ordered Kitts to investigate the details of Hank's passage through Knoxville. Kitts made a thorough investigation and filed a handwritten report which includes the details cited here. The report was made public, about a month before this book went to press, in a *Knoxville Journal* story of 15 December 1982.

In the last part of his report, Kitts makes these interesting comments:

Carr said he was driving Hank Williams. I noticed Williams and asked Carr if he could be dead, as he was pale and blue looking. But he said Williams had drank 6 bottles of beer and a doctor had given him two injections to help him sleep.

He asked me not to wake him up as he was very sick and looked that way. I had him (Carr) to stop at Rutledge. I wrote him a ticket (for reckless driving) at 12:30. He was tried before a Justice of the Peace, O. H. Marshall, and was fined $25 and costs.

I talked with him about Williams' condition in the presence of Sheriff J. N. Antrican and Marshall. I thought he (Carr) was a little nervous over paying the fine and he asked us not to bother Williams.

Carr had a soldier with him at the time he was in Rutledge. He paid the fine, thanked us and left at about 1 A.M.

After investigating this matter, I think that Williams was dead when he was dressed and carried out of the hotel. Since he was drunk and was given the injections and could have taken some capsules earlier, with all this he couldn't have lasted over an hour and a half or two hours.

A man drunk or doped will make some movement if you move them. A dead man will make a coughing sound if they [*sic*] are lifted around. Taking all this into consideration, he must have died in Knoxville at the hotel.[55]

Obviously, there is nothing scientific about Kitt's diagnosis of Hank Williams that night. But the officer's speculation reminds us of the terrifying possibility that Charles Carr, who checked out of a hotel less than three hours after he had checked in, frantically drove a dead Hank Williams out of Knoxville, picked up a still unidentified soldier along the way (a soldier who mysteriously disappeared before Carr got to Oak Hill), practically ran a patrolman off the highway, paid a quick fine, and then drove on until dawn finally convinced him to stop and face the situation. The other possibility has life slowly leaving the comatose body of Hank Williams somewhere between Knoxville and Oak Hill.

Many agree with Kitts that Hank died on 31 December 1952. Many others prefer to have Hank living into the early hours of New Year's Day of 1953. Though perhaps Kitts is closest to the truth, we will have to be content knowing only that the sad finish of Hank Williams either ended one year or began another.

DENOUEMENT

On her arrival in Oak Hill, Lillie Williams demanded an autopsy, which was performed by pathologist Dr. Ivan M. Malinin. The autopsy revealed alcoholic cardiomyopathy, heart disease traceable directly to excessive drinking. On 11 January 1953, the *Montgomery Advertiser* quoted the Fayette County coroner's jury report to Magistrate Virgil Lyons: "We the jury find on January 10 that Hank Williams died of a severe heart condition and hemorrhage. No evidence was found of foul play." The blood contained alcohol, but, according to Lyons, no indication of narcotics or other drugs. The hemorrhages were in the heart and in the neck; and because they were not consistent with the heart failure, one might suspect that they were the result of the Montgomery fight. But Hank had lived so carelessly that he could have died from any number of causes; and apparently the autopsy, performed on a body already embalmed, was neither very sophisticated nor very thorough.

Lillie sent the body home to Montgomery, to her place on North McDonough Street, and began planning the funeral for 4 January 1953. She wanted to have it at the Highland Baptist Church, but obviously the sanctuary was not large enough. The confusion was intense, with Audrey and Billie Jean both at the house, not to mention Lillie and Lon. Billie Jean was to have almost no say in the proceedings, and Lon would not even get to sit with the family. Fortunately, A. V. Bamford, the Nashville promoter who had booked Hank into Canton, showed up to arrange the funeral. The city donated use of its auditorium, and Bamford scheduled a two-thirty funeral for the fourth. About twenty-five thousand people showed up for what Roger Williams says "is regarded in Montgomery as the greatest emotional plunge that city has taken since the inauguration of Jefferson Davis as president of the confederacy."[56]

Some three thousand of the mourners went inside the auditorium when the doors opened at one-fifteen. A good many of those had time to file by and gaze at Hank Williams, laid out in an open silver casket, holding a small white Bible. Those who could not get in listened over loudspeakers outside or picked up the service on one of the two radio stations that carried it.

Ernest Tubb began by singing "Beyond The Sunset." A Negro quartet, the Southwind Singers, followed; they especially pleased the two hundred or so blacks seated in the auditorium's balcony. Dr. Henry Lyon of the Highland Baptist Church read the Twenty-third Psalm. He preached briefly, saying that Hank had gone to the last round-up, that his funeral sermon had actually been preached already in his songs. Roy Acuff—with Red Foley, Carl Smith, Webb Pierce, and many others in the chorus—sang "I Saw The Light." Foley sang "Peace In The Valley," and the Statesmen Quartet finished with "Precious Memories."

Hank was buried in Montgomery's Oakwood Cemetery Annex, an unpretentious place within easy walking distance of the state capitol building. A good bit of urban blight borders the cemetery. The police department and the city jail are nearby; bail-bonding companies cluster in the area. But Hank's plot, to which he was moved on 17 January 1953, is on a soft knoll that allows a fairly scenic view. His monument was unveiled during a Hank Williams Memorial celebration on 20-21 September 1954.

9. Hank's grave in Montgomery's Oakwood Cemetery Annex. The slab directly beside his plot is Lillie's. The last of the three slabs beyond Lillie's grave is Audrey's. *Photo by E. Denny.*

The affair, attended by an estimated sixty thousand, included dances played by Ray Price, Pee Wee King, and Jim Reeves; a huge parade with many Opry stars—but featuring Lillie in Hank's car, while the Alabama Air National Guard did some fancy flying overhead; and a memorial show starring Roy Acuff. Jimmie Davis, former governor of Louisiana and a good country songwriter, placed a wreath on Hank's grave at the unveiling of the tomb.

The marble monument, designed by Willie Gayle of the Henley Memorial Company, is distinct without being overwhelming. An upright slab is inscribed HANK WILLIAMS. Just below the name is the two-line refrain of "I Saw The Light." A cowboy hat rests at the foot of the slab near a number of marble squares inscribed with the names of some of Hank's songs. The Luke the Drifter square is in the center, as though Willie Gayle thought we should remember Hank as a moralist. On the back of the slab is the poem written by the divorcee, would-be widow, Audrey:

> Thank you for all the love you gave me
> There could be no one stronger
> Thank you for the many beautiful songs
> They will live long and longer
> Thank you for being a wonderful father to Lycrecia
> She loved you more than you knew
> Thank you for our precious son
> And thank God he looks so much like you
> And now can I say:
> There are no words in the dictionary
> That can express my love for you
> Someday beyond the blue
>
> Audrey Williams

A separate slab over the grave itself is marked simply with the name and the dates; a guitar and a pair of cowboy boots are carved into it. The slab, with all of its corners chipped away by souvenir hunters, is flanked by two urns and by two marble benches. The urns were originally cowboy boots, but vandals destroyed them.

Hank left no will, no life insurance. His estate was negligible; he had a cashier's check on the First National Bank of Montgomery for $4,000, and about $9,000 worth of personal items. He had been making little money, and Audrey was getting half of that. But his name and his songs were going to be worth quite a bit. The *Billboard* people were compiling their 1952 charts just as Hank died. He had three songs well ranked: "Jambalaya" (3), "Half As Much" (11), and "Honky Tonk Blues" (28). His music was to be even more popular during the first year after his death. The *Billboard* chart for 1953 had "Kaw-Liga" first, "Your Cheatin' Heart" second, and "Take

These Chains From My Heart" ninth. Obviously, the estate was going to call for a fight.

Billie Jean lost out fast. The *Alabama Journal* of 14 January 1953 reported that Louisiana Judge James Brolin, the judge who had put off signing Billie Jean's divorce decree, ruled that her marriage to Hank was illegal. But that did not keep her from going on the road as "Mrs. Hank Williams." Audrey went on the road under the same name; in fact, she was playing a "Kaw-Liga Day" celebration near Lake Martin on 19 March 1953. The two widows ended up in court that spring. Billie Jean, perhaps dismayed by Judge Brolin's decision, accepted a $30,000 settlement whereby she gave up all claims to the name and the estate. Audrey, who was sending a weekly FTD wreath to Hank's grave, had the widowhood to herself. In July, a Davidson County (Tennessee) Chancery Court gave her half of Hank's estate; near the end of August, Lillie was awarded the other half. Hank's child by Bobbie Jett was not granted a claim because Alabama does not allow illegitimate offspring to inherit from their natural parents, and the adoptive parents did not want to expose the child's identity in the law suits that would have been necessary to contest that law. Lillie was appointed administratrix of the estate and legal guardian of Hank Jr. when the boy was in Alabama. Otherwise, the child and his goods were in Audrey's care. Lillie, though, did not last long. She died in her sleep on 26 February 1955. She is buried to Hank's left, within inches of the border of his plot. She seemed to be anxious to beat Audrey to Hank's side, anxious to prove the statement she had made in her book: "Hank's mother was always his first girl and he never forgot it."[57]

Hank's sister, Irene Williams Smith now of Dallas, then became administratrix and Alabama guardian of Hank Jr. Her term was badly scarred. Audrey and Hank Jr. sued her in September 1966 for return of some of Hank's personal items. Then came another mess. Irene had sold the renewal rights for Hank's music to Acuff-Rose for $25,000 in March 1963. The original rights were not due to expire for another ten years, and many suspected that the price was ridiculous. Audrey and Hank Jr., just out of court on the first case, sued again in the fall of 1967. But Judge Richard Emmett upheld the original renewal contract in a decree of 30 January 1968. Irene's term as administratrix came to an end in August of 1969 when she was arrested crossing the border at Laredo with what the *Birmingham Post-Herald* on 2 August 1969 identified as "one of the largest amounts of pure cocaine ever to enter the U. S." She was sentenced to seven years in the federal jail in Alderson, West Virginia. Attorney Robert B. Stewart took over direction of the estate from that point.

The other jail sentence involved in the aftermath went to Toby Marshall. While prescribing for Hank, Toby had also prescribed for his wife, Fay, who lived in Albuquerque. She died on 3 March 1953. Governor Johnston

Murray sprang to action and revoked Toby's parole almost immediately. Toby stayed in jail for just over a year, until 1 May 1954. But the gates of the Oklahoma State Penitentiary were to swing open for him again in September 1956 when he started another year's sentence on two charges for unlawful possession of barbiturates.

Audrey had gone home to the place on Franklin Road and stayed busy being Hank's widow, adding to the house and directing the career of Hank Jr. by shaping the child into the image of his father. She taught him both Hank's voice and Hank's songs. Hank Jr. played his first show at age eight; he made The Grand Ole Opry at eleven and "The Ed Sullivan Show" at fourteen. He left his mother in 1967, but by that time he had assumed many of his father's problems as well as much of his talent. A very serious injury in a mountain-climbing accident in 1975 seemed to straighten him out.[58] He has, of course, successfully taken up his own brand of country music and seems to have adjusted well to his famous name. He lives in Cullman, Alabama, near his half-sister, Lycrecia Morris, who is married to a member of his band.

Billie Jean married Johnny Horton in 1954 and seemed to drop out of the Hank Williams picture for many years. She was widowed again in 1960 when Horton was killed in a Texas automobile accident. She got involved in the Williams estate in a suit over the MGM movie *Your Cheatin' Heart,* which had premiered at Montgomery's Paramount Theatre on 4 November 1964. Audrey had been the movie's technical adviser and, it seems, had allowed little footage to be wasted on the competition. Hank's marriage to Billie Jean was deftly ignored in the film, and the offended party sued MGM for $4.5 million in October 1969. She lost the case but sued again in March 1972. Her new case was against MGM, CBS, and Storer Broadcasting. CBS and Storer became involved because of television showings of the film (Storer owned WAGA, the CBS affiliate in Atlanta). In a peculiar decision, the jury declared Billie Jean the legal widow, said she was libeled, but awarded no damages. Billie Jean was persistent; she sued again on 4 May 1972. She took the 9 March decision for her widowhood into court against MGM, claiming that the studio showed malice in failing to destroy the movie and in continuing to market the sound track, neither of which acknowledged her legal status as Hank's second wife. She lost that case, too. But her flair for litigation may explain the notable scarcity of the film today. We can thank her for that.

Billie Jean did win one case, though. She sold her prospective interest in Hank's music to Hill and Range Publishers, and she and that company sued for a share of Hank's royalties. On 22 October 1975, U.S. District Court Judge L. Clure Morton ruled in Nashville that Billie Jean Berlin (she had since married N. Kent Berlin) had been Hank Williams's common-law wife and that she should have a part of the copyright renewals. Billie Jean is divorced from Berlin and lives now as Mrs. Johnny Horton in a Shreveport suburb.

Audrey died less than two weeks after the decision for Billie Jean. On 4 November 1975 she was found dead at the Franklin Road home; her death was of natural causes, but obviously drink and pills had done her considerable damage. Audrey had a small funeral in Troy, Alabama, and was then taken to Montgomery, where the Chaplain of Bourbon Street, Bob Harrington, read "Hey, Good Lookin' " at her interment. The most famous witness was George C. Wallace.

Audrey's burial plot is curious. Hank's dominates the scene, and Lillie is laid out snug to his left. To Lillie's left is the Smith family plot. The Smith's were the in-laws of Irene Williams. Their plot includes six graves, five of them now occupied. Irene's husband, J. T., and his parents are there, along with the infant of J. T. and Irene. The grave farthest from Hank's plot is Audrey's. The slab over it is as plain as Hank's. It carries the name and dates with the same guitar and boots that are carved on his stone. The overall view, then, is that Audrey got as close to Hank as she could, which was not very close; and she seems to have gotten that only through the good graces of the in-laws of Hank's sister.

One of the best stories for the relatives is Lon's. After spending about seven years in VA hospitals, he had a remarkable recovery when the aneurysm causing his problem burst; fortunately, it did not bleed into his brain, and he came away normal. Lillie, of course, was through with him by this time, so he moved back to McWilliams where, on 12 September 1942, he married Ola Till. Their daughter, Hank's half-sister, Leila, was born there on 19 June 1943. As an adult, Hank visited Lon regularly, and apparently the relationship was close. Lon was nearly eighty when he died on 23 October 1970 in Wilcox Memorial Hospital in Camden, Alabama. Carcinoma of the prostate had caused nephritis and uremia. He is buried in Hopewell Methodist Cemetery near McWilliams. Ola Till Williams lives in McWilliams; Mrs. Leila Williams Griffin lives in nearby Selma.

Memorials to Hank are, of course, numerous. The Sunday, 11 January 1953 *Montgomery Advertiser-Alabama Journal* was devoted to Hank, and it overflowed with testimonials by the news staff and by fans who had written in. Generally they were professions of grief and affection; sometimes they expressed the hopes of meeting Hank in another life. One was a spelling testimonial—"H" is for the heart for music, "A" is for his Alabama, "N" is for the nation's number one singer, "K" is for the king of the blues, "W" is for the will to be a success, "I" is for the island in the sky where he rests, and so on. Frank Walker wrote Hank a letter, in care of Songwriter's Paradise, wishing the deceased a happy New Year. Irene wrote him, too, and predicted their ultimate reunion. Freddie Hart and Eddie Dean wrote a poem in which Hank's guitar, deserted now, speaks of its loneliness. A group in Montgomery tried to raise money for a Hank Williams Memorial Auditorium to be built at the intersection of Interstates 65 and 85 in Montgomery. The project failed but has been renewed recently.

Not all of the recognition was so extravagant, though. On 10 March 1953, John M. Gallalee, president of the University of Alabama, announced the school's Hank Williams Music Scholarship. American Folk Publications had given the first one thousand dollars. The *Alabama Journal* noted the scholarship on 13 March, and one of its staff writers suggested some facetious though fairly sensible qualifications for the scholars. Recipients, he said, should have barely finished high school (he was unaware that Hank had not made it through), should have slept through classes (especially English), should not know one note from another, and should have a voice like an electric saw; applicants should be sorrowful and should have "a high-voltage compulsion for trouble and a revulsion for calm things and peace of mind." Finally, though, the recipient should be a "natural" and, "in his field, a genius." The first scholarship awards that I can identify went to Julia Mashburn and Max Camp in September 1954.

In 1974, the Butler County Historical Association marked Hank's birthplace with a plaque that is unaffected in its one-sentence statement that Hank was a "world famous composer and performer of country music." Unfortunately, quarrels among the various groups eager to be responsible for Hank's memory in Butler County have resulted in the moving of the plaque from the birth site to a small Hank Williams park nearby. The best-known memorial, and probably the most appropriate, is the one placed in the Country Music Hall of Fame in Nashville when Hank, Jimmie Rodgers, and Fred Rose became the first members in 1961. After the name and the dates, it reads:

PERFORMING ARTIST, SONGWRITER. . . . HANK WILLIAMS WILL LIVE ON IN THE MEMORIES OF MILLIONS OF AMERI- CANS. THE SIMPLE BEAUTIFUL MELODIES AND STRAIGHT- FORWARD PLAINTIVE STORIES IN HIS LYRICS OF LIFE AS HE KNEW IT WILL NEVER DIE. HIS SONGS APPEALED NOT ONLY TO THE COUNTRY MUSIC FIELD, BUT BROUGHT HIM GREAT ACCLAIM IN THE POP MUSIC WORLD AS WELL.

NOTES

1. The marriage license and certificate are available from the Butler County Courthouse in Greenville, Alabama. The license was taken out on 11 November 1916, the marriage performed on 12 November 1916. Several writers have assigned the wedding to 1918, probably because Lillie gave that date in her interviews.

10. Family and friends at the Hank Williams Memorial Picnic in 1982. (From left to right) Taft Skipper, Erleen Skipper, Walt McNeil (behind Erleen), J. C. McNeil, Ola Schuffert, and Braxton Schuffert. *Photo by E. Denny.*

2. Chet Flippo, *Your Cheatin' Heart: A Biography of Hank Williams* (New York: Simon and Schuster, 1981), p. 9.

3. John Temple Graves II, ed., *The Book of Alabama and the South* (Birmingham: The Protective Life Insurance Company, 1933), p. 58.

4. Jay Caress, *Hank Williams: Country Music's Tragic King* (New York: Stein and Day, 1979), p. 9.

5. Flippo, on p. 14 of *Your Cheatin' Heart: A Biography of Hank Williams,* seems to refer to Harry E. Rockwell's *Beneath the Applause (A Story About Country and Western Music and Its Stars—Written by a Fan)* (Published by Rockwell in 1973), p. 14.

6. The Alabama Bureau of Vital Statistics searched its files covering the years 1920 through 1929 and found no record of the birth of Irene Williams. A friend of the family gave me her birth date. Hank's birth certificate, not filed until 1 March 1934, is available through the bureau. His name on the certificate is spelled "Hiriam" instead of "Hiram."

7. James Agee and Walker Evans, *Let Us Now Praise Famous Men* (Boston: Houghton Mifflin, 1941).

8. Roger Williams, *Sing A Sad Song: The Life of Hank Williams,* second edition (Urbana: University of Illinois Press, 1981), pp. 7-8.

9. Ibid., p. 41.

10. Caress, *Hank Williams: Country Music's Tragic King,* p. 34.

11. Flippo, *Your Cheatin' Heart: A Biography of Hank Williams,* pp. 153, 208.

12. Williams, *Sing A Sad Song: The Life of Hank Williams, pp. 20-23.*

13. Flippo, *Your Cheatin' Heart: A Biography of Hank Williams,* p. 34.

14. Ibid., p. 37.

15. Williams, *Sing A Sad Song: The Life of Hank Williams,* pp. 39-40.

16. Lillie Williams, *Our Hank Williams: "The Drifting Cowboy"* as told by his mother to Allen Rankin (Montgomery: Philbert Publications, 1953), no pagination.

17. Ibid.

18. Ed Linn, "The Short Life of Hank Williams," *Saga,* January 1957, pp. 11, 86.

19. The Metro recording M572, "Mr. and Mrs. Hank Williams," is a good place to check on her talent.

20. The divorce decree of Audrey and Erskine Guy is available at the Pike County Courthouse in Troy.

21. The marriage license and certificate for Hank and Audrey are filed in the Covington County Courthouse in Andalusia.

22. Flippo, *Your Cheatin' Heart: A Biography of Hank Williams,* pp. 48-49.

23. Both books were published by WSFA in Montgomery; both are undated. Copies are rare. I found photo reproductions of them in The Country Music Foundation Library and Media Center in Nashville.

24. Bill Malone, *Country Music U.S.A. A Fifty-Year History* (Austin: University of Texas Press, 1968), p. 187.

25. Elizabeth Schlappi, "Roy Acuff," in *Stars of Country Music,* edited by Bill C. Malone and Judith McCulloh (Urbana: University of Illinois Press, 1975), p. 196.

26. Flippo, *Your Cheatin' Heart: A Biography of Hank Williams,* p. 58.

27. This letter, the other correspondence mentioned in this section, and the manuscripts of "Six More Miles" and "When God Comes And Gathers His Jewels" are available in The Country Music Foundation Library and Media Center in Nashville. Hank wrote this particular letter from 409 Washington Avenue, Montgomery 5. His previous address, 236 Catoma Street, had been crossed off Audrey's letterhead.

28. John W. Rumble, *Fred Rose and the Development of the Nashville Music Industry, 1942-1954,* unpublished Ph.D. dissertation, Vanderbilt University, May 1980, p. 164.

29. The divorce decree was signed by Eugene W. Carter of the Fifteenth Judicial Circuit Court in Montgomery. It is available from the Montgomery County Courthouse in Montgomery (Divorce Decree #19273).

30. Williams, *Sing A Sad Song: The Life of Hank Williams,* p. 74.

31. The decree amending the 1948 divorce is available from the Montgomery County Courthouse in Montgomery (Divorce Decree #19723).

32. Jerry Rivers, *Hank Williams: From Life To Legend,* second edition (Goodlettsville, Tennessee: Published by Jerry Rivers, no date but about 1981), p. 23.

33. Williams, *Sing A Sad Song: The Life of Hank Williams,* p. 149.

34. Rivers reproduces the letter in *Hank Williams: From Life To Legend,* p. 27.

35. Flippo, *Your Cheatin' Heart: A Biography of Hank Williams,* p. 164.

36. Rivers, *Hank Williams: From Life To Legend,* p. 28.

37. Hartnett T. Kane, *Louisiana Hayride: The American Rehearsal for Dictatorship 1928-1940* (New York: William Morrow, 1941), p. 4. The standard biography of Dudley LeBlanc is Floyd Martin Clay's *Couzain Dudley LeBlanc: From Huey Long to Hadacol* (Gretna, Louisiana: Pelican Publishing, 1973).

38. Rivers, *Hank Williams: From Life To Legend,* p. 33.

39. Flippo, *Your Cheatin' Heart: A Biography of Hank Williams,* p. 163.

40. Williams, *Sing A Sad Song: The Life of Hank Williams,* p. 75.

41. Caress, *Hank Williams: Country Music's Tragic King,* p. 100.

42. Linn, "The Short Life of Hank Williams," p. 89.

43. "MGM Publicist Recalls Hank Williams," in *Hank Williams The Legend,* edited by Thurston Moore (Denver: Heather Enterprises, 1972), p. 38. The article originally appeared in the 30 October 1965 issue of *Billboard.*

44. Williams, *Sing A Sad Song: The Life of Hank Williams,* pp. 176-177.

45. Ibid., p. 173.

46. Flippo, *Your Cheatin' Heart: A Biography of Hank Williams,* p. 150.

47. Ibid., pp. 152-153.

48. Rivers, *Hank Williams: From Life To Legend,* p. 17.

49. Minnie Pearl with Joan Drew, *Minnie Pearl: An Autobiography* (New York: Simon and Schuster, 1980), pp. 244-245.

50. The marriage license and certificate are available from the Bossier Parish Courthouse, Benton, Louisiana (Reg. No. 23624).

51. Wesley Pruden, "Ol' Hank: 'Widow Williams' Settles Old Score," *The National Observer,* 12 July 1971, p. 14.

52. The divorce decree is available from the Bossier Parish Courthouse, Benton,

Louisiana (Suit No. 11834). Several writers have spelled the last name "Eshlimar," but the divorce decree clearly indicates "Eshliman," as do the marriage license and wedding certificate.

53. Flippo, *Your Cheatin' Heart: A Biography of Hank Williams,* p. 198.

54. Caress, *Hank Williams: Country Music's Tragic King,* p. 194.

55. Doug Morris, "Hank Williams' Death Still Issue," *The Knoxville Journal,* 15 December 1982, p. C1.

56. Williams, *Sing A Sad Song: The Life of Hank Williams,* p. 223.

57. Williams, *Our Hank Williams: "The Drifting Cowboy,"* no pagination.

58. Hank Williams, Jr., with Michael Bane, tells the story well in *Living Proof* (New York: G. P. Putnam's Sons, 1979).

2

THE SONG:
AN EVALUATION

"Hank Williams, You Wrote My Life"

WRITING LIFE

One of the most persistent stories about Hank Williams is that the star clutched a lost song as he died. The crumpled number went like this:

> We met, we lived and dear we loved, then came that fatal day, the love that felt so dear fades away. Tonight love hathe one alone and lonesome, all that I could sing, I you you [*sic*] still and always will, but that's the poison we have to pay.[1]

We may want to read the song as Hank's last testimony to his love for Audrey and thus get into that debate about whether or not he was headed back to her. But a more important and more certain element shows here: We cherish the idea that the great songwriter always worked spontaneously, pulling fine music from his tortured experiences, even at the moment of death. Hank's composing as he died is one of the most romantic images in the history of American arts. And though the scene is not historical, it is deeply imbedded in the mind of country music.

It represents, I think, that authenticity which is the basis of genuine, or what many choose to call "hard," country music. At its best, the genre is absolutely straightforward and unpretentious. Ideally, the performer sings about his own life in his own songs. He allows none of pop music's fantasy and does not separate himself from his fans with the costumes and antics familiar to rock. In short, hard country is democratic; its performers do seem to be speaking to their equals of real and often shared experience. Thus the importance of knowing that Jimmie Rodgers worked for the railroads he sang about, that the "T.B. Blues" was about his own disease. And if Johnny Cash wants to sing about prison, especially if he wants to do so at Folsom, he will do well to have served a little time himself.

This demand for the connection of life and art may explain why country performers have to make so many personal appearances, why a performer as successful as Ernest Tubb has to show up in two hundred different places each year, and why he stays on after every show to shake hands and sign autographs. I think it also explains why country music generates so little criticism and so much biography and autobiography. To see the singers and comprehend their lives is to understand the music. The faces of Tubb, George Jones, Kitty Wells, and Merle Haggard are worth more than any number of producers and agents, the autobiographies of those stars worth more than most explorations of the folk origins of country music. Hank Williams is classic in this sense; telling whether his fans are more interested in his life or in his work is practically impossible. And I am not sure that anyone knows whether Hank's nickname, "Lovesick," came from his life or his art. The two items probably balance each other better in Hank than in any other singer, and they bring special satisfaction to hard country fans, who demand history, or mythology, with their music.

The clearest and most interesting illustration of my point involves Hank's songwriting. He was untutored, a composer who could not write a note and could therefore preserve songs only in his head or on demonstration records. He himself jested that he knew only two melodies, a fast one and a slow one, anyway. Like many great American naturals, he had learned much of his slight knowledge of music from a black, the character traditionally so sensitive to his own emotions. Like Jerry Lee Lewis's Old Sam, Hank's Tee Tot is music's equivalent of Uncle Remus, the unspoiled character who knows well because he is close to his feelings. And Hank himself has assumed Tee Tot's role for any number of country stars— Waylon Jennings, Charley Pride, Moe Bandy, and Johnny Paycheck among them—who want to claim the sincerity and spontaneity so basic in good country music. More than any other country songwriter, Hank is known as one who responded directly and immediately to his experience, as one who was so spontaneous that he composed even while he was dying.

Lillie Williams encouraged that kind of story as she claimed that Hank's songs simply sprang forth. Hank himself ventured that the songs burst out of him, that sometimes they were even divinely inspired. And he nurtured his connection to his audience when, in his preface to the second WSFA songbook, he said that many of his songs were responses to the cards and letters he received from his fans. More interesting than these claims is the mythology that flourishes around his composing; nearly every one of his best-known songs bears at least one good tale.

If he died writing that number for Audrey on his way to Canton, he supposedly had already sensed his approaching death and recorded the experience in "I'll Never Get Out Of This World Alive." The song, though, is not about last moments but about miserably bad luck, the kind involved in being written into a will only to have a fast lawyer prove that you had never been born. But "I'll Never Get Out Of This World Alive" was on the charts when Hank died, and the title seemed an appropriate remark for the passing of a writer who felt so intensely.

The Nashville part of his career, we hear, began when Hank composed "Mansion On The Hill" in response to a plot given to him by Fred Rose at their first meeting. The story, denied by the Roses, has it that the composition took an unusually long thirty minutes. "Jambalaya" was inspired by a menu in a Cut Off, Louisiana, restaurant, according to one tale. According to another, it came out of Hank's contacts with his Cajun friends on the Hadacol Caravan and was written in the back of Henry Cannon's Beechcraft Bonanza on one of Hank's returns to Nashville. The implication is that Hank suddenly came on the strange ways of the bayou folk and wrote a song about them. But we should remember that he spent some time in Shreveport and that he had written or collaborated on songs like "Bayou Pon Pon," "Cajun Baby," and "I'm Yvonne." Moreover, it seems fairly certain that Moon Mullican gave Hank a hand with "Jambalaya."

"I Saw The Light," a song that owes something to Albert Brumley's "He Set Me Free," was born when Hank saw the Montgomery Airport beacon, which let him know he was almost home. He may have gotten "Pan American" from the L&N railroad, which sent so many trains through Georgiana and Greenville, but only the wildest fan would discount the obvious influence of Roy Acuff's "Wabash Cannonball" on the song. Hank seemed equally inspired when he shifted settings for another railroad tune, "California Zephyr." He wrote the funereal "Six More Miles" just after his grandmother's death. Part of "Long Gone Lonesome Blues," that number about being left and having nothing to do but watch the fish swim, came from a fishing trip with Vic McAlpin. The Kowaliga Indians, who once lived outside Montgomery near where Lake Martin is now, inspired "Kaw-Liga." And a Nashville doctor supposedly got several songs, including "You Win Again" and "Jambalaya" again, by demanding that Hank sit down and write six numbers by way of sobering up.

Audrey, of course, inspired plenty. She herself said that Hank wrote "Cold, Cold Heart" after he and the children visited her in the hospital. She was angry with Hank and would not speak to him even though he gave her a fur coat on the occasion. He commented on her "cold heart" on the way home and struck up one of his best songs. "Move It On Over" came when Audrey changed the locks on him one night, leaving him to sleep in the doghouse. "Your Cheatin' Heart" materialized in a conversation about Audrey that Hank was having with Billie Jean. Tales have it that the same chat produced a number for his new love, "I Could Never Be Ashamed Of You," but the song is about forgiving a woman for cheating—not the best way to court fresh romance. The list could go on, and fancy would continue to dominate much of it.

As a major figure in Nashville, Hank had access to plenty of material by other writers; as a beginner, he himself had sold at least one song, "I Am Waiting For The Day That Peace Will Come," to Pee Wee King for twenty dollars.[2] So he knew of the commerce between established performers and aspiring writers well before he hit the city. In Nashville, he had the good help of skilled people like Vic McAlpin and of the various members of the Drifting Cowboys; Don Helms in particular has proved to be a gifted songwriter. And, of course, Fred Rose was there to help Hank polish his compositions. One of the best documents on this relationship is a song, "Hank And Fred," done recently by the reorganized Drifting Cowboys. The language of the number is rough enough to keep it out of print and off records forever, but Helms was good enough to give me a cassette copy. The song reveals the two composers at work on pieces like "Your Cheatin' Heart" and "Kaw-Liga" and then bickering over who is to get credit for them. Fred complains of how bad one of Hank's songs is and offers to do a rewrite, provided he can have half the credit. Hank says that Fred is welcome to all of it if he thinks he can sell it in the honky-tonks. And on it goes, with a lot of banter and the implication that the old pro was guiding a bright and rough talent, and with the implication that the two were dependent on each other and willing to accept that fact.

The spirit of "Hank And Fred" is real enough. Hank was a native genius who had written some good songs before he knew Fred Rose. He was also a ninth-grade dropout who could not write music, one who both needed and could take advantage of Rose's considerable ability. We might speculate that Fred would have taken more actual credit had he not been an ASCAP writer. Hank and Acuff-Rose were affiliated with BMI, and joint authorships with one writer from ASCAP and the other from BMI complicated things. But Fred Rose's reputation in Nashville is that of the patriarch, that of the talented and generous man who was good at helping writers develop in their own directions. Hank was fortunate to have had Fred's attention; Acuff-Rose, a profit-making outfit, was at least as fortunate to have Hank Williams.[3]

I am not certain that tracing Fred's hand in Hank's work is either possible or entirely crucial. Chet Flippo was a little too zealous when, in *Your Cheatin' Heart,* he set out to run it all down and debunk the myth enveloping Hank's songwriting. In effect, he was arguing what many knew anyway—that Hank did not find his songs under cabbage leaves. History tells us that Hank got help. But the myth cannot be thrown out with the bath water because it tells us accurately that Hank was inspired. It also tells us, more importantly than anything else, that Hank performed with such sincerity that it was easy for his audiences to believe that he had written his songs during dramatic moments in his life. He performed so convincingly that he seemed to be the sole proprietor even of songs not his own. He opened on the Opry with "Lovesick Blues," by Cliff Friend and Irving Mills, and he closed his recording career with "Take These Chains From My Heart," by Hy Heath and Fred Rose. As everyone knows, much of Hank Williams fell between the two; as most would agree, even the first and last songs have come to belong to Hank as well as to anyone. The mythology of his songwriting, then, is as much the product of his best performances as of his finest writing.

Thus he falls into the category with great blues performers like Billie Holiday and Janis Joplin, with great country performers like George Jones and Tammy Wynette—artists who seem inseparable from their art. As audience, we can suspend disbelief and accept what these people sing as absolute truth; or better, we can understand that they perform so well that what they sing could be true. For the literary mind, the process is like that of admiring the passion and immediacy of Wordsworth's "Tintern Abbey" or Coleridge's "Kubla Khan" without accepting the myths that claim that each poem was written in a single draft but realizing that these same myths of complete spontaneity tell us much both about the poems and the poets. Hank does not belong in the Lake Country; the simple argument is that he does belong to the old tradition of the romantic writer. One of the great illustrations of that tradition lies in Hank's 22 December 1952 performance of "The Log Train" for neighbors and relatives in Taft Skipper's store. The song was Hank's: it was about his father; it was done for people who understood it well because most of them had been associated with the Smith Lumber Company. Hank did not record the song commercially, and in fact it was lost at MGM until the *Time/Life* people found the demonstration record as they were preparing their recent issue on Hank. This moment, which is historical, is complete in its representation of hard country music, the perfect conclusion of Hank's career.

Such is the primary significance of Hank Williams, the writer/performer, to country music. He embodied the authenticity that comes when life and art blend, an authenticity that hard country and the blues cling to, one that demands basic instruments, minimal production, and spontaneous (or apparently spontaneous) composition and performance. This authenticity may explain the popularity of The Country Music Hall of Fame manuscript exhibit that reveals the basics of any number of good country songs written on scraps of stationery and cocktail napkins. Most of these songs went through some pretty fancy and professional hands before they hit wax, but their rudiments seem to have been spontaneous. Such is what hard country fans prefer to remember about them. The same spontaneity is the basis of Dorothy Horstman's good book *Sing Your Heart Out, Country Boy,* a collection of country classics, in which each song is introduced by the story of its composition. Almost invariably Horstman's notes connect the lyrics to some specific event or moment in the composer's life.

All of this suggests a kind of innocence, a lack of concern with fashion, an impression that the songs are being sung because they are felt and need singing. Maybe this is why a good nasal twang is so necessary to hard country. For in its way it says that the music is what it is, that it is real and untutored, without any desire to be otherwise, a point that George Jones makes with his recent LP, "I Am What I Am." Thus hard country fans may be put off by Nashville's increasing sophistication, by things like its tuxedoed awards shows, which are often self-consciously imitative of more cosmopolitan show business. The same fans may be disappointed when they hear Hank overdubbed with the strings of an MGM orchestra; they may be disappointed when Charley Pride does Hank's "Honky Tonkin' " with the full production of a television show like "Solid Gold." And when the Oak Ridge Boys, so inspired by the gospel at one point, suddenly find new and more profitable inspiration in a brand of country/rock, they seem exploitative. One even suspects that Nashville has handicapped itself with the sophisticated, multitrack recording systems that can eliminate some of the authenticity that Hank and the Drifting Cowboys achieved when all at once they cut a number directly into an acetate disc.

Without forgetting that Nashville's new ways produce plenty of fine music and without getting too crossly conservative, I want to suggest that Hank's type of authenticity can be violated as well by performers who, realizing the renewed popularity of hard country, suddenly start reclaiming country origins. Moe Brandy and Joe Stamply, who have in their time tried not to be so rural, are hard at proving now that they are just a couple of good old boys. Barbara Mandrell, as glossy as any pop star, is busy singing "I Was Country When Country Wasn't Cool." And Tom T. Hall—who has come from the country to be most recently a fiction writer—seems to be straining a point when he sings "Country Is." The good hard country performer simply does not pause to define his art.

The "Outlaw" performers—people like Willie Nelson, Waylon Jennings, Johnny Paycheck, and Hank Jr.—have a lesser version of the same problem. To some extent, Hank belongs with this group in their general disregard for society's norms. And these performers are certainly eager to claim him. They sing of him regularly, in songs like Jennings' "Are You Sure Hank Done It This Way," Paycheck's version of "Mansion On The

Hill," and Hank Jr.'s "Family Tradition." Peter Guralnick reports that Jennings believes that Hank haunts his tour bus, and that Waylon actually keeps an extra bunk for Hank's spirit.[4] On the 1980 television show, "A Tribute To Hank Williams: The Man And His Music," Hank Jr. called his father "the most wanted outlaw in the land." These stars seem to pursue Hank for his authenticity; and because Nashville has lost touch with some of that element, some performers have even moved their bases of operation out of that city. One mark of their music is its debauchery—its steady celebration of sex, drink, and drugs. One sees the connection with Hank Williams easily. But the link breaks down—and as it does I hope it makes my point—when we realize that Hank thought he was supposed to avoid these things rather than recommend then. His debauchery could compete with that of the "Outlaws," and it becomes more convincing because it was not so deliberately pursued and promoted. The "Outlaws," though admirable for their talent and for their awareness of the necessity to prove Hank's authenticity, sacrifice some of both by being self-conscious in their pursuit of it.

Flannery O'Connor used to talk about how the South and its fiction had "manners." She referred less to courtesies and more to identifiable characteristics—distinctness, perhaps idiosyncracy, in things like conversation, religion, politics, and so forth. This distinctness has separated the region and its fiction from the mainstream of American life. The object here is not to compare Hank to O'Connor but to say that hard country has a similar set of "manners"—things like its considerable emotionalism, its particular themes, its sincerity, and maybe even its nasality. Like the region itself, the fiction and the music are being diminished steadily as major currents of national life pull at them. But stubborn types, like O'Connor from one art form and Williams from another, become attractive for their resistance to conformity and strident commercialism.

Appropriate recognition does not always come to these kinds of artists. Society has a way of sweeping by them. But when the mainstream does discover them, it seems to cherish them all the more, perhaps because we enjoy the sense of discovery or perhaps because we like to see the apparently insignificant character have his day. And the appreciation becomes especially sweet when it has not been sought out. One takes pleasure in watching a writer like O'Connor—who seemed not to worry much that the literary establishment looked upon her as a quaint, if not bizarre, southern lady—become a mainstay of American letters. Long-term fans of country music can take a similar pleasure in knowing that the general public now realizes that country music is not just something to burn tires by. Without ever becoming anything except the boisterous country boy that he had always been, Hank Williams certainly gained the attention of mainstream America.

I think this is why the stories about outdoing Bob Hope or putting Milton Berle in his place have become such popular parts of his life. The once obscure Hank Williams, America's "little man," was overtaking two of popular culture's most highly regarded stars. Country fans take fierce pleasure in the triumph. I also believe that this was the importance of Hank's being invited to Hollywood. The invitation was a sign of his considerable appeal. That he turned down one contract and botched another, apparently by insulting Dore Schary, suggests that Hank was not too worried about promoting himself. His alcoholism may explain part of his lack of interest, but nonetheless the image of Hank as a country original who did not care about Hollywood glamour is vivid. Whether it was intentional or not, avoiding film was probably smart; Hank would have sacrificed much of his authenticity by becoming a singing cowboy on a Hollywood horse.

Popular music was more successful than was Hollywood in its notice of Hank Williams. Its tributes to him have been made by Marty Gold, Connie Francis, Del Shannon, Buddy Greco, Connie Stevens, and even Spike Jones. BMI gave pop awards to "Cold, Cold Heart," "I'm So Lonesome I Could Cry," "Jambalaya," and "Your Cheatin' Heart." Tony Bennett made a career with his million-selling version of "Cold, Cold Heart." Frankie Laine and Jo Stafford did well with "Hey Good Lookin'." Stafford became known by her rendition of "Jambalaya." I am sure that Rosemary Clooney could explain what "Why Don't You Love Me" meant to her career. Rhythm and blues man Ray Charles understands the importance to him of "Your Cheatin' Heart." And if Perry Como put Hank on television as a rural oddity in the early 1950s, it was probably Hank and country music that brought the crooner to the South in the early 1960s to wax a Nashville version of "Dream On Little Dreamer."

A particular irony here is that rock, the music that did so much to push country aside in the 1950s and 1960s, made good use of some of Hank's material. Bill Haley, the first white rocker, got to jumping with "Too Many Parties And Too Many Pals." The song was not Hank's, but it was Hank's 1950 version of it that the rocker was trading on. Haley had been a country picker—one who called himself "Yodeling" Bill Haley and who had called his band "The Four Aces of Western Swing" before he dubbed them "The Comets."[5] He was sacrificing a small country career to bolt to the point of rock and roll. And he was making use of Hank in the switch. In 1952, the year after Hank's "Cold, Cold Heart" had been such a hit, Bill thought up a rocker called "Icy Heart." Thus Hank played a part in the founding of rock and roll, a part that would get support soon when the Pearls did "Your Cheatin' Heart," when Fats Domino did "Jambalaya," and when a wild country rocker called Jerry Lee Lewis started pounding his way to the big time with "You Win Again."

Robert Shelton is on target, therefore, when he says that Hank "was the first country song writer to have become solidly entrenched with the pop singers of Tin Pan Alley, almost single-handedly bringing about the union of pop and country which followed his death."[6] In spite of all of his appeal to broad audiences, all of his potential for pop stardom, Hank Williams did not cross over after his songs. Again and again in doing this research, I have heard the story of Hank's stopping to play Tony Bennett's "Cold, Cold Heart" on the jukebox. The story is a good one because it indicates the willingness of the country singer/writer to be a paying customer for his own song as it made its way among pop singers. Hank just did not change.

I have to keep in mind, of course, that Hank's career was extremely brief and not very well designed. Had he lived longer and fallen among smooth promoters, he might eventually have turned up with a permanent, a saxophone, and a less nasal sound. But I doubt it. He felt that he was doing all right, that tampering with a good thing was pointless. If we can be glad that he did not make movies, we can be just as glad that he did not become a Haley rocker or a Como/Bennett crooner and that his authenticity survived as long as he did. If we are concerned that some of his numbers have drifted into the music that was going to stall country for a decade or so, we might enjoy knowing that Hank's infiltrations of pop and rock have helped to broaden the tastes of a nation eager to listen to country music today.

THE LOVER

The good Calvinistic South has always known how to enjoy its despair. A war lost to the North, hard work, and some poverty are not bad topics for sweet misery; but no subject suits the purposes better than the broken love that proves that even the best thing we have cannot survive in a fallen world. Without much doubt, failed romance is the major subject of country music today, and country fans have long heard plenty about it. A. P. Carter dealt with the theme early on in numbers like "Wildwood Flower" and "I'm Thinkin' Tonight Of My Blue Eyes." Jimmy Davis and Charles Mitchell had a classic in "You Are My Sunshine." Jimmie Rodgers sang about being wrecked by a woman in his first blue yodel, "T For Texas." Bob Wills's "San Antonio Rose" still gets plenty of attention, as does Bill Monroe's "Kentucky Waltz."

In her essay on the subject, Dorothy Horstman quotes Webb Pierce on the subject: "It's different things that make a song a hit. One of the things is you sing about the things they think about most, but don't talk about. That becomes an emotional outlet for the people, and they feel they have a friend in the song."[7] Horstman sees World War II as an important factor here because it separated so many people from their lovers and because it gave many women some independence by sending them to work. The war brought the era of the "Dear John" letter, and it brought some sad hits like Ted Daffan's "Born To Lose" and Ernest Tubb's "Walking The Floor Over You."

Hank Williams, his career taking hold as the war came to an end, was certainly ready to pitch in on the subject, ready to make love-gone-wrong part of the grain of country music. One of country's great scenes has him leaning into a microphone and breaking his voice over a song of shattered love, a song powerful on its own but even more powerful because looming behind it were Hank's crazy romances. "Lovesick" Hank Williams knew enough about messed-up passion; and with his melancholy streak, he brought the music a pathos especially appealing to those away from home and from loved ones. The result, as Horstman puts it, is that "Williams remains to this day the most sympathetic and successful figure in the musical expression of unrequited love."[8]

Hank came to the theme without much trouble. His mother had shown him something of the comings and goings of love while he was still a child. Lillie and Lon were not the best match. Chet Flippo has them slugging it out in *Your Cheatin' Heart.* And though Flippo tends to exaggerate, Lillie seems to have shed little grief when Lon left in 1929 for his long stays in VA hospitals. She evidently received some male attention in his absence and made no real effort to retrieve him from his sickbed. Certainly she did not welcome Lon to her home in Montgomery when he showed up after many years of hospitalization. No one seems certain of the number of Lillie's husbands, and records are hard to find; friends and relatives have told me that "several" plighted their troth to Lillie and received some rough treatment in return. Wherever they are, W. W. Stone and the Mr. Bozzard referred to earlier—not to mention Lon—could testify to that.

Like his mother, Hank seemed to require romance. He learned from her that it rarely went smoothly and that its terms generally were dictated by women. Audrey reinforced his lessons. She and Lycrecia had moved into Lillie's boardinghouse while her husband, Erskine Guy, was overseas; ironically, Guy would be the perfect audience for those songs of broken love that Hank was to write and sing so well. Audrey may not have been on Hank's trail when she arrived at Lillie's, but she was to be after him soon. And it seems that she knew how to get into his tough heart quickly. She became his lover at home, his partner on the road.

If that sounds ideal, it was not. Togetherness may have been too much, or maybe the romance was not very well founded to begin with. But Hank and Audrey never had it easy. Lillie stretches things in her book, once more, when she says that "You could know just how Hank and Audrey were getting along at all times by listening to his latest hits on records and radio."[9] Neither Hank nor the media was always agile enough to keep up with the turnings of that love. But Audrey generously supplied the tension that seemed to inspire Hank's writing. Life with Hank left no shortage of things to quarrel over. Lillie's boardinghouse was not exactly a honeymoon suite; Audrey was frustrated, a would-be star who could not carry a tune; Hank got no slight attention from other women, and rather obviously, he drank too much. Audrey was not far from her parents, and she furled the flag many times at Lillie's. Hank's job with the Alabama Drydock and Shipbuilding Company in Mobile made for similar charges and retreats on his part.

The entire affair was impetuous. If they got married in a filling station during a road trip, they fought on others. Supposedly, one such tift had Hank pulling Audrey out of the car by her hair to leave her by the roadside only to find her waiting for the crew at the next place that sold Falstaff. Obviously, the 1948 divorce was extemporaneous. The terms of the split were cordial enough to allow the conceiving of Hank Jr. Nashville and the baby meant more separations, probably more infidelities, and certainly more jealousies. All of this led to the very real and permanent divorce of 1952, a divorce that marked the end of Hank's career about as well as his being fired from the Opry.

Friends of the couple in both Nashville and Montgomery acknowledge America's fascination with tempestuous but sincere romance because they almost invariably say that Hank and Audrey loved each other deeply but could not get along. Hank made the matter even more interesting and titillating with his extra women. Bobbie Jett had turned up at Lillie's house heavy with Hank's child, and Hank apparently took that connection seriously. Erleen Skipper recalls that he brought Bobbie out to her home near Georgiana although he left her in the car while he went in to visit his cousins. Erleen is fairly certain that the woman accompanied Hank and Bob McKinnon on the little vacation at Lake Martin that eventually produced "Kaw-Liga." Hank's other passion was Billie Jean, the married woman he had taken from Faron Young at gunpoint. One wonders why Hank never got a song out of the occasion when Billie Jean and Bobbie Jett collided at Lillie's in 1952.

Hank's stage weddings to Billie Jean were fundraisers. Hank needed cash, and he was going commercial with some private business, no doubt. He sang, got married, and made nearly $15,000 at once. But the moment has some symbolic value as well. Singing love songs—"Jambalaya" was the hit of the festivity—and getting married suggest something about Hank's sense of weaving his life with his music. The audience knew the whole story—of Audrey and Hank Jr. in Nashville, of Hank and his new "ma cher amio" in Shreveport. Some people were happy to see Hank have a new romance. Many more just could not believe that Hank and Audrey were finally finished. Like Hank's good Montgomery friends, Braxton and Ola

Schuffert, they were convinced that Hank was going to straighten himself out and work his way back to Audrey. Some believed that Hank invited Audrey to the wedding, met her at the airport, and then sent her back to Nashville when she refused to reconcile. Another story has him totally ineffective as Billie Jean's lover; another has him desperately trying to call Audrey during that last trip to Canton in 1952. Fans just would not give up on the drama of Hank and Audrey.

That drama would not have been so sharply etched if Hank had not sung about it with such feeling. Once again he performed so well that the music seemed to be unmistakably about events that had just happened. His response to his experience was direct; he spent little time developing the elaborate conceits or metaphors popular in today's country music. He seemed to be just too involved to unravel studied comparisons like that in a recent hit, "I Just Cut Myself On A Piece Of Her Broken Heart," or those parodied by Jack Clement in "Flushed From The Bathroom Of Your Heart." One of the chief qualities of Hank's music is a simplicity that suggests that the song is coming straight out of experience and not from a producer's office or a writer's study. "Your Cheatin' Heart" is one of the most unadorned and one of the best pieces ever to come out of country music.

The simplicity did more than emphasize authenticity. Hank had a considerable gift for very sharp visual images, and the directness of his songs heightened their effect. The sleepless nights of the treacherous lover in "Your Cheatin' Heart" are as vivid as the memory of a happy past that steals through the mind of a man who sees his woman with a new lover in "I Can't Help It [If I'm Still In Love With You]." I'm So Lonesome I Could Cry" contains one of the most striking images in country music as it tells how the silence of a shooting star lights up the night. Hank might not have been interested in my point, but his image is synesthetic, the kind that mixes the senses. The Romantic poets, so dependent on their emotions, produced the type regularly. In "Ode To The West Wind," for example, Shelley describes reflections of flowers in the Mediterranean as being "So sweet, the sense faints picturing them." The reflection is so clear that we seem to be able to smell the flowers; we picture sweetness, see an odor. The subject of Hank's sentence is "silence"; the verb is "lights." So we get one image of sound, another of sight as quietness brightens the dark. The two images do not make sense together except that, for some reason, the night is almost always quiet when we see falling stars and we are almost always lonely when we stare into the dark. The simplicity of the lines keeps the image from seeming self-conscious just as it makes it so startling.

Hank made some other contributions to country's sad love songs. He must have been one of the first to hint at divorce when he recommended splitting up over putting up with half-hearted love in "Why Should We Try

Anymore.'' But he did not usually have such an easy solution to problems of the heart, and his best situations involved that potentially fine romance that, for one reason or another, does not work out. He sang less about love that has ended and much more about one-sided love, the kind that lingers even when it cannot possibly be fulfilled. The result was a pathos, a kind of self-pity, that Hank mastered; with the help of fiddler Jerry Rivers and steelman Don Helms, he could practically get a tear on command. The early number, "Mansion On The Hill," works at the idea as it reveals the poor boy who can never have his rich girl because of the obvious social differences. The boy pining away in his cabin in the valley simply could not miss with an audience sensitive to snobbery. That same theme has received recent voice in Mike Huffman's "Tight Fittin' Jeans," the number about the country boy who could love the rich girl right, if he could have her.

The pathetic lover, who offers more affection than his beloved can bear, turns up over and over. If she could love him only "Half As Much" he could be happy. His love goes on beyond hers in "I Can't Help It [If I'm Still In Love With You]." "Take These Chains From My Heart," by Hy Heath and Fred Rose, may suggest divorce again as it speaks of losing faith and needing escape. But as it discusses lingering heartaches, it has the fine ambiguity of wanting to be rid of a woman and wanting to keep her at the same time. "You Win Again" catches the same ambiguity. She abuses him, and he should leave; but he just cannot stop his passion. Ray Charles picked up on that idea in "I Can't Stop Loving You"; and the same pathetic situation turns up in a Tom T. Hall number, done well by George Jones, "I'm Not Ready Yet," where the lover knows it is time to go but just cannot leave. Hank found more pathos in Claude Boone's "Wedding Bells," a hit second only to "Lovesick Blues" in 1949. Here the lover watches his love marry another. He did it again in Leon Payne's "They'll Never Take Her Love From Me," where, to prove love, the singer steps aside so his beloved can marry another. And she does, leaving his testimony of affection to feed on itself. "I'd Still Want You" is about pretending not to care, about not letting friends know just how much one loves an abusive woman. In "My Heart Would Know," Hank could feign that his affection had died, but his crying heart would know the truth.

Hank's best expressions of love hopeless in spite of great potential probably lies in his best-known songs, "Your Cheatin' Heart" and "Cold, Cold Heart." In the former, the lover seems to be having some revenge on a faithless woman as he imagines the sleepless nights she will get for doing him wrong. But then he gives his true emotions away by admitting that his nights are just as restless as he imagines hers to be, and the subtle indication is that most of the misery belongs to him. In "Cold, Cold Heart," Hank loves intensely, but his beloved has been hurt before and does not trust his affection. The more he tries to express his love, the more suspicious of him she becomes. Because she has been hurt, she needs the love that she just cannot accept. The song tells us everything about the sadly ironic view of love that dominated the life and work of Hank Williams.

Thus love for Hank and for more than a few in his audiences ran its absurd course. And thus through Hank, country came to work out one of its sustaining themes—the perplexing business of lovers and beloveds, of needing love and rejecting it at the same time. Whatever the love song, Hank always seemed to be indicating that he and Audrey could have been great lovers had they been able to stay in the same household long enough. The good fan has to see Hank behind country's great songs of lost love—behind numbers like "The Tennessee Waltz" that Patti Page made famous, behind George Morgan's "Candy Kisses," behind the "Faded Love" of Bob and John Wills, behind the synoptic "Dear John," behind Barbara Mandrell's " 'Til You're Gone," behind George Jones's "He Stopped Loving Her Today." And Hank and Audrey practically haunt those stages occupied by the good duos like George Jones and Tammy Wynette, Conway Twitty and Loretta Lynn, Dolly Parton and Porter Waggoner, perhaps even David Frizzell and Shelley West—all of them fully aware of what Hank's authenticity has meant to country music.

SIN AND SALVATION

Hank heard much of the music of his early years at Mt. Olive Baptist Church, where his mother played the organ. The story goes that he sat with her at the instrument. If this makes Hank seem remarkably pious, we might note other gossip around Georgiana and Mt. Olive to the effect that Hank was a bit of a rapscallion who called for supervision while his mother was occupied with the church's music. Thus his perch in the front. Whether for discipline or devotion, Hank was prominent in church in those first years, and Mt. Olive's congregation has memorialized with a plaque the little wooden bench he stood on to sing his first songs.

Hank's musical heritage was not all sacred, though. His aunt, Mrs. McNeil, no doubt taught him some hymns when he lived with her and her family during the school year of 1934-1935. But the lumber camp that was his home that year taught him plenty of tunes that got no one into heaven. Tee Tot must have known some sacred numbers, but he was a man of the street and had a few notions about the secular world. By the time Hank arrived in Montgomery in 1935, ready to start his own career, he had a grasp of both kinds of music and an awareness that sincerity carried a blues number as well as it carried hymns. He could put that awareness to work on the radio shows and in the schoolhouse concerts that allowed a certain amount of rowdiness but insisted on a sacred closing.

But Hank was to make his way in the honky-tonks fairly soon; and the joints, which had been given such a fine air of evil by Prohibition, did not make much room for spirituality. In trying to define honky-tonk music, Nick Tosches talks about the "small-group sound that developed in redneck bars" and then cites the "lyrics of sex and whiskey." To give this music its setting, he quotes Al Dexter, who defines the honky-tonks as "these beer joints up and down the road where the girls jump in cars and so on."[10] By talent and temperament, Hank Williams was well suited to the joints. As Peter Guralnick puts it, "Unless you were a schooled musician and could read and play with some of the larger groups, the small honky-tonk bands were the path of least resistance, and what they were playing then, same as now, was boogie music for dancing with a country-oriented beat and instrumentation."[11] Hank served much of his apprenticeship in these places, working there steadily from about 1938 until he hit the Opry in 1949. And he made plenty more stops among them after he was an Opry regular.

Much of his music was from, or for, those scenes. In the little known "I've Been Down That Road Before," Hank laments the risks of being a smart aleck, the type he tended to be at times, among rowdy boys. He complains of some knots on his bald head and of some missing teeth before describing a time when he was so beat up that his mother did not recognize him after he was hauled home. A more memorable song, "Honky Tonk Blues," follows suit as Hank sings about leaving a good country home to hit the night spots of the city. In the end he claims to have had enough and to be heading back to his daddy's farm.

Not all of his juke joint songs come to such moral conclusions. In "Honky Tonkin'," a man invites someone else's wife to party. If she has some money, he claims, he can show her some wicked places. "Hey Good Lookin' " is from the same cloth. It attempts to lure the lady from her stove, from her good domestic life, to cook up something with him, something, one assumes, having little to do with fat back and green beans. Hank offers her no commitment beyond two dollars, plenty of soda, and some free dancing. He is just as blunt in "I'll Be Bachelor 'Till I Die," where he gallantly offers to hold the girl's hand, to pet her when she cries, to let her cool him with her fan (that great southern euphemism for ardency in polite parlor courtship), and to take her honky-tonkin'. Marriage, as the title makes plain, is not part of the program.

Hank even found ways to get hound dogs, those critters that have always fascinated country, into his honky-tonk tunes. "Move It On Over" is about sleeping with the dog after coming home late to an angry wife. "Homesick" concerns the errant lover who jokingly says he will do anything to get back into his lover's house; if she wants a new dog, he claims, he will learn to bark. "Howlin' At The Moon" is even more whimsical as it describes a man going happily after a coy woman. She has him so confused that he wears socks for neckties, tries to eat steaks with a spoon, and, of course, howls at the moon. In fact, he claims to have become the best hound in the county for want of her.

"Long Gone Lonesome Blues" is not quite as mournful as its title suggests, and the number went well with the rowdy crowds. Here Hank talks about being so lonesome that he tries to drown himself. Fortunately, the river was dry. Hank would break his voice over the refrain, creating a kind of witty despair that was not to be taken too seriously. In "Why Don't You Love Me," he just cannot understand why the beloved is so cold; he allows that he is as handsome as ever, the same trouble she has always known, and that he just cannot fathom the cooling of her passion. "No, Not Now" comes from the old jokes about wives resisting their husbands. They make their men wait during courtship, and for some strange reason they make them wait even after they are married.

This jesting at the passionate lover made Hank's honky-tonk music unique. For the genre has often focused on lost lovers drinking away their miseries. Songs like "City Lights," "Lost Highway," "There Stands The Glass," "The Wild Side Of Life," "Honky Tonk Angel," "After The Fire Is Gone," and "She's Acting Single [I'm Drinking Doubles]" are typical. They are also typical in that they generally mix broken love with carousing; bad romance becomes license for drinking and running around. Hank's songs of broken love played well in the joints, and he played them there plenty. But, remarkably, he rarely set his songs of serious romance in those places. He did not let missed love anticipate affairs and hard drinking. His keeping separate the two types of music worked well for him because it marked the sincerity of his approach to real love and allowed one type of song to heighten the other. Hank understood the value of working up an audience's deep agony only to turn the emotion to an amusing romp, a romp that meant good times and not drinking away sorrow. Thus his honky-tonk music belongs to the spirit of that fine and raucous number by Lefty Frizzell and Jim Beck, "If You've Got The Money, I've Got The Time," a piece that is just short of being sentimental about romance. And one suspects that his honky-tonk music was successful at least partially because it was so happy and because it was so happily played against the songs of broken love.

The good times that he captured in that music helped make his concerts such blasts. And stories of his performances have become legend. Perhaps the best known of those occasions involved his attempt to sing "My Bucket's Got A Hole In It" on The Grand Ole Opry. Hank had scheduled the number, but Opry officials balked when they realized that it included the word "beer." Hank could sing the song, they decided, but the "beer" had to go. Supposedly, the star complained that he did not see why he could not say "beer" on stage since he was going on full of the golden elixir anyway. But finally he obliged the officials, dropped the "beer," and went out to wail about a leaking bucket that kept him from buying "buttermilk." The crowd, familiar with the song and with wicked Hank as well, loved it. A Dallas audience waited for him until after midnight and then cheered a tipsy

Hank when he opened the show with "good morning." Another crowd may have been angry enough when he stood them up in Richmond, but they were back the next day to get their money's worth during the show in which he made fun of a reviewer, Edith Lindeman, by dedicating "Mind Your Own Business" to her. He practically became a hero for being drunk and missing a show. The "bad boy" was just a part of Hank and his music, and his audiences seemed to understand that in his rowdy ways he was just showing them what he was. George Jones enjoys Hank's privileges today.

Hank was just as real in his religion. For all of his iniquity, he never shook off those beginnings back at the Mt. Olive Baptist Church. If the three-year-old child sang his first notes there, the adult returned to a similar setting just before he died. As indicated in the biographical essay, Hank and Billie Jean went to the Chapman Methodist Church with Taft and Erleen Skipper on the night of 21 December 1952. Hank sang with the congregation, but he turned down the invitation to perform individually even though he was willing to sing for the same friends and acquaintances the next morning in Taft's store. He may have been too weary to go before the Methodists that night, but Erleen thinks that Hank just did not feel that his recent life allowed him to lead church music. Believing that he was so serious about his religion, at least at the moment, is easy.

He knew the reality of "I Saw The Light" as well as that of "Honky Tonkin'." The latter may have dominated, but a full 20 percent of the songs he wrote are sacred. Apparently he had felt some urge to moralize when he took the persona of Luke the Drifter. Numbers like "Pictures From Life's Other Side" tell us that people who seem to be bad can have good hearts, and "Be Careful Of The Stones That You Throw" contains another warning of hypocrisy. These songs were popular enough, but they are not major, perhaps because of their sentimentality or perhaps because the persona separated Hank from himself in its contriving to help the honky-tonk lover get at an additional audience. Hank did not need help; he was fine as the Hank Williams who could sing wrenching love songs, hot-blooded juke-joint numbers, and his very sincere religious songs.

Much of that religious music is fairly standard. "The Angel Of Death," "Are You Walking And A-Talking For The Lord," "Calling You," "Jesus Is Calling," "Ready To Go Home," "When The Book Of Life Is Read," and "I'm Gonna Sing" are traditional in their sentiments about whether or not we are prepared to die and what heaven will be like. "A Home In Heaven" concerns those who build good homes here without preparing for one above. "A House Of Gold" and "Wealth Won't Save Your Soul" are similar in their comments on materialism. "Last Night I Dreamed Of Heaven" is about meeting loved ones above.

Several of Hank's hymns are more striking, however. "How Can You Refuse Him Now," "Jesus Died For Me," and "We're Getting Closer To The Grave Each Day" are all simple, but each deals vividly with the crucifixion. Each song details Christ on the cross, the nailed hands and the crown of thorns, as sinners are called to recognize the importance of Christian sacrifice. "Jesus Remembered Me" is just as graphic as it depicts the lost sinner, not far from Hank, who finally looks up and is greatly surprised to find that Jesus recognizes him.

The easy acceptance of the details of biblical history and the sincere rendering of them are the marks of Hank's great sacred songs, the marks of most good hymns. These songs bring the events of salvation out of what often seems to be the vague past into the distinct present thus connecting directly the sinner and his salvation. Few hymns do this better than "I Saw The Light," a convincing song, as it links Christ's healing of the blind man with His healing of the modern sinner. The sinner comes to realize that Christ spans history. Hank captured here the full meaning of the biblical story, and he presents it simply as history and without the sermonizing that might have gone into it. The hymn becomes particularly moving when we know its stories, the one about his seeing the beacon that meant he was almost home, the other about how Hank, so deep in his problems late in life, would not sing the hymn with Minnie Pearl because, as he put it, "there ain't no light. It's all dark."[12]

In spite of Hank's gift for sacred music, I think Lillie Williams was wrong to suggest in her little book that her son "was a sort of preacher at heart." Mothers can be forgiven that sort of thing. But Al Bock makes the same error, at greater length, in *I Saw The Light: The Gospel Life of Hank Williams,* in which he tries to argue that Hank was a major religious figure. And Jay Caress may have over-Christianized Hank in *Hank Williams: Country Music's Tragic King.* Hank was not a pious man trying to push aside a corrupt world; he pursued sin at least as hotly as he pursued Jesus. If he was a rounder, he knew all along that he should have behaved better. The tension created thereby is an important one. The South has long known how to mix a little Saturday night hell raising with some Sunday morning piety; writers like Flannery O'Connor, William Faulkner, and Tennessee Williams have always cut respectability with debauchery in their fine realizations of the way things are. Hank was to bring the tension to a Grand Ole Opry that had been intent on preserving a happier view of human nature. Generally, its subjects were the wholesomeness of dogs, biscuits, work, trains, and religion. The audiences were from clean-cut, well-scrubbed families. They would stand in line for a day at the ticket window of Ryman Auditorium, formerly a church, without even imagining a riot. The performers appeared to be nearly as wholesome; and if they did drink and carouse a bit, they did so out of sight. An old-time group like "The Fruit Jar Drinkers" had actually felt compelled to change their wreckless name to "Dixie Sacred Singers" when they recorded religious numbers. And when Roy Acuff brought Rachel Veach into his band, he got considerable mail complaining about the image created by a woman's traveling with all those men. Acuff

solved the problem by turning band member Beecher Kirby into Bashful
Brother Oswald by way of suggesting that Rachel was family and quite safe
after all.

Opry officials did not know what to do with Hank Williams, except to try
to keep him from singing "beer" on stage. He was obviously a threat to the
hallowed grounds of Nashville. In their widsom, or in their eagerness to
seize hot property, they let him into Ryman for a few years until he became
too outrageous to keep. While he was there, he taught the Opry to allow a
little misbehavior in its music, if only to point out the wages of sin.

The idea certainly took hold; misbehavior has become apart of country,
and generally it has been tempered with some kind of disapproval or
justification. Kenny Rogers's Ruby does take her love to town. Dolly Parton
has become something of a sex symbol, one who splits out of her dress as
she goes up to receive another country award, one who had recently starred
in the film version of *The Best Little Whorehouse In Texas.* Helen
Cornelius and Jim Ed Brown have sung of spreading blankets on the
ground. But when we look past the sensual, we find a backdrop of morality.
Ruby, as she spreads her love, is betraying a badly wounded veteran of Viet
Nam, in a sense betraying the country itself. Jim Ed and Helen can spread
blankets because they are married, at least in the song. And because of her
giggles and taffeta, the vampish Dolly Parton still seems capable of
believing that the stork brings babies. She and Porter Waggoner know that
they will get caught if they keep meeting at "The Dark End Of The Street."
George Jones and Tammy Wynette know that "God's Gonna Get 'Cha For
That." And we understand that Shel Silverstein's queen of the Silver Dollar
is really unhappy in spite of all the action.

The lives of many country stars have come from Hank's pattern. Sin and
salvation pull at Jerry Lee Lewis. And Nick Tosches tells us that Jerry Lee
could get powerfully repentant at times about songs like "Great Balls Of
Fire."[13] Old Johnny Cash lets it be known that he spent a few years in sin.
He wears those black suits as if he might be doing a little Protestant
repentance; and he calls on his wife, June Carter, when he seems to need a
little help with his wholesomeness.

"Hee Haw," the long-running show that was country's major television
vehicle in the 1970s, certainly understands the point. The program brings on
all sorts of flesh, most of it concentrated in what is known as an "All Jug
Band." I am not convinced that "jug" refers to the instrumentation in this
all-female outfit. But "Hee Haw" always closes with a religious note, clean
overalls and a good a cappella version of some familiar four-square hymn,
something an audience that has been tempted by the flesh can sing along on.

Among the "Outlaws," Willie Nelson seems capable of repentance,
probably because he is likely to follow songs like "Whiskey River" or
"Bloody Mary Morning" with a vigorous rendition of "Amazing Grace."
His film, *Honeysuckle Rose,* allows a good bit of hard drinking (some of it

done by drivers weaving down the highway in a bus), a good bit of womanizing, and the feature attraction—Willie seducing the twenty-year-old daughter of his best friend. The film might need an "R" rating if wholesomeness did not envelop the licentiousness. There are happy family scenes, sad partings, and touching reunions as Willie and his band come and go on their tours. And in the end, the wayward hero comes home, chastened a bit but forgiven, convinced finally that he loves only his wife, the fairly sexy Dyan Cannon. All comes to be right with the world, and we leave the theatre feeling that maybe Walt Disney had produced the film.

Country music is gradually eliminating the moral tension that Hank Williams brought to it. Its consistent innuendoes—the references to sex, booze, and drugs— do not call for so much repentance in the 1980s. We hear a lot now about lovers leaving love all over each other, about laying me down and not to sleep, about getting stoned. But this move, I am sure, can be read as part of the slide away from country and into pop, a crossover that seems to be an obsession with a recording industry always looking for broader markets. And if we want to blame Hank for pulling down some old barriers, we should note that his singing of sin probably helped country move into the more liberated last half of the twentieth century.

Hank, then, stands as a turning point between an older and more straitlaced country music and the more liberated type we hear today. His approach to sin survived in the short run because it helped the industry admit a little titillation without completely violating its wholesome image. Unfortunately, country has sometimes allowed hypocrisy to replace Hank's authenticity in the matter. We may well find it hard to put up with a song like the Billy Sherrill and Glen Sutton hit "Almost Persuaded," in which we get to see an illicit romance shape up only to have one of the lovers flee in a fit of conscience. Titillation is served as a kind of pious morality wins out. Yet I think I can say that, regardless of the trend he may have started, Hank's songs of sin and salvation have survived in the long run because of the very realistic tension they created. Hank's struggles with good and evil were as genuine as his broken loves. Those struggles, presented so convincingly by Hank Williams, brought country music around to a more complete understanding of human experience, an understanding that has old-time religion tugging at afternoon delights. I would like to think that the best and most important country show had Hank bending into "Cold, Cold Heart," "Honky Tonkin'," and "I Saw The Light."

THE SHRINE

While I was in Nashville checking the last details of this volume, *The Tennessean* reported a strange tale. During the television taping at the Opry House of "That Good Ole Nashville Music," Gary Gentry was singing his new song, "The Ride." The number tells of a hitchhiker, on his way to

Nashville, who gets picked up by a man in a Cadillac. As they approach the city, the driver turns around to head for his home in Alabama. He lets his passenger out and asks him to call him "Hank." When Gentry sang that last "Hank," the lights all over Opryland went out. Electricians found a burned open switch. Gentry, along with everyone else on hand, was fast to claim the mechanical failure as Hank's guiding hand in the song.[14] Perhaps the freakish moment that supplied such good publicity for a young singer tells us something of the pervasiveness of Hank's spirit in Nashville.

A sign from Hank seems capable of making a career, for country music simply venerates him. It has given him all of its significant prizes, and a *Down Beat* poll has voted him the "most popular country and western singer of all time." In 1961, Hank joined Jimmie Rodgers and Fred Rose as the first members of the Country Music Hall of Fame. By 1969, "Your Cheatin' Heart" had had its millionth broadcast performance, and BMI recognized the occasion with a "Special Citation of Achievement." "Jambalaya" received the same citation in 1971.[15] Long before Gary Gentry got his break at Opryland, country singers were making tributes to Hank. Elvis may have generated more souvenirs and more printed words, but certainly Hank Williams has caused more music—from his own kind, the professionals who knew him best and perhaps appreciate him most—than any other American singer. The long list of tributes could start with songs like Jimmy Logsdon's "Hank Sings The Blues No More," Arthur Smith's "In Memory Of Hank Williams," and Ernest Tubb's "Hank, It Will Never Be The Same Without You." It would run right up to the present as it takes in Waylon Jennings's "Are You Sure Hank Done It This Way," Mike Cross's "Thanks Hank," Travis Pritchett's "Hank's Home Town," Bob McDill's "Good Old Boys Like Me" (the good old boys are Hank and Tennessee Williams), Kris Kristofferson's "If You Don't Like Hank Williams," and Paul Craft's "Hank Williams, You Wrote My Life."

Albums of Hank's songs, or of songs about Hank, are nearly as plentiful. They are by everyone from Floyd Cramer and Hank Locklin to Stonewall Jackson and Roy Acuff to George Jones. Even Charley Pride, the black country star, has cut a Williams album, "There's A Little Bit of Hank In Me." The lengthy discography at the end of this book indicates that MGM still perceives Hank Williams as hot property. Many of his records are still available; they almost always go for full price. Sneezy Waters and Jim Owen, the two Williams impersonators, still thrive. At least three Alabama festivals go on in his name. Radio shows devoted to Hank still play. And a good movie, *The Last Picture Show*, marked an entire era with a sound track made up basically of his songs.

Celebrating and selling Hank Williams has grown into its own industry, and Hank's music is so prominent that it has become the subject of parody. In a piece called "Hippie Boy" by Chris Hillman and Gram Parsons, The

Flying Burrito Brothers sent up "The Funeral," a number Hank had done as Luke the Drifter. Hank's Luke speaks of coming across the Savannah funeral of a black child and is condescending and sentimental as he discusses the general ignorance and simplicity of the blacks gathered to mourn the passing. He goes on to suggest that, in spite of his color, the child was good and is with God. The Hillman/Parsons version is about the death of a little drug courier, a child who, on a mission for a few dollars, had tried to eat the drugs when he got caught. As unseemly as he may be, he, too, is with God, long hair and all. Roy Blount pokes gently at the industry with his "Why Ain't I Half As Good As Old Hank [Since I'm Feeling All Dead Anyway]."[16]

The good fun does not dampen the spirits of the fans who come to Hank Williams. They buy millions of dollars worth of his music. They flock from considerable distances to see his things at the Country Music Hall of Fame and in the state archives in Montgomery. They visit his grave in that city's Oakwood Cemetery Annex—a graveyard marked by a sign carrying a drawing of Hank's boots and guitar—to such an extent that caretakers have had to replace the grass around the grave with artificial turf. They seek him out with such vigor that his cousins, Taft and Erleen Skipper, practically have to run a Hank Williams clearinghouse out of their home near Georgiana. Erleen says that they get so many calls that they have to sleep with the phone off the hook. In no research that I have done have I run into so many people who know so much about a particular person and who are anxious to know so much more about him.

Hank did come to Nashville at the right time. Country music was quickly getting popular; it had its own recording experts at Castle, its publisher in Acuff-Rose, its protector in BMI. Hank thrived with the industry and died just as rock and roll was beginning to vibrate across the nation. But to see him simply as the creature of history would be a mistake, for he shaped and substantiated country music at least as much as it shaped and substantiated him. He was a natural who, both as writer and performer, either initiated or magnified the basic characteristics of a genre that was just realizing itself as a phenomenon of American culture. Because of his particular life and his particular talent, he was able to show country music the importance of authenticity more dramatically than any writer/performer before or since. He articulated at least as clearly as anyone the full emotional range of broken romance, an old theme that World War II and Hank Williams made especially poignant. As he cut his melancholy loving with some loose, juke-joint tunes, he showed country that plain wholesomeness just was not enough, that human experience involved a little more than home cooking. And he tempered it all with some deeply religious feelings that gave his life and his music a tension that is irresistible to fans who knew him well. He came and went with one of country music's great moments, that period bordered roughly by World War II and Elvis's start with Sun Records in 1954, or bordered just about as well by Hank's arrival in Nashville in 1946 and his death on New Year's Day in 1953.

NOTES

1. Chef Flippo prints the song in *Your Cheatin' Heart: A Biography of Hank Williams* (New York: Simon and Schuster, 1981), p. 206. Hank's physical condition after the stop in Knoxville on the night of his death rules out the chance of his writing at the time, and one suspects that the fragment is one of many like it that Hank left behind.

2. Minnie Pearl with Joan Drew, *Minnie Pearl: An Autobiography* (New York: Simon and Schuster, 1980), p. 210.

3. John W. Rumble works out the complications of the relationship in *Fred Rose and the Development of the Nashville Music Industry 1942-1954,* unpublished Ph.D. dissertation, Vanderbilt University, May 1980, pp. 90-93.

4. Peter Guralnick, *Lost Highway: Journeys and Arrivals of American Musicians* (Boston: David R. Godine, 1979), p. 211.

5. Nick Tosches is good on this subject in *Country: The Biggest Music In America* (New York: Stein and Day, 1977), p. 31ff.

6. Robert Shelton, *The Country Music Story: A Picture History of Country and Western Music* (New York: Bobbs-Merrill, 1966), p. 91.

7. Dorothy Horstman, *Sing Your Heart Out, Country Boy* (New York: Dutton, 1975), p. 137.

8. Ibid., p. 139.

9. Lillie Williams, *Our Hank Williams: "The Drifting Cowboy"* as told by his mother to Allen Rankin (Montgomery: Philbert Publications, 1953), no pagination.

10. Tosches, *Country: The Biggest Music in America,* p. 24.

11. Guralnick, *Lost Highway: Journeys and Arrivals of American Musicians,* p. 98.

12. Pearl, *Minnie Pearl: An Autobiography,* p. 215.

13. Nick Tosches, *Hellfire* (New York: Delacorte Press, 1982), pp. 129-133.

14. Walter Carter, "Hank Williams's Ghost Blacks Out Opry House," *The Tennessean,* 28 July 1982, p. 29.

15. The best statistics on Hank's recording successes are in Thurston Moore, ed., *Hank Williams The Legend* (Denver: Heather Enterprises, 1972), p. 36.

16. Roy Blount, *Crackers* (New York: Knopf, 1980), p. 170.

3

INTERVIEWS

Barbara Walters may be able to get some startling confessions out of Dolly Parton, but even that famous interviewer would have had trouble with Hank Williams. He simply did not talk much to the press; and when he did, he told them only what he thought they expected to hear. He almost never revealed any of the personal details that we have come to expect of great interviews.

Part of the problem was Hank's insecurity. He did not come from behind his facade for the media, probably because he did not want to talk about his personal life and because he did not have any really elaborate theories about his skill as writer and performer. He saw nothing interesting in growing up in rural Alabama, and he was content to let people think that his songs simply sprang forth, that he knew they were no good if they took more than fifteen minutes to write.[1] He was content to promote his records with some down home generalizations. Another problem was that in his prime Hank was doing two hundred one-nighters a year. Time for interviews was short because he was often pulling into town just before a show and pulling out just after it. There was no journalist to travel with him to record intimate details. Hank's drinking did not always leave him in the best shape for chitchat anyway.

Ray Jenkins, of the *Alabama Journal,* tried to interview him when he was in Columbus, Georgia, with the Hadacol Caravan. The newsman told Roger Williams: "I couldn't figure out if he was drunk or what, but he didn't say much, and I couldn't make sense out of what he did say. I didn't even write a story about him ."[2] Hank's answers, when they came, did not go too deep. In a *Country Song Roundup* interview, he revealed that his favorite record was "Cold, Cold Heart," that his favorite food was chicken, that his favorite color was blue, that his favorite entertainers were Johnny Ray and Moon Mullican, and that he did have a record collection.[3] Jerry Rivers reports that California disc jockey Cottonseed Clark asked Hank why his songs were so sad. Hank replied: "Well, Cottonseed, I guess I always have been a sadist."[4] When Allen Rankin asked him about a Luke the Drifter number, Hank replied: "Don't know why I happened to of wrote that thing. Except somebody that's fell, he's the same man, ain't he, as before he fell? Got the same blood in his veins, ain't he? So how can he be such a nice guy when he's got nothin'? Can you tell me?"[5] Hank was more relaxed and more garrulous in a Melvin Shestack interview conducted near Rochester, New York, in 1948. Shestack says he was doing the interview for his high school newspaper and that the faculty adviser refused to print the piece. He tells of meeting Williams and of having hot dogs and soft drinks with him. The interview is atypical, and those who knew Hank's travels well are convinced that he was not even in New York at the time.[6]

Hank said so little that many of the interviews turn out to be articles with a sprinkling of quotes from him. Ralph Gleason's June 1952 interview is like that. Gleason was working for the *San Francisco Chronicle* when he went out to the Leamington Hotel in Oakland to talk to the singer. When Gleason went into the hotel room, Hank was in the lavatory. When he came out, according to Gleason, he "went over to the top of the bureau, swept off a handful of pills and deftly dropped them, one at a time, with short, expert slugs from the glass." They then went down to the coffee shop for breakfast, where Hank recalled his singing at Mt. Olive Church, his following Tee Tot, and his first recording session. He called his music "folk music" and explained that "the tunes are simple and easy to remember and the singers, they're sincere about them." He cited Johnny Ray for his sincerity and said that Roy Acuff is "the biggest singer this music ever knew." Gleason intended to follow up the interview at intermission and after the show that night, but he says that "At the intermission, it was impossible to talk to him. He was a little stoned and he didn't seem to remember our conversation earlier in the day and the party was beginning to get a little rough. They were whiskey drinkers and so I gave them room, looked around a while and then went on back out."[7] Gleason's squeamishness, remarkable in a newspaperman, especially in one who would later write for *Rolling Stone*, left him without much of an interview. So the good journalist wrote about how he tried to interview Hank Williams.

Fortunately, Rufus Jarman was a little harder to frighten, and he got some good quotes with which to finish off a *Nation's Business* article on the urbanization of country music. His interview took place not long before Hank died, and it includes the most often quoted statements by the star. Hank emphasized the sincerity of the good country singer and said that "when a hillbilly sings a crazy song, he feels crazy. When he sings, 'I Laid

My Mother Away,' he sees her a-laying right there in the coffin.'' The reason for the sincerity is that the hillbilly singer was brought up in tough circumstances; he knew about life, about hard work. In Hank's words, ''you got to have smelt a lot of mule manure before you can sing like a hillbilly. The people who had been raised something like the way the hillbilly has knows what he is singing about and appreciates it.'' His songs, he added, are for the common people, American or otherwise. And he argued that the music revealed quite a bit about American life.[8]

I do not have a great ''Walters'' type interview to offer here; I do not think there is such a creature. What I do offer is a short unpublished interview of Hank and Audrey by disc jockey Bob McKinnon. Following that are my own interviews with Bob Pinson, who is probably the best expert on Hank's music, and with Don Helms and Jerry Rivers of the Drifting Cowboys.

HANK AND AUDREY WILLIAMS

Bob McKinnon was a popular disc jockey for WRFS in Alexander City, Alabama. He was on daily with shows like the ''Cowbell Club,'' the ''1050 Club,'' and ''Bob's Ballroom.'' He was a friend of the Williams family; and at the request of Lillie Williams, he took Hank to Lake Martin for recuperation in the middle of August 1952, just after the firing from The Grand Old Opry. McKinnon lives now in Wetumpka, Alabama. His interview of Hank and Audrey aired in 1950 in Alexander City and is typical of the radio promotions made by the couple as they toured. Hank is in good spirits here and seems remarkably eager to promote Audrey. The taped interview was generously contributed by Bruce Gidoll of Provo, Utah.

B.M. It's mighty fine to have all these best-selling records. But this morning, man, we got something better than that. We have *the* man himself Hank Williams. Hank, how are you?

H.W. Aw, fine Bob; it's awfully good to see you again, fella.

B.M. It's mighty good to see you. The world's being nice to you, I suppose.

H.W. Aw, just fine. How's every body in Alex City getting along?

B.M. They doing fine, Hank. The way your records are selling all over the country and the way that *Billboard* and all these magazines write you up, I can say that you're doing O.K.

H.W. Well, we're eatin', about three times a day, I reckon.

B.M. Who's this really attractive young lady you have here with you?

H.W. That's my War Department. That's my boss there. That's Mrs. Hank.

B.M. Can't we get her to say a few words?

H.W. She'd be glad to.

B.M. Might I ask you first, Mrs. Hank, how did he ever get such an attractive wife? May I say that or would that be the wrong thing to say?

A.W. I'll tell you, we just won't go into that. Thanks anyway.

B.M. It certainly is nice to have you on our program, too. I understand that sometime ago you did some numbers with Hank. Is that right?

A.W. Yes, that's right. We did a couple, I believe, for MGM.

B.M. Well that's fine. It certainly is a pleasure to have both you folks here. Hank, what's up for the future? What records have you got coming out? What can you tell us about the future?

H.W. Well, you got this new one called "Long Gone Lonesome Blues"?

B.M. I reckon I have, boy. Spinning it every day.

H.W. Well that's fine. I don't know what's comin' up next. They don't tell me. Everybody else finds out before I do. By the way, Audrey's gonna make some records here a little later. They talkin' to her about recording. She's gonna record for Decca. You ought to have some of them before long.

B.M. I sure do, ah, ah. . . . I'm gonna look for 'em Hank. I don't have any of 'em now. but.

H.W. They haven't made 'em yet.

B.M. Maybe that's why I haven't got any.

H.W. That's possible.

B.M. How was this overseas trip you took here a while back?

H.W. Aw, that was a fine deal. We went to . . . where did we go honey? We went to Berlin, we went to Vienna, we went to Wiesbaden [Hank is very careful with the pronunciation, which brings a good bit of laughter] we strictly went to Wiesbaden. We went all over the occupied zone over there. Where we had any boys at all we went to see 'em. And by the way, on the nineteenth, me and the boys are goin' to Alaska and see all the boys up there, gonna go up and pick them a few tunes, that is, if we can get thawed out enough.

B.M. Well, Hank, that's mighty fine. I tell you, there is another thing, too, I'd like to ask you right now. How is that young fella Randall Hank gettin' along?

H.W. You mean "Bocephus," huh?

B.M. "Bocephus," is that what it is?

H.W. Yea, I got to calling him that when he was first born, and he's got to where he won't answer to nothin' else.

B.M. So, Hank Williams, it's been nice being with you once again. I'd like to tell you that I still think you're number one in friendliness and the number one hillbilly artist today. It's a pleasure to play your records because you are such a nice guy and because your records are so good. Anything you'd like to tell the good folks in Alabama?

H.W. Yea, that's awful kind of you, Bob. You know, Alabama is my home. Well, it's both our homes; me and my wife both come from Alabama. And we're sorta partial to the folks in Alabama. In fact, we are always talking about Alabama everywhere we go. I get back down to Montgomery about, say, every two or three months—see my mother; she lives down there. My wife's people live down below Troy, Alabama. We go down quite often; we stay in pretty close contact with Alabama. I'd like to say thanks to everybody for requesting these tunes, and we really appreciate it. And everytime you buy one of these records, remember that it's not that I need the money so bad, but the folks I owe need it awfully bad.

B.M. Thank you, Hank Williams. And Mrs. Hank, mighty glad to have you with us today. And we'll be looking for those records you're going to make.

BOB PINSON

Bob Pinson is head of acquisitions at the Country Music Foundation Library and Media Center in Nashville. A native of Wichita Falls, Texas, he moved to California in 1947 in what he calls the "post-war Okie rush." He began collecting records at the age of eleven and eventually accumulated over fourteen thousand volumes. The Country Music Foundation bought that collection in 1972, shortly before Pinson came to work for the Foundation, and it became the basis for a current disc inventory of over one hundred thousand volumes. Pinson is one of country music's finest scholars, one of its best discographers, and certainly one of its most devoted fans. Two of his particular interests are Bob Wills and Hank Williams. This interview took place in Pinson's office in The Country Music Foundation Library on 16 February 1982.

Q. Bob, do you think Hank Williams's greatness was as writer or as performer?

B.P. I give him credit for both. But to me, performing was the main thing. More than anyone else, he put sincerity into the song; he put the guts in honky-tonk music. I don't think anyone before him could put such a hard drive in a vocal, unless it was Roy Acuff, an idol of Hank's.

Q. So Mitch Miller's comment that Hank was another Stephen Foster is not so much to the point? We'll remember Hank as performer for the most part?

B.P. I will remember him both ways. But the gutty performance was the thing. The catalyst for my great interest in him was "Lovesick Blues," and Hank did not write that one. I had heard other records by him, but I did not start buying his records until I heard "Lovesick."

Q. When did you see Hank perform?

B.P. I saw him in San Jose, California, at the Civic Auditorium in 1950.

Q. What were the remarkable characteristics of his performance?

B.P. Again, the sincerity, the real pouring out of the heart. And there was an interesting physical characteristic. I had gone early and gotten a front row seat, looking up at the stage about twelve feet away. When Hank would hit the high note in a yodel, it appeared that his height would expand about an inch. His neck stretched with the note. It looked like he would actually grow with the high notes.

Q. A few have contended that Hank had some contempt for his audiences, that he remembered the demeaning work he had to do as a kid and just did not like to perform for anyone. Would you comment?

B.P. I didn't detect any of that. I met him backstage before he came out, and he received me cordially. He signed my program, and I naively said, "I hope you'll perform 'Lovesick Blues' and 'Long Gone Lonesome Blues' tonight.'' He said he didn't think he'd be letting me down on those two requests.

Q. Was he drinking?

B.P. I did not detect it if he was. He was perfectly gracious. I went back after the show and got the autographs of the Drifting Cowboys, who were just as gracious.

Q. If Hank were working today, would he be drawn to the Opry or to the so-called "Outlaw" group?

B.P. That would have to be pure conjecture, of course. I tend to think he would have been drawn to the outlaw thing. However, you do have to remember that he died before the "rockabilly" phase came in. But, on the other hand, he did have a high regard for Moon Mullican, with whom he apparently collaborated on writing "Jambalaya," and Moon's piano stylings had quite an influence on such rockabillies as Jerry Lee Lewis. Another hint might be his recording session in August of 1947. This seems to be the only session Hank controlled to any degree in terms of musician personnel, and Hank brought in, among others, L. C. Crysel, a jazzy fiddler from Montgomery. Fred Rose was so upset that he substituted fiddler Tommy Jackson for the session's last song. Rose could simply not tolerate Crysel's jazzier licks. When a performer is so closely controlled by his producers, it is hard to tell what his real inclinations are. But Hank had some real interest in other musical forms.

Q. You have studied a few of Hank's show itineraries. What would a typical week in 1950 be like? A Saturday night performance on the Opry in Nashville and then?

B.P. Well, let's take an itinerary from August 1950. On August 12 Hank performed on the Opry. On August 13, he was in Springfield, Ohio. On the 14th, it was Youngstown, Ohio. Then Akron on the 15th and probably New Lewistown, Pennsylvania, on the 16th. On the 17th, he appeared in Richmond, Virginia. And he most likely appeared somewhere else on the 18th before returning to Nashville for the Opry on the 19th. The schedule could be very grueling.

Q. Nashville's recording industry was very young when Hank came up in 1946. I have read that the first record was cut here in 1945. Do you think Hank was important in establishing that industry?

B.P. I think Eddy Arnold did a session at WSM here for RCA in December of 1944. The engineers who opened Castle Studios recognized the potential for recording in Nashville. Artists were having to go to Chicago, Atlanta, or New York to record. And these engineers did not know about Hank when they started. So, instead of starting an industry, Hank came in on one that was just getting under way. Obviously, he gave it a considerable boost.

Q. Just about every country musician today claims some of Hank's influence. Is that just a way of indicating a kind of sincerity, or is Hank's influence that considerable?

B.P. I give them the benefit of the doubt; most of them really loved the man. Ferlin Huskey, George Jones, Faron Young, and Ray Price were probably the most directly influenced. Merle Haggard falls into the Williams category as a singer of the hard life. John Anderson and Ricky Skaggs are more recent examples of real good, hard country singers, with Anderson approaching from the honky-tonk side and Skaggs more from his Bluegrass background.

Q. What is your response to the considerable gossip about Hank?

B.P. It makes no difference to me; the personal life is a separate issue. The music is my major interest.

Q. Hank's music crossed over into pop. But Hank was always content to be a country singer. Is there any reason that he did not try to go popular as a performer?

B.P. Back then, the performers and/or the industry were generally content to let pop artists cover their songs rather than water down their own performances to make them palatable to both audiences. I think Hank was perfectly content to have Tony Bennett record "Cold, Cold Heart" or Rosemary Clooney record "Half as Much"—he would carry the country field and they could carry the pop market. There was not so much a push then for the crossover artist. The whole crossover phenomenon is a complex issue and a book could and, perhaps, should be written on the subject.

Q. I think George Jones is like Hank in that regard. Isn't he content to be a hard country singer?

B.P. There's no doubt on that score. I saw Jones before he ever recorded. He was in the Marines and would perform in a joint called Forester's Hall in Redwood City, California. He came in uniform and sang only Hank Williams songs. This was around 1952. George is certainly cut from Hank's pattern in more ways than one.

Q. Do you think that the Hank/Audrey relationship is somehow reflected in the relationship of George Jones and Tammy Wynette? We seem to know who Hank and George are singing about, and maybe this gives their songs even more authenticity.

B.P. I think there may be some truth in that. Jones was certainly a Hank Williams fan before he had his own domestic problems. But his later songwriting could certainly have been influenced by similar personal problems.

Q. How much talent do you think Audrey Williams had?

B.P. I don't put her on a very high pedestal. She sang flat, but even so she sounded o.k. with Hank. She was not a good performer and to some extent he was indulging her. She was, at first, a regular on one of his early morning radio shows. But someone—Hank, a sponsor, a station manager—decided to drop her. And it was just Hank and the Drifting Cowboys from then on.

Q. Is there anything particular in recent literature on Hank that you would like to comment on?

B.P. I still look on Roger Williams's *Sing A Sad Song* as being the best book. But others have strong points. Jay Caress's book was strong in detailing the night of Hank's death. Flippo's book includes information on dates when Hank was drying out. His book, of course, was a fictionalized biography. And I'm a little reluctant to put quotes around what someone "probably" said. I think he had Hollywood in mind, that he was writing a kind of screenplay. Caress was too willing to accept this Melvin Shestack interview of Hank when Hank was on the Louisiana Hayride and supposedly appeared in the Northeast. That's all fiction; it never happened. And I have some doubts about Caress's use of M. C. Jarrett. Jarrett supposedly had some original tapes. I went to see Jarrett when I read that, and the tapes that were played for me on that visit were not originals. Jarrett had merely overdubbed his own steel guitar on some earlier recordings where steel was nonexistent or at least not very prominent.

Q. You have been in the Williams country there below Montgomery. Did you draw any conclusion about how hard his childhood might have been?

B.P. Not really. That "Black Belt" part of Alabama is a tough area, and I can see how times might not have been easy. I certainly believe the accounts of Hank's having to sell peanuts and shine shoes.

Q. For a singer who was so sincere, that background must have been extremely important?

B.P. Maybe so, but don't overlook the intensity in the singing of hymns at church either. The sincere outpouring of one's soul in shouting out the old church hymns is quite similar. Hank could have been, consciously or unconsciously, carrying that sincerity a step further. Of course, his singing in church as a child has been well documented. And it's also interesting that for his very first recording session Hank performed four of his own compositions, three of which were sacred songs.

Q. Has any country performer ever been as good as Hank Williams?

B.P. Well, when you say "country performer," I immediately think of the whole spectrum. And when I think of these various country music categories, I'd have to say "yes." Bob Wills was for western swing what Williams was for honky-tonk. Then, in a similar view, you'd think of Bill Monroe in bluegrass music, the Sons of the Pioneers or Gene Autry for the cowboy field, old-time groups like the Carter Family, the Skillet Lickers or Charlie Poole, Elvis for rockabilly. Others are more difficult to pigeonhole, such as Jimmie Rodgers or even Johnny Cash. Overall, the list is lengthier than one might initially think.

JERRY RIVERS AND DON HELMS

Jerry Rivers and Don Helms, Hank's fiddler and steel player, respectively, were the backbone of the Drifting Cowboys; their performances gave the band the wailing blues sound that made its music so distinctive. Don, a native of New Brockton, Alabama, joined the band in 1943 and was to meet Hank in Canton, Ohio, for the New Year's performance of 1953, on the day Hank died. He was, then, with Williams practically from beginning to end. Jerry is from Nashville, Tennessee. He turned down an offer to join the Drifting Cowboys when they were playing on The Louisiana Hayride in Shreveport. But he accepted a 1949 offer when Hank was reorganizing his band just after his first appearance on The Grand Ole Opry. Bob McNett, lead guitarist, and Hillous Butrum, on bass, were the other members of the band. Both left the group in 1950, to be replaced by Sammy Pruett and Howard "Cedric Rainwater" Watts. Pruett has returned to his native Alabama after working in Nashville for the Gibson Guitar Company. Watts died in 1972. Butrum has a record sales/promotion business on Music Row in Nashville. McNett lives in Pennsylvania but still plays with Helms, Rivers, and Butrum in the recently reorganized version of The Drifting Cowboys. When not on the road with the band, Rivers and Helms are booking executives with Buddy Lee Attractions, an agency that handles everyone from the Carter Family to Johnny Paycheck to Adam and the

Ants and the Allman Brothers. This interview took place in Rivers's office, on Music Row in Nashville, on 16 February 1982.

Q. Hank Williams, Jr., called you two "fossilized outlaws" on TV recently. Would Hank Sr. and the Drifting Cowboys be more at home with the outlaw movement of today than with The Grand Ole Opry of 1950?

A. (*Jerry*) Junior was making fun of our beards. But, seriously, he might like to think his daddy was the first cowboy/outlaw type. He says that in some of his songs. But Hank was fighting to be part of the established country music world, not to reject it like the outlaws.

(*Don*) Hank was a rebel to some extent, but basically he was just trying to find his place in country music, not start a new phase of country music.

Q. Did Hank ever show any resentment of the way he grew up?

(*Don*) I can't say he ever complained about it. He didn't gripe about those hardships. He was pleased with what he accomplished and knew that he had come a long way from his Alabama childhood.

(*Jerry*) His childhood may have been hard, but he did not resent it. In fact, he may have had problems because he wanted to hold on to that part of his life, to continue being a good old Alabama boy. If other successes were going big-time hunting and fishing, Hank wanted to fish with a pole and worms, or go squirrel hunting. His associates were going to Reelfoot lake with the vice mayor to shoot ducks out of a private, heated blind. Hank was shooting rabbits just outside of Nashville. The problem was that Audrey was climbing the social ladder of country music. None of this impressed Hank. He worked with Fred Rose but didn't want to go out to Fred's mansion for cocktails. All this contributed to his discontent, his insecurity and fear about where he was going. He was country's first superstar and didn't have any patterns to follow. He didn't have some sharp agent to take care of him and tell him how to behave.

(*Don*) I remember going down to pick up a new Cadillac with him, the one he died in, and he looked it over and said, "I got to go to the Belle Mead Country Club tonight. But I ain't goin' by myself; you got to ride with me." So we rode out there with the top down and pulled up in front. The black attendant came out and parked the car, and Hank just marveled at that.

Q. Did he talk about his musical background, about Rufe Payne in particular?

A. (*Don*) He mentioned it. But it seems like its been played up too much. He also mentioned singing in church. But he didn't sit around talking about where he got his start.

(*Jerry*) The general fact that Rufe and the church influenced him is about all anybody really knows.

Q. What about Lillie? Was she as tough as she gets credit for?

A. (*Don*) Aunt Lillie? She pushed Hank very hard. As far back as I knew him, Hank had a little bit of a drinking problem. She'd try to stay on top of that. Hank would get on a tear once or twice a year, several days at a time. And she was strict about watching him. I lived in the boardinghouse on Catoma and saw that.

(*Jerry*) I didn't know her real well, but we'd stop when we went through

Montgomery and she'd cook dinner for us. Naturally, her marital situation wasn't typical of the deep south mother—she was married several times. Otherwise, she was average—well-liked at the boardinghouse. Hank would comment on her from time to time, the way you comment on your wife.

(*Don*) Something like "Boy, don't get her started.'"

Q. Don, you knew Hank when he was courting Audrey. Was it general knowledge that she was still married to Erskine Guy at the time?

A. (*Don*) I didn't know Guy. I was with Hank and Audrey when they married—in a Texaco Station in Andalusia, Alabama.

Q. Was it awkward for the band that Audrey wanted to sing?

A. (*Jerry*) Well, yes. It wasn't comfortable having a woman along, especially the boss's wife. We had to watch what we said. And not only that, she wasn't a good singer. You could kick off a song, and she might not sing in the same key. Who was I to say, "Hey, you got it in the wrong key"? It was uncomfortable.

(*Don*) She just wasn't professional. She cramped our style; she cramped Hank's style. He told me one time, "It's bad to have a wife who wants to sing, but it's hell to have one who wants to sing and can't."

(*Jerry*) But he didn't make an issue out of it the way others have. Her singing wasn't their problem; they had trouble because they got where they didn't trust each other.

Q. Did you know of their divorce of 1948?

A. (*Don*) No. They split plenty of times, but I never heard of a divorce before 1952.

Q. Did Hank talk about Lycrecia?

A. (*Don*) He thought a lot of Lycrecia.

(*Jerry*) There was a strong tie between them before and after the birth of Hank Jr.

Q. Did you ever sense that Hank had any contempt for his audiences?

A. (*Don*) Only toward the few people who came to heckle, to see if he was drunk. Generally, he seemed to thrive on performing.

(*Jerry*) When he picked up his notebook and went on stage, he was determined that they were going to like him. He seemed to draw them to him, and it seemed that everybody felt related to him, like he's one of ours.

Q. What about the Hadacol tour? Was it a good time?

A. (*Don*) It was an extravaganza—the biggest show I'd ever seen. When you're eighteen or nineteen and want to play music, nothing could be better. We were traveling on a private train, all the food you wanted was free, the cleaning was free, a lot of pretty girls, hobnobbing with big names. It was a combination of circus, concert, and comedy.

(*Jerry*) We did not know how big Hank was until we saw him with Bob Hope and Jack Benny.

Q. Was Hank a spontaneous songwriter? Did songs just pop forth?

A. (*Don*) Not always. Sometimes they would. Sometimes he'd struggle with one for an hour and have to shelve it. Then a month later he'd have it. Sometimes he'd write one or two in a night. He wrote a good bit in the car while we were traveling.

Q. Fred Rose worked on some of those songs. Did that bother Hank?

A. (*Don*) No. It was Hank's idea. He worshiped Fred Rose and used him as a sounding board. They'd argue about songs. But Hank always gave him his credit.

(*Jerry*) People make too much of the collaboration. Today they got a dozen producers around telling a songwriter how to write a song. But Hank did not always give in to Fred. Fred didn't want him to record "Lovesick Blues."

(*Don*) Fred told him he [Hank] wrote better stuff than that ["Lovesick Blues"], said the "damn thing was out of meter," and it was. They fussed through the whole recording session. Hank said, "Them damn people down there, I been singing that thing, they like it, they don't know it's out of meter; they think a meter is something you put a nickel in." Fred would walk out and say, "O.K., sing that out-of-meter damn thing then." And he did.

Q. Did Hank talk much about his back problem?

A. (*Jerry*) Yea, we had to cancel some dates when he had his operation. He fell when we were squirrel hunting and that's the first I knew he had such an extensive problem. He was really hurt and I had to carry him. He'd say, "Oh boy, I've done it now." My understanding was that an earlier accident had left him in bad shape. This definitely affected his life. It got him into drugs and he abused his medical privilege. You have to understand that there was no real underground drug traffic here then. It wasn't a matter of getting up for a show with some pills or some cocaine. Hank's drug problem involved prescriptions, stuff he was taking for pain. He'd say, "It says take one every four hours; maybe I ought to take four every hour; that's four times as good, ain't it?" It was a lot more serious than he thought it was. We'd get on him about it, remind him of how he was the day before. But he'd just say that he hurt.

(*Don*) Some writers have tried to bring his drug problem into a more recent setting. But Hank would have been startled by the drug traffic that Nashville knows today. The drug habits of a 1980s rock band have little connection to Hank's habits.

Q. Did Hank ever drink to get happy?

A. (*Don*) If he drank at all, he would just go until he got nasty. He was a binge drinker.

(*Jerry*) In those days, almost every artist on the Opry drank more than Hank. They'd drink every day and go on and be happy. I bet you that Hank drank less than any drinking artist on the Opry. But he wasn't a social drinker.

(*Don*) For five or six days, sometimes eight or ten, boy would he drink, just stay wiped out, till we put him in to dry out.

Q. Would he cooperate when you took him out to Madison Sanitarium?

A. (*Don*) He'd cooperate after you got him in there and got the door closed behind him. He'd fight on the way. He called it "the Hut." They had some little outbuildings with bars on the windows, special dry-out tanks. One time we brought him in off the road; he didn't know where we were going. We pulled up and said, "Come on, Hank; let's get out." And he said, "Oh no, oh no, I ain't goin' in there; that's that fucking hut." The attendants would get him in there and he'd sit and look at us like, "Well, you have screwed me again." He'd stay in three or four days, sometimes a week. I'd take him candy bars and comic books every day and check on him. I lived pretty close. About the third day he'd perk up and say, "reckon when they gonna let us out of here?"

Q. Jerry, in your book you talk about some of Hank's depressions. How did they show themselves?

A. (*Jerry*) He'd withdraw—and it wasn't because of a break with us. We'd tease him a little, call him "lovesick."

(*Don*) He quit going hunting and fishing—quit listening to the ball games on the radio. We'd be ready to take off somewhere and he'd say, "Ya'll go on, I'll meet you there" rather than pile in the car with us the way he used to.

Q. Jerry, you said in your book that Hank's death was shocking but not unbelievable.

A. (*Jerry*) He'd gone on several binges right in a row. We'd come up on him in the Tulane Hotel, where he'd been three or four days without eating. We knew he was acting like this. So though we hadn't seen him for a month or more before he died, we couldn't be completely overwhelmed when we heard he was dead.

(*Don*) I've gone to his room when he was on those binges, and when I'd start in I'd get the feeling like, "Well, what am I going to find. There might be a window open and him out it."

Q. What performer today do you think is most in his tradition?

A. (*Jerry*) George Jones, except that George is not as interested in writing as Hank. George can make an audience love him the way Hank could, and they forgive him the way they forgave Hank.

(*Don*) Merle Haggard has to be considered. I hear some of Hank's sincerity in Merle's work. And he's getting to be a pretty good writer, too.

Q. You reorganized the Drifting Cowboys in 1976. How have they been received?

A. (*Jerry*) It was 1977 before we actually got on the road. It's going well. We worked over one hundred and thirty dates last year [1981]. Most of what we have done has been in tribute to or somehow related to Hank Williams. That's what we are best known for. We just did a two-record set, a tribute to Hank, specifically for TV sales. We are working now with Delta records. We did a Hank Williams record for them. But we have just finished a record for Delta that has no Hank Williams on it. We'd like to work toward some of our own identity.

Q. Did you know Billie Jean?

A. (*Jerry*) She was a knockout—and naive—she couldn't ring a doorbell then. But she's smart and tough now.

Q. Did Hank marry her to spite Audrey?

A. (*Don*) I've thought about it—rebound.

(*Jerry*) She was a beautiful young girl; it was an ego trip for Hank, and he was trying to get Audrey out of his mind. But he really did love Audrey, and she loved him.

(*Don*) Yes, he loved her. Hank loved Audrey; he really did.

(*Jerry*) I think there were times when he wished he hadn't loved her because they did get crossways on a lot of things.

Q. Any closing remarks?

A. (*Don*) Just it was a pleasure to have been associated with someone immortalized, someone they still write about and seek information on. I'm pleased to have been associated with Hank Williams.

Q. Is there any comment you want to make on the history of Hank Williams?

A. (*Jerry*) It was brief, probably more so than the books and movie have implied.

NOTES

1. Allen Rankin, "Rankin File," *Montgomery Advertiser,* 4 April 1948, p. 3B. In a discussion of writing a song, Hank said, "If it takes any longer than 15 minutes I know the idea is no good and throw it away."

2. Roger M. Williams, *Sing A Sad Song: The Life of Hank Williams,* second edition (Urbana: University of Illinois Press, 1981), p. 184.

3. The interview is reprinted in Thurston Moore's *Hank Williams The Legend* (Denver: Heather Enterprises, 1972), p. 48. It appeared originally in the June 1953 issue of *Country Song Roundup,* p. 12.

4. Jerry Rivers, *Hank Williams: From Life To Legend,* second edition (Goodlettsville, Tennessee: Published by Jerry Rivers, no date but about 1981), p. 22.

5. Rankin, "Rankin File," *Montgomery Advertiser,* 4 February 1953, no pagination.

6. "Hank Williams" by Melvin Shestack in *The Country Music Encyclopedia* (New York: Thomas Y. Crowell, 1974), pp. 301-306. The interview is reprinted in "Hank Williams: He Had Country Soul," in *The Songs of Hank Williams* (New York: Barnes and Noble, undated), pp. 7-26.

7. Ralph J. Gleason, "Perspectives: Hank Williams, Roy Acuff and Then God!!" *Rolling Stone,* 28 June 1969, p. 32.

8. Rufus Jarman, "Country Music Goes to Town," 41 (February 1953), 49. The interview is reprinted in Linnell Gentry's *A History and Encyclopedia of Country, Western, and Gospel Music* (St. Clair Shores, Michigan: Scholarly Press, 1972), pp. 115-124.

4

BIBLIOGRAPHICAL ESSAY
AND BIBLIOGRAPHY

BIBLIOGRAPHICAL ESSAY

Establishing a standard biography and evaluation of Hank Williams is difficult. One problem is that myth intervenes constantly, and the point where the human character ends and the nearly divine one begins is unclear. Hank left little behind other than his songs and recordings to tell about himself. His mother, Lillie, was relentless in her romanticizing of her son and of her part in his success. Audrey, Hank's first wife, was so eager to capitalize on the myth that she gave little really dependable information. Billie Jean Jones, his second wife, knew him only briefly. Hank's sister, Irene, has not yet published the book she announced long ago. Toby Marshall supposedly wrote a two-hundred page manuscript on the last months of Hank's life, but Toby, who would be eighty-two now, has disappeared, his manuscript with him. And Hank Jr. was only three when his father died; his autobiography, *Living Proof,* has more to do with living with Hank's myth than with Hank.

Another problem is that Hank's behavior clashed with the wholesome image cultivated by the world of The Grand Ole Opry. The inner circle of country music has not been anxious to expose the entire man. Some liked Hank well enough to want to let myth protect him; others know that the myth still helps bring in hard cash. Nashville is loosening up, but the shrine of Hank Williams is still well guarded. Scholars were not especially quick to besiege it anyway because neither country music nor the South that has been its stronghold was entirely respectable in the early 1950s.

When I started this project, the author of an earlier biography told me that finding Hank Williams would be rough. He was right; Hank will elude us for a long time to come, perhaps even for good. Nonetheless, I offer the following essay and bibliography to those who want to search or to those who are simply curious about where I have been and what use I have made of my sources.

Fortunately for those working on the life and work of Hank Williams, a good bit of research has been done already, much of it very recently. The most timely and most conspicuous book is *Your Cheatin' Heart: A Biography of Hank Williams* (1981) by Chet Flippo of *Rolling Stone*. As his preface indicates, Flippo has done what may be the most extensive research into Hank's life. He has ransacked the usual sources; additionally, he has researched Toby Marshall, studied Hank's medical record and autopsy report, investigated the relationship between Hank and Paul Gilley "who sold Hank some of his best-loved songs," and seen a private collection of papers belonging to Audrey Williams.

But Flippo resisted the idea of the critical biography that he seems so well qualified to write. Instead, in an attempt to give the life "immediacy and fire," he takes a narrative approach. The facts are plentiful, but the book, for the most part, goes after an accurate feeling for the man. Flippo is a good writer, and he is shrewd in taking this narrative approach, for it gives him the freedom to go after what he believes to be the real Hank Williams, while it may give *Your Cheatin' Heart* an especially broad audience. Like much of Nashville's music, the book is designed to be a crossover hit—one that country fans will not miss, one that those who know little about country music can still enjoy. Many of Hank's fans will be put out by the laid-bare version of the man that Flippo presents. Those pursuing history are going to be frustrated because Flippo's kind of writing does not admit a means of separating fact from interpretation. But no one, including those who have never heard of Hank Williams, is going to be denied a good read in this volume. Flippo's view of the singer/composer as a hard, depressed, and largely antisocial character may be a necessary slant in the search for Hank Williams.

The appeal that Flippo seems to want calls less for the ordinary and more for the shocking, and sometimes he overdraws his characters and situations. For example, we see Lillie, who was huge at two hundred and twenty-five pounds, snatching the five-pound Hank from her own womb, holding him up like a rabbit to be chopped behind the ears. Lon, meanwhile, was drunk on the porch. He was well-versed on dodging his wife's right-cross. Young Hank was to learn quickly from his dad and, according to Flippo, spent time hiding out in the graveyard. If this is fiction, it is heavy-handed; if it is fact, surely it could be put more subtly. The point, though, is good enough; these broadly drawn opening scenes show us the bases of Hank's weakness, the ease with which women would always dominate him and the deceptive solace that he would find in a jug. Flippo's research on the alcoholism reveals many of Hank's stays in sanitariums, beginning with the one in Prattville, Alabama, in 1945; his speculation about Hank's growing up under Lillie's thumb is that it explains why Hank had so much difficulty forming real friendships with men.

Flippo's version of Hank's early years is sensible, and it moves well. He identifies the spinal problem, the "spina bifida occulta of the first sacral segment of the lower spine" (p. 153), and his medical research here is convincing. He gives an interesting version of Miss Audrey, a passionate country girl who started sleeping with Hank long before she was divorced from her first husband. Her devious use of sex to get her way is certainly a major thread winding through Flippo's view of the marriage. Like Lillie, Audrey takes plenty of lumps from Flippo, who sees her infidelity as one of Hank's major problems. He is, moreover, the first to identify in print Audrey's divorcing of Hank on 26 May 1948, exactly a year before the birth of Hank Jr. He notes, of course, that the divorce was amended *Nunc pro tunc* on 9 August 1949.

Another issue that Flippo takes up is that of the amount of collaboration involved in Hank's songwriting. We may like the image of Williams as spontaneous composer, as one whose sensitivity to the world around him overflowed into fine songs. Evidently, Hank had as much of that gift as anyone; but at the same time, many writers, among them Ed Linn and Roger Williams, have discussed the help he got from Fred Rose and Vic McAlpin. Without giving us too much evidence, Flippo dwells on this issue, implying that Hank may have received more help than we knew about and arguing that Paul Gilley, a Moorehead State College basketball player, wrote versions of "I'm So Lonesome I Could Cry" and "Cold, Cold Heart." This view is an interesting one that shows the easy commerce between young songwriters and established stars. But I wish we could have had more specific facts here; and I wish, like many of Hank's fans I suspect, that Flippo had not given this quite so much the air of an exposé.

A few other points need mentioning. Flippo has an interesting view of Hank's relationship with his audiences. Roger Williams in *Sing A Sad Song* has said of Hank that "had life required only that he sing to loving crowds of people, he'd be singing to them still" (p. 147). Hank knew how to entertain crowds. But as Flippo notes, late in his career and deep into his alcoholism, Hank could be contemptuous of an audience and surly on stage. Flippo's idea is that the alcohol brought out a truly antisocial streak in Hank that perhaps had its basis in Hank's street peddling and shoeshining. He was, Flippo implies, willing to accept the money and praise of a shoeshine customer, but he was resentful of those who would put him through his paces in such a way. I am not sure that the parallel between shining shoes and performing for adoring throngs holds up, but perhaps it suggests accurately a facet of Williams's personality.

Flippo goes into some detail with regard to Hank's sex life, with Audrey and Billie Jean and a few others, including at least one fifteen-year-old. Once again, footnotes would be interesting, though documenting the deeds of darkness has never been easy. Another point that gets attention concerns Hank's death, which has been shrouded in the mystery of what and how much Hank was taking and drinking at the time. Flippo gives this a turn by speculating that Hank had been in a barroom fight shortly before his death. His other addition here is what he takes to be Hank's last song, the love note perhaps to Audrey, that he supposedly clutched as he died. Most readers should be cautious about accepting the last item as fact.

Your Cheatin' Heart reads well enough. Obviously, though, it will dismay some of Hank's best fans while leaving others to long for more information. It cannot be counted as traditional biography; such, according to its author, was not the intent, although the subtitle and the documentary photographs imply historicity. I think it is one of the more popular treatments of Hank's life, and I think as well that it could go into film easily. If this turns out to be the case, I hope the filmmakers will temper it with the calmer presentations of writers like Roger M. Williams.

Roger Williams—a New York writer who has worked for *Sports Illustrated, Time,* and *Saturday Review*—is probably the best-known Hank Williams scholar, and practically all work on the singer/composer in the past ten years is deeply indebted to him. Doubleday published his *Sing A Sad Song: The Life of Hank Williams* in 1970; Ballantine Books put out a paperback edition of it in 1973; and the University of Illinois Press published the second edition of the volume as part of its Music in American Life series in 1981. This second edition is the most accessible, and it is the most valuable of the three because it includes a fine discography by Bob Pinson of The Country Music Foundation Library and Media Center. Unfortunately, it does not include the photographs that are a part of the paperback. And perhaps more unfortunately, the book was printed from the plates of the 1970 edition; so Roger Williams's very brief afterword is the only updating. The anachronisms are no major problem. But the book does miss out on ten years of information. *Sing A Sad Song,* though, is a good work; and, at least partially because of Pinson's discography, it might be called the standard book on Hank Williams.

The biography's particular strength is its treatment of Hank's youth. The coverage is extensive, the mythology is kept in its place, and the credibility is strong because of the author's numerous interviews with Hank's family and acquaintances. These interviews may turn out to be the most valuable part of the book because the memories of family and friends fade and the immediate family dwindles. Another strength, certain to appeal to country fans in general and Hank Williams fans in particular, is the calm and nonsensational perspective. Hank Williams here is a wild enough character, but he is not quite so bizarre as he is in Chet Flippo's version.

As this book gives the basic facts of the biography, it also shows some of the basic problems of dealing with Hank Williams. Roger Williams misses the date of the marriage of Lillie and Lon Williams; he assigns the 1916 wedding to 1918, probably because Lillie herself always gave 1918 as the year. In trying to work out the source of Hank's back problem, Roger Williams is reduced to suggesting that the star might have fallen off ice skates as a child, an improbable episode south of Montgomery. And he is a little uneasy about the region he is dealing with, a little skeptical about Hank's native South. His discussions of Alabama lynchings and the slayings of civil rights workers by way of backdrop may have seemed necessary to a writer at work in the late 1960s, but they seem a little self-conscious now.

A related problem is that Roger Williams is not certain of just how much the general public knows about the South and country music. In order to keep it all clear, he drifts into digressions on whiskey stills, the southern connection between politics and country music, the role of radio stations, the social strata of Nashville, and the origins of musical instruments. Sometimes these wanderings are interesting; often they seem like padding. I think that Roger Williams, had he been writing a few years later when both the South and country music had become a little more respectable, could have avoided most of this. The other problem that this author, like everyone else writing on Hank, has is in the chronology of the Nashville part of Hank's career. All of Hank's moves in the era will never be charted. Pinson's discography dates Hank's recording sessions and thus helps with the chronology. Ironically, Roger Williams includes Pinson's discography without being able to use its information in his own text because he could not revise it for his 1981 edition.

But in spite of my bickering, *Sing A Sad Song* will continue as a major part of Hank Williams scholarship. It is, as I have said, both thorough and sensibly calm. I would recommend that readers, as they finish the book, turn to Roger Williams's recent essays on Hank. One is in the 1975 volume, *Stars of Country Music: Uncle Dave Macon to Johnny Rodriguez,* which is edited by Bill C. Malone and Judith McCulloh. The other is *Hank Williams,* a 1981 booklet that comes with the first issue of the *Time/Life* "Country and Western Classics," a three-record set of Hank Williams's music. Both of these essays reflect the work of a writer who has done very careful scholarship and then has had quite a bit of time to think about it and to temper it with more recent work. Both of these essays have good evaluations of Hank's artistry and influence, and the *Time/Life* booklet has a particularly good and succinct biography along with good notes, by Charles K. Wolfe and Bob Pinson, on the background of the forty songs on the records. This booklet, taken with the records, is a fine introduction to Hank Williams.

Another book generally considered to be important is *Hank Williams: Country Music's Tragic King* by Jay Caress, a country disc jockey, singer, editor, and recently converted Christian from Illinois. Caress does not add a great deal to our knowledge of Hank. For the most part, he works with materials presented by Roger Williams, extrapolating them with some curious ideas and some purple prose. Hank gets compared to King Saul, King Lear, and Van Gogh, all in one paragraph (p. 7). Hank's marriage to Audrey, in the hands of Caress, comes to be like that of Lincoln to Mary Todd. Another padded discussion points out that "Every great and popular artist has been an unknown at one point" (p. 61). A discussion of "the art of pain" suggests that "It's almost as if one night Edgar Allan Poe had delivered by cosmic mail his invisible mantle of pain's dark hidden wisdom to some iron bridge down on some back-country creek between Montgomery and Shreveport" (p. 91). Later we find that audiences were "slapped into Silly Putty by Hank Williams" (p. 122). Hank, I'm afraid, was born too soon for Silly Putty.

Caress writes better prose when he is sure of his subject. He is good on Hank's death and the circumstances surrounding it. He is helpful, too, with a concluding summary of what has happened to the story's major characters since Hank's death. But otherwise, the book is just not up to the subject. Some confused facts and the acceptance of some of the mythology as fact spoil its credibility. The conclusion, which sees the deceased Hank heading for his eternal reward, is almost bizarre. All of us wish heaven for Hank Williams; few though have visualized it as clearly as Jay Caress, who has God watching Hank "take his solitary ride into eternity." Caress goes on to describe Hank's view of the world from various heights as Hank travels upward. Finally, the departed hero has "this sense of, of *glory.* . . . There was a magnetic presence, an energizing aliveness to the space he floated in, yet the perfection he felt was still nothing he could see—it merely affected the way he saw everything else" (p. 231). The spirit of Hank, gazing down on the world below, realizes that it will burn itself out just as he did. Thus Hank becomes parable for the earth itself.

Jerry Rivers's *Hank Williams: From Life to Legend* adds another dimension to the materials on Hank. Rivers, Hank's fiddler from 1949 to 1952, deals less with scholarly detail and much more with the impressions and anecdotes appropriate for a memoir. This reminiscence, begun ten years after Hank's death, sticks mostly to the period during which Rivers knew Hank. The book, then, is a useful resource for The Grand Ole Opry part of Hank's life. Rivers is obviously affectionate about Hank; and although he brings up the problems of drugs and drink, he does not allow them their full role. *From Life To Legend* is particularly good in describing the Hadacol tour, and its collection of photos of Hank's funeral is the best in print. The discography in this book has been superseded by Bob Pinson's, but Rivers does list some of the records in tribute to Hank. In his second edition, he includes a discography of the reorganized Drifting Cowboys.

Another reminiscence is of value, but perhaps for the wrong reasons. Lillie Williams's *Our Hank Williams: "The Drifting Cowboy"* as told by his mother to Allen Rankin—an eighteen-page booklet that sold for a dollar mainly through the mails—is often wrong about details and is generally self-serving. Lillie's comment that Hank was only five when Lon left belongs more to the wronged wife than to history. She is much further off as she claims to have left Hank in Mobile for only three weeks instead of the nearly two years indicated by the Alabama Shipbuilding and Drydock Company. She is right to emphasize Hank's religious songs but probably wrong to say that "Hank was a sort of preacher at heart." Apparently she misunderstood Hank's back problem completely; she describes it this way: "With all of his traveling he had developed a spinal injury. He had to have an operation. Some people thought that the way Hank trembled and 'suffered' over a song was part of his act but his friends knew that the 'act' was real. He was suffering continuously." Lillie has her best moment as she describes the relationship of Hank and Audrey: "They say the course of true love never runs smoothly. Certainly it didn't in this case."

The chief value of the book is that it identifies the sources of some of the Hank Williams myths as it reveals a good share of his mother's personality. Lillie is the one who tells the tale of Hank's writing "Mansion On The Hill" by way of proving his songwriting ability to Fred Rose. If history has Hank and Audrey calling on Fred, Lillie has Fred hearing "Move It On Over" and calling Hank in for a contract. Apparently Lillie was eager to keep Audrey's part minimal. She was just as eager to give herself a major role in practically everything her son did; and *Our Hank Williams,* I think, really is Lillie's Hank Williams.

Much less fanciful than Lillie's work is Robert K. Krishef's *Hank Williams* (1978). This sixty-four page biography for children, ages from about ten to fourteen, is direct and well written, accessible without being condescending. Krishef does not avoid Hank's drinking or his marriage to Billie Jean Jones, two items that Lillie steers carefully around.

A few other books call for mention. Thurston Moore's *Hank Williams The Legend* (1972) is a collection of articles that range from maudlin fan rag stuff to good scholarship. For example, Bill C. Malone's good introduction, "Hank Williams: Voice of Tradition in a Period of Change," is followed by Irene Williams Smith's Ouija board approach to Hank's death, "My Treasured Life with a Beloved Brother." The volume reprints John Stephen Doherty's "Hank Williams Won't Die," an article better than its title, especially in its treatment of Hank's adult life and his involvements with women. A good collection of liner notes, written by everyone from Paul Ackerman to Nat Hentoff, is included along with a good many sentimental reminiscences, a recipe for crawfish pie, a discography, an interview, and a useful assortment of news clippings. Obviously, the book is irregular, but a careful reader can benefit by noting

The Legend's facts and its reflection of the popular response to Hank Williams.

Hank As We Knew Him (1982) is a helpful little booklet published by the Three Arts Club of Georgiana and Chapman, Alabama. It lists no author but is copyrighted in the name of Sherry Bowers. The twenty-four pages focus on Hank's local reputation and include some good photos of his boyhood haunts along with some clippings from *Butler County News*. Mr. and Mrs. Burton Odom prepared a similar booklet, *The Hank Williams Story* (1974), for the Butler County Historical Association. Largely dependent on Roger Williams, this volume gathers the essentials of Hank's life and adds a few new comments by acquaintances of Hank's. Harry E. Rockwell's *Beneath the Applause (A Story About Country and Western Music and Its Stars—Written by a Fan)* (1973) is an account of a fan's pilgrimage through Hank's world. Its particular interest is an interview with Lon Williams and some good details gathered from those in Oak Hill, West Virginia, who were associated with Hank's death.

Of much less use are Jim Arp's *The First Outlaw: Hank Williams* (1979) and Al Bock's *I Saw The Light: The Gospel Life of Hank Williams* (1977). Arp, a North Carolina disc jockey and musician, obscures a worthy idea, that Hank was the precursor of today's "outlaw" singers, in this little volume. His rambles through country music and over Hank Williams are sometimes entertaining, but they are almost always too general to be of much help. The book is not easy to find but can be ordered from A&B Enterprises, 403 Phifer Road, Kings Mountain, North Carolina 28086. Al Bock works over Hank's religious inclination mercilessly as he tries to prove the obvious, that Hank's "gospel songs were consistent with the fundamental Christian faith which was at the root of his life" (p. 5). In making his case, Bock does recount the basic facts of Hank's life, but his apologies for Hank's drinking and honky-tonking are inappropriate; and his garrulous discussion of "I Saw The Light" dwells on how electricity has diminished our appreciation of light as an image of God. His discography is basically the same as the one by Jerry Rivers in *Hank Williams: From Life To Legend*.

Several books offer some good background that is of help in establishing Hank's context. Paul Hemphill's *The Nashville Sound: Bright Lights and Country Music* (1970) is good reading and gives us a fine if now slightly dated taste of Nashville's atmosphere. Hemphill's Hank is a rounder who did much to give the wholesome Music City a more worldly tint. Michael Bane's *White Boy Singin' the Blues: The Black Roots of White Rock* (1982) finds Hank caught between the heavy influences of blues and the primarily white world of country music. Peter Guralnick's *Lost Highway: Journeys and Arrivals of American Musicians* (1979) places Hank nicely into the world of the blues and honky-tonk. The very readable and outrageous

Country: The Biggest Music In America (1977), by Nick Tosches, is good on Hank's influences, especially on rock and roll. And since Minnie Pearl was so closely associated with Hank, her autobiography (1980) is important. Her story contains an abundance of sweetness and light; but her chapter on Hank (22) is tough and accurate as it focuses on her friend in the last part of his career.

The most scholarly books on the Nashville music scene are John W. Rumble's Vanderbilt University dissertation, *Fred Rose and the Development of the Nashville Music Industry, 1942-1954* (1980) and Bill C. Malone's *Country Music U.S.A. A Fifty-Year History* (1968). Rumble explains better than anyone the intricacies of music publishing, and he includes many details about Hank's relationship with Acuff-Rose. He notes that Hank often "depended on Rose to complete compositions he [Hank] had begun" (p. 126) and that the association with Hank "largely accounted for Rose's recognition and commercial prosperity" (p. 116). I trust that the dissertation will soon be available from a commercial publisher. Malone's book, published for the American Folklore Society's Memoir Series, is a thorough work that finds that "Williams was the symbol of country music's postwar upsurge, and his sudden death in 1953 signified the ending of the boom period" (p. 232). Like Rumble, Malone is sure that Hank was important in establishing Acuff-Rose as a prosperous business.

Dealing with the articles in newspapers and magazines is nearly impossible. Much of that material is of the "fan" variety and is not of special help to researchers. And most of the material that is substantially historical has been absorbed by the many books on Hank. Those who want to sample this material should see the clippings files at the Country Music Foundation Library and Media Center in Nashville and at the Department of Archives and History in Montgomery. The Nashville file draws from broad sources, while the Montgomery version concentrates on Alabama papers. However, the Montgomery collection includes a scrapbook of clippings on Hank, *Hank Williams Scrap Book,* collected by Charles B. McKee. A Montgomery band leader, McKee clipped articles from many sources, especially *Variety*, and donated his scrapbook to the Archives on 11 January 1966. Most major newspapers have files on Hank; I found some good information in the morgue of the *Atlanta Journal-Constitution,* for example. Another representative source is Thurston Moore's collection of articles and clippings in *Hank Williams The Legend* mentioned earlier. The 11 January 1953 issue of the *Montgomery Advertiser-Alabama Journal* is filled with articles and letters about Hank and includes the article by Lillie (as told to Allen Rankin) that became the basis for the booklet *Our Hank Williams.* The June 1953 issue of *Country Song Roundup* is devoted to Hank as is the March 1975 issue of *Country Music Magazine,* which includes articles by Hank Jr., Nick Tosches, and Dave Hickey. This same issue prints a number of good photographs. One might also check the significant dates in Hank's life against the appropriate issues of *Billboard*.

Any number of "encyclopedic" books mentions Hank. Charles K. Wolfe does a good brief comparison of Hank and Jimmie Rodgers in *Tennessee Strings: The Story of Country Music in Tennessee* (1977). Henry E. Pleasants's essay on Hank in *The Great American Popular Singers* (1974) is a readable introduction that is largely dependent on Roger Williams. Robert Shelton includes a similar introduction in *The Country and Music Story: A Picture History of Country and Western Music* (1966). Linnell Gentry's brief statement on Hank in *A History and Encyclopedia of Country, Western, and Gospel Music* (1972) is good only for the basic facts. But Gentry's book does reprint Rufus Jarman's *Nation's Business* article, "Country Music Goes To Town" (February 1953). Jarman includes some fine quotes from Hank. By far the most handsomely produced essay on Hank is in Jack Hurst's *Nashville' Grand Ole Opry* (1975). A number of folio-size photographs accompany the concise introduction to Hank.

Probably the most often cited articles are the Ed Linn piece in *Saga* (January 1957) and the two pieces by Eli Waldron in the *Reporter* (19 May 1955) and in *Coronet* (January 1956). Waldron accepts a good bit of Lillie Williams's information, which is not very dependable. He repeats the mother's story about retrieving Hank from Mobile as well as her tale about Hank's writing "Mansion On The Hill" for Fred Rose. Linn's work is more thorough and more accurate; it belongs in the category with John Stephen Doherty's "Hank Williams Won't Die" as a good early article. Doherty's work, which originally appeared in the May 1959 issue of *Climax,* is one of the strongest parts of Moore's *Hank Williams The Legend.* I think, though, that the Roger Williams essays mentioned already will continue to be the best short works done on Hank Williams.

The many tribute articles are usually very personal statements by those who have had some brush with Hank and his music; few are of particular use in the search for historical details. But several are very articulate and well worth reading. The best among them is probably David Halberstam's clean summary of Hank's life and unsentimental evaluation of his music in *Look* (13 July 1971). David Mankelow's "Legend," which appeared in the April 1973 issue of *Country,* is a good twenty-years-after appraisal that discusses Hank's rural origins, his sincerity, and his popular appeal. Mankelow concludes that Hank is the father of modern country music. John Mortland did a similar story for the April 1973 issue of *CREEM.* Melvin Shestack discusses the survival of Hank's work in a commemorative piece for *Country Music* (January 1973). Nick Tosches gets down to some close analyses of Hank's music in the special Hank Williams issue of *Country Music* (March 1975). He praises Hank's simplicity and then makes this important point: "Simplicity in song-writing is no virtue by itself: the trick is to convey profound moods or thoughts in a simple manner. Hank did that'' (p. 30).

Not every writer, though, has been so thrilled with Hank Williams and country music. A *Variety* staffer was not very kind in a piece, "Hank Williams Immortal to Cornball Fans," that talks about the "hinterland folk" who admire Hank (29 April 1953). Wesley Pruden is more than a little snide in his *National Observer* article, "Ol' Hank: 'Widow Williams' Settles Old Score," which concerns some of Billie Jean Horton's litigation against the Williams estate. Frank Clayton was not especially kind in his depiction of Hank's August 1952 arrest in Alexander City, Alabama. *The Alabama Journal* story of 20 February 1971 bares a gaunt and dying Hank in the midst of the D.T.s. Ralph Gleason was no gentler in his *Rolling Stone* story of 28 June 1969 as he recounts the difficulties of interviewing a Hank Williams strung out on booze and pills.

But to find Hank at his worst, one should turn to the Edith Lindeman story in the *Richmond Times-Dispatch* (30 January 1952). Her review of Hank's Richmond performance is titled "Hank Williams Hillbilly Show Is Different: Star Makes Impression of an Unexpected Kind," and it is scathing. Ray Price opened the show and performed for about thirty minutes before bringing on an obviously inebriated Hank Williams who had trouble remembering his songs and staying on key. Lindeman goes on to describe a disgruntled crowd that could find no one in the box office to make refunds. The ticket salesman, she says, had left to take the proceeds to B. C. Gates, "promoter of the show, who was reported to be ill at home" (p. 18). Hank made a second appearance after the intermission and opened, according to the reviewer, with the following statement to the crowd: "I wish I was in as good shape as you are. Hank Williams is a lot of things but he ain't a liar. If they's a doctor in the house, I'll show him I've been in the hospital for eight weeks and this is my first show since then. And if you ain't nice to me, I'll turn around and walk right off" (p. 18). Lindeman ends with some faint praise for Ray Price. Faulting the writer for her tough comments is difficult, but fans of Williams might well prefer the more sympathetic account of one of his bad performances given by Minnie Pearl in her autobiography. If Lindeman found a drunk hillbilly, Minnie Pearl found a sensitive and tragic man.

Most of Hank's music remains in print and is easy enough to find. The two WSFA songbooks present the only difficulty; they are very rare, and unfortunately they include only the words of the songs because Hank hoped his fans would tune in to pick up the melodies from his radio shows. The first one—*Songs of Hank Williams "The Drifting Cowboys"*—came out in about 1945. The uncopyrighted book sold for thirty-five cents and included the words of the following ten songs: "Grandad's Musket," "Mother Is Gone," "Won't You Please Come Back," "Six More Miles," "I'm Not

Coming Home Any More," "You'll Love Me Again," "A Tramp On The Street," "I Am Praying For The Day That Peace Will Come," "Honkey-Tonkey," and "Take Away Those Lonely Memories." The second book—*Hank Williams and His Drifting Cowboys, Stars of WSFA Deluxe Song Book*—came out in about 1946 and is a little fancier than its predecessor. Reprinting all but one of the songs from the first book, it includes words for the following thirty songs: "I Bid You Free To Go," "Never Again Will I Knock On Your Door," "The Days Are So Long," "I Am Praying For The Day That Peace Will Come," "Singing Water Fall," "Forever Is A Long, Long Time," "You Always Seem To Go The Other Way," "Back Ache Blues," "I'm Not Coming Home Any More," "The Last Message," "I Don't Care If Tomorrow Never Comes," "When God Comes And Gathers His Jewels," "I Never Will Forget," "There's A New Light Shining In Our Home," "In Dreams You Still Belong To Me," "Mother Is Gone," "Some Day You'll Be Lonely Too," "I Watched My Dream World Crumble Like Clay," "Calling You," "Am I Too Late To Say I'm Sorry," "Six More Miles," "Won't You Please Come Back," "My Darling Baby Girl" (with Audrey), "Grandad's Musket," "I Just Wish I Could Forget," "Let's Turn Back The Years," "Honkey-Tonkey," "I Loved No One But You," "A Tramp On The Street," and "You'll Love Me Again." The deluxe edition carried prefaces by Hank and WSFA Program Director Caldwell Stewart. The book is uncopyrighted. These two collections are important because they show us the work Hank had done before he met Fred Rose and because they demonstrate the basic characteristics that would always be a part of Hank's work—the simplicity, sincerity, and directness that he never gave up. That the books are so hard to come by is unfortunate. I found photostats of them in The Country Music Foundation Library and Media Center in Nashville and a few random pages from them in the Alabama Department of Archives and History in Montgomery.

The sheet music for Hank's better known songs is available in several forms. *Hank Williams' Favorite Songs, Hank Williams' Country Music Folio,* and *Hank Williams' Country Hit Parade* are "souvenir" songbooks. Each one includes a short introduction by Fred Rose, several photographs, and twenty songs. However, one should keep in mind that the sixty songs covered by the series come to fewer than half of Hank's complete work. *The Best of Hank Williams* collects thirty songs; and *The Songs of Hank Williams* includes fifty-five numbers, a brief essay on Hank by Melvin Shestack, and a twenty-two entry discography. There is, of course, the inevitable *E-Z Way Edition,* which simplifies twenty-six of Hank's songs for organ, guitar, and piano. The music from the George Hamilton film of Hank's life is available in *Songs from YOUR CHEATIN' HEART.* In addition to the music, the book has a brief introduction by Sam Katzman, producer of the MGM picture, and includes a series of shots from the film.

By far the best source of Hank's music is *The Complete Works of Hank Williams: A 129 Song Legacy of His Music.* Outside of the music itself, the most interesting facet of this volume involves the composer credits, which clearly indicate Hank's various collaborations.

All of the songbooks except the WSFA volumes are available from Thurston Moore Country, Ltd., P.O. Box 1829-30, Montrose, Colorado 81401. All of the books except the WSFA volumes, *The Best of Hank Williams,* and the *E-Z Way Edition* can be ordered from Acuff-Rose International, 2510 Franklin Road, Nashville, Tennessee 37204. Those wishing to quote Hank's songs should be certain to request rights from the publisher, for the country music industry is zealous in protecting its material. As I indicated before, the two WSFA songbooks are uncopyrighted, but some of that music is copyrighted in later editions of Hank's work.

The arts have had a difficult time dealing with Hank. Their versions of him are valuable to researchers only as they reflect the problems involved in dramatizing a life that was so intensely romantic in its own right. Whether or not this observation can be accepted as a general rule, turning the truth to fiction almost always seems to diminish the dramatic qualities of Hank Williams's life. Another problem is that most artistic treatments of the South and of country music have been simpleminded in their depiction of good old boys and girls and their antics—until recently, when we got a sensible film version of Loretta Lynn's life in *Coal Miner's Daughter.*

Your Cheatin' Heart (1964), a low budget MGM film, is typical in both regards. Its little drama pales beside the reality, and the very idea that George Hamilton could play Hank Williams is farfetched. Roger Williams offers amusing praise when he says that Hamilton was perhaps a better choice to play Hank than Sammy Davis, Jr. (*Sing A Song,* p. 241). And Susan Oliver's Audrey makes one think he is watching a Sandra Dee movie, something on the order of *Tammy Goes to Nashville.*

The plot is no stronger than the cast. Hank sings "Jesus Loves Me" as Tee Tot dies in his arms. Then he deserts a medicine show to join *Audrey's* band, the Drifting Cowboys. Hank plays out his part as the mischievous drunk, falling off a horse while celebrating the birth of Hank Jr., singing with backup music reminiscent of Ray Coniff, and finally drying out only to pass away in the back of his car. Notably absent from the film are Hank's divorce from Audrey and his marriage to Billie Jean. That Audrey was MGM's technical adviser may explain the oversights.

The $1.2 million film premiered at Montgomery's Paramount Theatre on 4 November 1964. Stars like Johnny Cash, Tex Ritter, and Roy Acuff put on a two-hour stage show for the occasion; Governor George Wallace contributed by declaring "Hank Williams Week." The film went on to produce a good return for its backers until Billie Jean filed the suits discussed in the biographical essay.

Paul Schrader—who wrote *American Gigolo, Taxi Driver,* and *Raging Bull*—prepared a script for a more recent film based on Hank's life. But the film has never been made. During his research for *Your Cheatin' Heart,* Chet Flippo discussed the script with Schrader and called it "explosive" and then suggested that "It's too raunchy for Hollywood" (*The Greenville* [South Carolina] *News,* 24 April 1981). The only real evidence of Hank in Hollywood, then, continues to be in his songs, which dominate the sound track of *The Last Picture Show.*

The TV special, *A Tribute to Hank Williams: The Man and His Music,* which aired in Nashville on 12 April 1980 (it played at various times elsewhere), included a respectable film biography. Jim Owen, who has long performed a one-man Hank Williams show, is good enough as Hank. Laney Smallwood does not look much like Audrey, but she plays the part well. And the script, by Nashville's Billy and Pat Galvin, is far more realistic than that of the MGM movie. Audrey is not the ever-loving wife this time out; she is cruel enough to leave an ailing Hank at home in bed while she goes out on the town. And Hank is mean enough to take a few shots at her for her trouble. The TV film, however, is really just a series of clips cut into basic entertainment supplied by a series of distinguished singers. Hosted by Hank Jr., the special features such stars as Brenda Lee, Faron Young, Kris Kristofferson, Johnny Cash, Waylon Jennings, Teresa Brewer, and Roy Acuff. It is much more a series of highlights and not a complete document. And it does get sentimental, especially as it approaches Hank's death. Nonetheless, the show is important in that it does not entirely ignore the seamy side of Hank's life.

Two fairly well-known stage productions, both one-man shows, continue to thrive. Jim Owen performs Hank's songs well and has become a standard part of the "Hank Williams All Day Picnic" at Sherling Lake Park in Greenville, Alabama. Parts of his performance are available on the gold record "Jim Owen as HANK" (0102). The Canadian performer Sneezy Waters performs "Hank Williams: The Show He Never Gave" based on what would have been the New Year's Day performance in Canton, Ohio. In November 1981, Albert Harris, a playwright at the University of Tennessee in Knoxville, announced that his *Jambalaya* would open in New York in the fall of 1982. I do not believe that the play has been produced yet.

Alabama writer Babs Deal was the first to try a novel based on Hank's life. His *High Lonesome World: The Death and Life of a Country Singer* (1969) claims no historical reference, but the book is obviously about Hank in almost every detail. It includes the familiar characters—Wade Coley is a pale Hank, who dies on his way to an engagement in Memphis; Miss Audrey becomes Lorene, the divorcee who wanted to be the widow; Billie Jean is Kitty, the new wife; Lillie is Maud, the distressed mother; Luke the Drifter turns up as The Wanderer; and Tee Tot is the shuffling and talented darkey, Linc Smith.

The novel starts with Wade's death and tries to get back through his life by having the various characters respond to the death. Though received reasonably well in 1969, *High Lonesome* seems very dated now, especially in its two-dimensional picture of Hank and country music. And the book is just too busy; its three hundred pages are divided into thirty-seven chapters (three twelve-chapter sections and then a coda called "The Last Long Day"). All the characters focus on the death, and they simply run together as they give us thirty-six versions of the same event.

Probably the most interesting literary treatment of Hank Williams is in Roy Campbell's *Hustler* story, "Little Skeeter's Gotta Learn" (March 1978). In this story a girl named Candy is seduced on the day of Hank's death. She is so pleased with herself, and so anxious for more, that she leaves home, pretending that she is going to Hank's funeral. Actually, of course, she is off to be a hooker. Skeeter, her young admirer, learns of how Candy has abused the sacred memory of Hank, beats her senseless, and then starts his own pilgrimage to Hank's grave. Campbell may have the right idea in letting Hank be more a presence than a character here.

What is left to be done with Hank? From the world of the arts we might like a good novel, one that treats Hank and country music unselfconsciously, without implying that they are aberrations of American life. The point is not so much that the world has to have a particular novel but that such a novel would indicate that the nation has recognized country music and its figures as major and acceptable elements of its culture. We might like a good movie as well, but it may be a long time coming. *Coal Miner's Daughter* might seem to set the right precedent; Hank's life, though, did not have the upbeat aspects of Loretta Lynn's. We need to be sure that we are ready for a treatment of Hank similar to that of Elvis in the more or less documentary *This Is Elvis*.

As for scholarship, the biography can use more documentation, more verification of fact. Much could be done in plotting Hank's various travels and performances out of Nashville and The Grand Ole Opry. The reconstruction of his professional life for those three years would be invaluable for the biography itself and as a mark of the life of the well-known country performer. One hopes that eventually Hank Williams Jr., and his half sister, Lycrecia Guy Morris, will be willing to sit for extended interviews. The other major project is evaluative; just where does Hank fit in the scheme of country music? That, too, may be a while in coming because country music has produced so many offshoots. The many blends of country, with various other types of music, especially rock, may have to settle for a while before we can follow Hank's influences and identify his place.

Those who want to pursue these projects would do well to start with a trip to the Country Music Foundation Library and Media Center at 4 Music Square East in Nashville. The library has complete holdings of literature on country music; it has a record collection of over one hundred thousand volumes; it has a large collection of films about or involving country music figures; and it has a collection of videotapes of many country music television shows, along with a variety of home movie type films involving important figures.

Those working on the life of Hank Williams will find the recordings and literature there. They will also find a print of *Your Cheatin' Heart,* the MGM film; a kinescope of Hank on "The Kate Smith Evening Hour" in 1952; a home movie of one of Lycrecia's birthday parties; a film of the September 1954 "Hank Williams Memorial Day" celebration in Montgomery; and the TV show, "A Tribute to Hank Williams: The Man and His Music." Another valuable resource here is the Armed Forces Radio Service Transcriptions collection of recordings of The Grand Ole Opry done for the military abroad. Unfortunately, Hank's premiere on the Opry on 11 June 1949 was not on the network portion of the show and thus is not on one of the sixteen-inch records. But Hank can be heard on the Opry the following week and for many weeks thereafter.

Some of the literature on Hank is extremely rare and is probably most accessible at the Foundation Library. The photocopies of the two WSFA songbooks are among the holdings as are a copy of *How To Write Folk And Western Music To Sell* by Hank and Jimmy Rule, a copy of Lillie's *Our Hank Williams: "The Drifting Cowboy,"* a copy of Harry E. Rockwell's *Beneath the Applause,* a copy of *The Hank Williams Story* by Mr. and Mrs. Burton Odom, and a copy of *Hank As We Knew Him.* The library also owns a set of the ten Good Vibrations records, *Hank Williams. . . .The Man, The Legend.* These records, made primarily for radio play, blend Hank's music with a number of interviews and with a narrative of Hank's life. The interviews with the Drifting Cowboys, with Faron Young, and with Charles Carr (Hank's driver on the fatal trip to Canton), are particularly valuable. Most of the material on these records concerns Hank's life in Nashville.

The library, as I have indicated, maintains a clipping service and therefore has a good file of news stories about Hank. It owns a copy of John W. Rumble's Vanderbilt dissertation on Fred Rose, a copy of the Souvenir Program for the 1954 unveiling of Hank's tomb, and copies of the two Hank Williams *Family Photo Albums* put out by the Hank Williams Memorial Foundation. The notes for Thurston Moore's *Hank Williams The Legend* are there, as are the documents involved in my own research. Chet Flippo has indicated that his papers will end up in the library. The staff's knowledge of country music makes it one of the archive's best resources.

Those wishing to do research at the Foundation Library should write the reference librarian in advance. Because the stacks are closed, the library can accommodate only a limited number of patrons at any given time. Those working in the library should take time to go upstairs to the Country Music

Hall of Fame and Museum, where they can see Hank's Hall of Fame plaque and portrait, one of his guitars, and an exhibit that includes some of Hank's correspondence with the Roses, the manuscripts of "Six More Miles" and "When God Comes And Gathers His Jewels," and a copy of Hank's first Sterling recording.

Until recently, the Hank Williams Museum, which housed a good many of Hank's personal effects along with the Cadillac in which he died, was less than a block from the Foundation Library, at 115 16th Avenue South. It has been closed, and the rumor is that it is being moved to Cullman, Alabama, the home of Hank Williams, Jr. A few of Hank's personal items, an oil portrait of Hank, the McKee scrapbook on him, and a fine file of news clippings are available at the State of Alabama Department of Archives and History in Montgomery, Alabama, 36310.

The Hank Williams Appreciation Society International offers a good membership package of information and photos from its headquarters at P.O. Box 121 Station A, Flushing, New York 11358. Hank Williams Memorial, Inc., is a group dedicated to building a museum in Montgomery. The organization publishes a newsletter and can be contacted at P.O. Box 5051, Montgomery, Alabama 36101. Bruce Gidoll of Provo, Utah, has a fine private collection of Williams memorabilia. Among many other items, his collection includes numerous foreign pressings of Hank's music, more than two hundred photographs, taped interviews and radio shows, some footage of Hank's funeral, quite a bit of the original sheet music, one of Hank's guitars, an unopened bottle of Hadacol, and a life-sized bronze bust commissioned by Gidoll. George Merritt of Huntsville, Alabama, owns a good collection of photographs and taped interviews.

BIBLIOGRAPHY

Agee, James and Walker Evans. *Let Us Now Praise Famous Men.* Boston: Houghton Mifflin, 1941.

Arp, Jim. *The First Outlaw: Hank Williams.* Kings Mountain, North Carolina: A&B Enterprises, 1979.

"A Tribute To Hank Williams: The Man and His Music." A television special aired in Nashville on 12 April 1980 and at various times elsewhere, written by Billy and Pat Galvin.

Bane, Michael. *White Boy Singin' the Blues: The Black Roots of White Rock.* New York: Penguin Books, 1982.

Blount, Roy. *Crackers.* New York: Knopf, 1980.

Bock, Al. *I Saw The Light: The Gospel Life of Hank Williams.* Nashville: Green Valley Record Store, Inc., 1977.

Campbell, Roy. "Little Skeeter's Gotta Learn." *Hustler,* March 1978, pp. 68-70, 78-80, 88-90.

Caress, Jay. *Hank Williams: Country Music's Tragic King.* New York: Stein and Day, 1979.

Carter, Walter. "Hank Williams's Ghost Blacks Out Opry House." *The Tennessean,* 28 July 1982, p. 29.

Clay, Floyd Martin. *Couzain Dudley LeBlanc: From Huey Long to Hadacol.* Gretna, Louisiana: Pelican Publishing, 1973.

Clayton, Frank. "Remembering Hank." *Alabama Journal,* 20 February 1971, p. 4.

Country Music Magazine, 3 (March 1975).

Country Song Roundup, 1 (June 1953).

"Court To Air Late Singer's Marital Status." *Atlanta Journal,* 23 October 1969, p. 2A.

"Damages Denied to Williams' Widow." *Atlanta Journal,* 6 March 1972, p. 2A.

Deal, Babs H. *High Lonesome World: The Death and Life of a Country Music Singer.* Garden City, New York: Doubleday, 1969.

E-Z Way Edition [of Hank Williams' music]. Wenona, Minnesota, and Milwaukee, Wisconsin: Hal Leonard Publishing, 1982.

Flippo, Chet. "Hank Williams Hits the Opry: 1949." *The Journal of Country Music,* 8, #3 (undated), 5-17.

_____. *Your Cheatin' Heart: A Biography of Hank Williams.* New York: Simon and Schuster, 1981.

Gentry, Linnell. *A History and Encyclopedia of Country, Western, and Gospel Music.* St. Claire Shores, Michigan: Scholarly Press, 1972.

Gleason, Ralph J. "Perspectives: Hank Williams, Roy Acuff and Then God!!" *Rolling Stone,* 28 June 1969, p. 32.

Graves, John Temple II, ed., *The Book of Alabama and the South.* Birmingham: The Protective Life Insurance Company, 1933.

Guralnick, Peter. *Lost Highway: Journeys and Arrivals of American Musicians.* Boston: David R. Godine, 1979.

Halberstam, David. "Hank Williams Remembered." *Look,* 35 (13 July 1971), 42.

Hank As We Knew Him: Memories of the Early Life of Hank Williams As Recalled by Some of Those Who Knew Him. Georgiana and Chapman, Alabama: The Three Arts Club of Georgiana and Chapman, 1982.

"Hank's Widow Illegally Wed." *Alabama Journal,* 15 January 1953, pp. 1A, 7A.

Hank Williams and His Drifting Cowboys, Stars of WSFA, Deluxe Song Book. Montgomery: WSFA, no date but probably about 1946.

"Hank Williams Immortal to Cornball Fans." *Variety,* 190 (29 April 1953), 10, 52.

Hank Williams' Country Hit Parade. Nashville: Fred Rose Music, undated.

Hank Williams' Country Music Folio. Nashville: Fred Rose Music, undated.

Hank Williams Family Photo Album No. 1. Nashville: The Hank Williams
 Memorial Foundation, undated.
Hank Williams Family Photo Album No. 2. Nashville: The Hank Williams
 Memorial Foundation, undated.
Hank Williams' Favorite Songs. Nashville: Fred Rose Music, 1953.
Hank Williams Memorial Souvenir Program. Montgomery: The Alcazar
 Temple, September 1954.
Hank Williams . . . The Man, The Legend. Nashville: Good Vibrations,
 1977. This ten-hour recording was written and narrated by Jim Owen
 and produced by Ron Huntsman.
"Heart Condition Killed Hank, Coroner's Jury Says in Report." *Mont-
 gomery Advertiser,* 11 January 1953, pp. 1A, 8A.
Hemphill, Paul. *The Nashville Sound: Bright Lights and Country Music.*
 New York: Simon and Schuster, 1970.
Horstman, Dorothy. *Sing Your Heart Out, Country Boy.* New York:
 Dutton, 1975.
Hurst, Jack. *Nashville's Grand Ole Opry.* New York: Harry R. Abrams,
 1975.
Jarman, Rufus. "Country Music Goes To Town." *Nation's Business,* 41
 (February 1953), 44-49. This article is reprinted in Linnell Gentry's *A
 History and Encyclopedia of Country, Western, and Gospel Music*
 (pp. 115-124) listed above.
Kane, Hartnett T. *Louisiana Hayride: The American Rehearsal for
 Dictatorship 1928-1940.* New York: William Morrow, 1941.
King, Larry. "The 'Hillbilly Shakespeare' Left 'em Sobbing in their Beer."
 TV Guide. 5 March 1983, pp. 42-45.
Krishef, Robert K. *Hank Williams.* Minneapolis: Lerner Publications, 1978.
Lindeman, Edith. "Hank Williams Hillbilly Show Is Different: Star Makes
 Impression of an Unexpected Kind." The *Richmond Times-
 Dispatch,* 30 January 1952, p. 18.
Linn, Ed. "The Short Life of Hank Williams." *Saga,* January 1957,
 8-11, 86-91.
Malone, Bill C. *Country Music U.S.A. A Fifty-Year History.* Austin:
 University of Texas Press, 1968.
_____ and Judith McCulloh, eds., *Stars of Country Music: Uncle Dave
 Macon to Johnny Rodriguez.* Urbana: University of Illinois Press,
 1975.
Mankelow, David. "Legend." *Country,* 2 (April 1973), 30-32.
McKee, Charles B. *Hank Williams Scrap Book.* Alabama Department of
 Archives and History, Montgomery. Donated by McKee on 11
 January 1966.
Montgomery Advertiser-Alabama Journal, 11 January 1953.
Moore, Thurston, ed., *Hank Williams The Legend.* Denver: Heather Enter-
 prises, 1972.

Morris, Doug. "Hank Williams' Death Still Issue." *The Knoxville Journal,* 15 December 1982, p. C1.

Mortland, John. "Hank Williams," *CREEM,* April 1973, pp. 68-69.

Odom, Mr. and Mrs. Burton. *The Hank Williams Story.* Butler County, Alabama: The Butler County Historical Association, 19 May 1974.

"Oklahoma Committee Told Phony Physician Prescribed Sedative For Hank Williams." *Montgomery Adviser,* 12 March 1953, p. 10A.

Pearl, Minnie with Joan Drew. *Minnie Pearl: An Autobiography.* New York: Simon and Schuster, 1980.

Pleasants, Henry E. *The Great American Popular Singers.* New York: Simon and Schuster, 1974.

Porterfield, Nolan. *Jimmie Rodgers: The Life and Times of America's Blue Yodler.* Urbana: University of Illinois Press, 1979.

Pruden, Wesley. "Ol' Hank: 'Widow Williams' Settles Old Score." The *National Observer,* 12 July 1971, pp. 1, 14.

Rankin, Allen. "Rankin File." *Montgomery Advertiser,* 4 April 1948, p. 3B.

_____. "Rankin File." *Montgomery Advertiser,* 29 December 1952, no pagination.

_____. "Rankin File." *Montgomery Advertiser,* 4 February 1953, no pagination.

Rivers, Jerry. *Hank Williams: From Life To Legend.* Denver: Heather Enterprises, 1967. Second edition published by Rivers in about 1981; available from him at Rt. 1, Box 20, Goodlettsville, Tennessee 37072.

Rockwell, Harry E. *Beneath the Applause (A Story About Country and Western Music and Its Stars—Written By a Fan).* Published privately by Rockwell in 1973.

Rumble, John W. *Fred Rose and the Development of the Nashville Music Industry 1942-1954.* Unpublished Ph.D. dissertation, Vanderbilt University, May 1980.

"Sadly the Troubadour." *Newsweek,* 41 (19 January 1953), 55.

Shelton, Robert with photos by Burt Goldblatt. *The Country Music Story: A Picture History of Country and Western Music.* New York: Bobbs-Merrill, 1966.

Shestack, Melvin. *The Country Music Encyclopedia.* New York: Thomas Y. Crowell, 1974, pp. 301-306.

_____. "The World's Not Yet Lonesome For Me." *Country Music,* 1 (January 1973), 38-46.

Songs from YOUR CHEATIN' HEART. Nashville: Fred Rose Music and Milene Music, undated.

Songs of Hank Williams "The Drifting Cowboy." Montgomery: WSFA, no date but probably about 1945.

The Best of Hank Williams. Wenona, Minnesota, and Milwaukee, Wisconsin: Hal Leonard Publishing, 1982.

The Complete Works of Hank Williams: A 129 Song Legacy of His Music. Nashville: Acuff-Rose International, 1980.

The Songs of Hank Williams. New York: Barnes and Noble Books, undated.

Tosches, Nick. *Country: The Biggest Music In America.* New York: Stein and Day, 1977.

_____. *Hellfire.* New York: Delacorte Press, 1982.

Waldron, Eli. "The Death of Hank Williams." The *Reporter,* 12 (19 May 1955), 35-37.

_____. "The Life and Death of a Country Singer." *Coronet,* 39 (January 1956), 40-45.

"Widow of Singer Loses 2nd Suit." *Atlanta Journal,* 1 August 1972, p. 9B.

Williams, Hank and Jimmy Rule. *How To Write Folk And Western Music To Sell.* Nashville: Harpeth Publishing, 1951.

Williams, Hank Jr. with Michael Bane. *Living Proof.* New York: G. P. Putnam's Sons, 1979.

Williams, Lillie with Allen Rankin. *Our Hank Williams: "The Drifting Cowboy."* Montgomery: Philbert Publications, 1953. The basic materials of this book are in a long *Montgomery Advertiser/ Alabama Journal* article of 11 January 1953.

Williams, Roger M. "Hank Williams," in *Stars of Country Music: Uncle Dave Macon to Johnny Rodriguez,* edited by Bill C. Malone and Judith McCulloh. Urbana: University of Illinois Press, 1975.

_____. *Hank Williams,* with notes on the music by Charles K. Wolfe and Bob Pinson. Alexandria, Virginia: Time/Life Books, 1981.

_____. *Sing A Sad Song: The Life of Hank Williams.* Garden City, New York: Doubleday, 1970.

_____. *Sing A Sad Song: The Life of Hank Williams.* New York: Ballantine Books, 1973.

_____. *Sing A Sad Song: The Life of Hank Williams.* second edition with discography by Bob Pinson. Urbana: University of Illinois Press, 1981.

_____. "Writing About Hank." *Country Music,* 1 (May 1973), 58-61.

"Williams' Widow Loses Suit." *Atlanta Constitution,* 2 August 1972, p. 13A.

"Williams' Widow Again Sues MGM." *Atlanta Journal,* 4 May 1972, p. 4B.

Wolfe, Charles K. *Tennessee Strings: The Story of Country Music in Tennessee.* Knoxville: The University of Tennessee Press, 1977.

Your Cheatin' Heart. An MGM film written by Stanford Whitmore, directed by Sam Katzman, starring George Hamilton, Susan Oliver, Red Buttons, and Arthur O'Connell. Hank Jr. sings his father's songs, 1964.

APPENDIX I

CHRONOLOGY

22 December 1891	Birth of Elonzo Huble Williams, father of Hank Williams, in Lowndes County, Alabama, near the small town of Braggs.
24 August 1897	Birth of Fred Rose in Evansville, Illinois.
12 August 1898	Birth of Jessie Lillie Belle Skipper, mother of Hank Williams, in Butler County, Alabama.
20 March 1901	Birth of Horace Raphol "Toby" Marshall in Michigan.
12 November 1916	Marriage of Jessie Lillie Belle Skipper and Elonzo Huble Williams.
9 July 1918– 26 June 1919	Lon Williams' military service, part of it in France, with the 113th Regiment of Engineers, 42nd Division.
8 August 1922	Birth of Irene Williams, Hank's older sister, to Lillie and Lon Williams in Mt. Olive Community, Alabama.
28 February 1923	Birth of Audrey Mae Sheppard, Hank's first wife, in Pike County, Alabama.
17 September 1923	Birth of Hiram "Hank" Williams to Lillie and Lon Williams in Mt. Olive Community, Alabama.
28 November 1925	Beginning of the WSM ("We Shield Millions") Barn Dance, sponsored by National Life and Accident Insurance Co., in Nashville. The Barn Dance became The Grand Ole Opry in 1927.
November 1929	Lon Williams entered the VA Hospital in Biloxi, Mississippi, and was not to live with Lillie, Irene, and Hank again.

1930	The family moved to Georgiana, Alabama, where Lillie ran a boardinghouse. Hank may have met Rufe "Tee Tot" Payne here.
1934-1935	Hank spent the school year with his cousins, the McNeils, at the Pool Lumber Camp near Fountain in Monroe County, Alabama.
1935	The Williams family moved to Greenville, Alabama.
10 July 1937	The Williams family moved to Montgomery. That fall, Hank won the Empire Theatre talent contest, singing his own composition, "The WPA Blues." He began making appearances on radio station WSFA.
13 August 1941	Birth of Lycrecia Ann Guy to Audrey Sheppard Guy and James Erskine Guy in Pike County, Alabama.
12 September 1942	Elonzo Williams, now fully recovered, married Ola Till in McWilliams, Alabama.
1942	Fred Rose and Roy Acuff established Acuff-Rose Publishing Company, the first for Nashville.
	Hank probably met Audrey Sheppard Guy in this year.
	After being rejected by the Selective Service because of his back, the nineteen-year-old Hank dropped out of the ninth grade and went to Mobile, where he took a job with the Alabama Drydock and Shipbuilding Company.
19 June 1943	Birth of Hank's half-sister, Leila Williams, to Elonzo and Ola Till Williams.
Fall 1944	Hank returned from Mobile to Montgomery.
5 December 1944	Audrey divorced Erskine Guy. The decree stipulated a sixty-day reconciliation period before remarriage.
15 December 1944	Audrey and Hank were married, in a Texaco Service Station near Andalusia, Alabama, by Justice of the Peace M. A. Boyett. The wedding took place fifty days before the end of Audrey's reconciliation period.
1944-1945	Hank was a regular on WSFA and was touring the area with the Drifting Cowboys. He published his first songbook in this period: *Songs of Hank Williams "The Drifting Cowboy,"* which included ten songs and sold for thirty-five cents.
1945	Hank's first hospitalization for alcoholism, in Prattville, Alabama.
14 September 1946	Hank and Audrey traveled to Nashville to meet Fred and Wesley Rose and to establish Hank's songwriting and recording career.
Fall 1946	Sterling Records in New York asked Fred Rose to

	recommend some country and western talent. Fred recommended the Oklahoma Wranglers and Hank Williams.
11 December 1946	Hank's first recording session, at WSM Studio D, Castle Recording Company. He cut four of his own songs for Sterling: "Calling You," "Never Again [Will I Knock On Your Door]," "Wealth Won't Save Your Soul," "When God Comes And Gathers His Jewels."
1946 (ca.)	Hank published his second song book: *Hank Williams and His Drifting Cowboys, Stars of WSFA, Deluxe Song Book.* It included thirty songs.
13 February 1947	Nashville recording session, which included "Honky Tonkin'," for Sterling.
21 April 1947	Nashville recording session, which included "Move It On Over" and "I Saw The Light." This was Hank's first session for MGM and Frank Walker.
4 August 1947	Nashville recording session, which included "On The Banks Of The Old Ponchartrain."
6 November 1947	Nashville recording session, which included the best known version of "Honky Tonkin'."
7 November 1947	Nashville recording session, which included "Mansion On The Hill."
3 April 1948	Opening of The Louisiana Hayride in Shreveport.
26 May 1948	Audrey divorced Hank for the first time, in Montgomery.
22 December 1948	Cincinnati recording session, which included "Lovesick Blues."
August 1948	Hank became a regular on The Louisiana Hayride.
25 February 1949	MGM released "Lovesick Blues," which was to become *Billboard*'s number one hit of the year. It was on the charts for forty-two weeks and, without doubt, helped get Hank onto The Grand Ole Opry.
1-2 March 1949	Nashville recording session, which included "Mind Your Own Business" and "You're Gonna Change [Or I'm Gonna Leave]."
20 March 1949	Nashville recording session, which included "Wedding Bells."
26 May 1949	Randall Hank Williams, "Hank Jr.," was born in Shreveport, Louisiana. Hank called him "Bocephus" after a puppet used by Rod Brasfield, an Opry comedian.
11 June 1949	Hank made his debut on The Grand Ole Opry, singing "Lovesick Blues" to six encores.
9 August 1949	The divorce of 26 May 1948 was amended *Nunc pro tunc*.

30 August 1949	Recording session in Cincinnati, which included "I'm So Lonesome I Could Cry" and "My Bucket's Got A Hole In It." The latter includes Hank's only guitar solo on record.
August 1949	Hank and Audrey purchased their home at 4916 Franklin Road, Nashville.
Fall 1949	Hank's first trip to "The Hut," Madison Sanitarium in Nashville.
October 1949	Hank recorded eight radio shows on sixteen-inch records for the LeBlanc Corporation. The records were for radio stations and not for sale to the general public, but many of the cuts turned up later on MGM records.
13 November 1949	Hank and Audrey began a tour of Armed Forces bases in Germany with Red Foley, Roy Acuff, Minnie Pearl, Jimmy Dickens, and others. The tour ended at Thanksgiving.
9 January 1950	Nashville recording session, which included "Long Gone Lonesome Blues" and "Why Don't You Love Me." This was the first session with the Drifting Cowboys.
10 January 1950	Nashville recording session, which included the first four cuts by "Luke the Drifter."
14 June 1950	Nashville recording session, which included "They'll Never Take Her Love From Me."
31 August 1950	Nashville recording session, which included "Moanin' The Blues."
11 November 1950	Nashville recording session, which included "Nobody's Lonesome For Me."
21 December 1950	Nashville recording session, which included "Cold, Cold Heart."
December 1950	March of Dimes recording session in Nashville. The fifteen-minute show was aired the following month.
1950	Hank had three songs on *Billboard*'s yearly retail sales chart: "Why Don't You Love Me" (4), "Long Gone Lonesome Blues" (5), and "Moanin' The Blues" (30).
16 March 1951	Nashville recording session, which included "I Can't Help It [If I'm Still In Love With You]" and "Hey Good Lookin'."
23 March 1951	Hank and Audrey recorded "The Pale Horse And His Rider" and "A Home In Heaven" in Nashville.
21 May 1951	Hank was admitted to the North Louisiana Sanitarium in Shreveport to be treated for his alcoholism and his back problem. He was released on 24 May.
1 June 1951	Nashville recording session, which included four sides by "Luke the Drifter."

25 July 1951	Nashville recording session, which included "Baby, We're Really in Love."
10 August 1951	Nashville recording session, which included "Half As Much."
15 August 1951	The Hadacol Caravan began in New Iberia, Louisiana. It was supposed to last forty days, until 2 October, but it ended after thirty-four shows on 18 September in Dallas.
9 October 1951	"Toby" Marshall was paroled from Oklahoma State Penitentiary, where he had been serving a three-year sentence, which began 15 October 1950, for second-degree forgery (Ottawa County Case #2858).
24 September 1951	The *Nashville Banner* announced that Hank had signed a movie contract with MGM. Hank was never involved in the production of a movie, however.
1951	*How To Write Folk And Western Music To Sell,* by Hank and Jimmy Rule, was published by Harpeth Publishing Company. It sold for one dollar.
	"Hank and Audrey's Corral," a western wear store, opened on Commerce Street in Nashville.
	Hank had three songs on *Billboard*'s yearly retail sales chart: "Cold, Cold Heart" (1), "Hey Good Lookin' " (8), and "Crazy Heart" (29).
3 January 1952	Hank moved out of the Franklin Road home.
10 January 1952	Audrey filed for separate maintenance.
29 May 1952	The divorce from Audrey was final. Hank may have spent some time in the federal narcotics hospital in Lexington, Kentucky, shortly thereafter.
13 June 1952	Recording session in Nashville, which included "Jambalaya," "Settin' The Woods On Fire," and "I'll Never Get Out Of This World Alive."
Summer 1952	Hank met Billie Jean Jones Eshliman, a telephone operator from Bossier City, Louisiana, who moved to Nashville in July 1952.
11 July 1952	Nashville recording session, which included "You Win Again."
11 August 1952	Jim Denny fired Hank from The Grand Ole Opry. "Jambalaya" was on its way to being the number one song at the time. Hank went home to Montgomery.
15 August 1952	Hank and disc jockey Bob McKinnon went to Lake Martin, not too far from Montgomery and near the Creek Indian town called Kowaliga, the inspiration of the title, "Kaw-Liga."

17 August 1952	Hank was arrested in Alexander City, Alabama, for being drunk and disorderly.
20 September 1952	Hank appeared on The Louisiana Hayride.
23 September 1952	Nashville recording session, which included "Your Cheatin' Heart," "Kaw-Liga," "Take These Chains From My Heart." "Take These Chains From My Heart" was Hank's last commercial recording. It was on the charts for only twelve weeks, but it was number one for four of those weeks.
18 October 1952	Hank married Billie Jean Jones Eshliman in Minden, Louisiana.
19 October 1952	Hank married Billie Jean twice, once in the afternoon and again in the evening, at the New Orleans Civic Auditorium.
28 October 1952	Billie Jean's divorce from Harrison Holland Eshliman, whom she had married in 1949, became final.
31 October 1952	Hank was admitted to the North Louisiana Sanitarium.
27 November 1952	Hank was admitted to the North Louisiana Sanitarium.
11 December 1952	Hank was admitted to the North Louisiana Sanitarium.
21 December 1952	Hank and Billie Jean visited Taft and Erleen Skipper in Georgiana. They went on to Montgomery before Christmas. On Christmas day, they tried to visit Lon, but he had gone to Selma.
27 December 1952	Hank and Billie Jean attended the Blue-Gray football game in Montgomery with his cousins, Taft and Mary Skipper.
28 December 1952	Hank performed for the Montgomery chapter of the American Federation of Musicians.
30 December 1952	Hank left Montgomery for a New Year's Day show in Canton, Ohio.
1952	Hank had three songs on *Billboard*'s yearly retail sales chart: "Jambalaya" (3), "Half As Much" (11), "Honky Tonk Blues" (28).
1 January 1953	Hank was dead on arrival at the Oak Hill, West Virginia, hospital. "Jambalaya" was the number one song in the *Billboard* poll.
4 January 1953	Hank's funeral at the Montgomery City Auditorium at two-thirty P.M. He was buried later that day in the Oakwood Cemetery Annex. His body was moved to its present grave in the Annex on 17 January 1953.
3 March 1953	Fay Marshall, wife of Toby Marshall, died in Albuquerque, New Mexico.
10 March 1953	University of Alabama President John M. Gallalee announced the Hank Williams Memorial Music Scholarship.

13 March 1953	Governor Johnston Murray of Oklahoma revoked Toby Marshall's parole.
1953	Lillie, with Montgomery writer Allen Rankin, published *Our Hank Williams: "The Drifting Cowboy."*
	Billie Jean Jones Williams forfeited all claims to the name and the estate of Hank Williams for $30,000.
	Hank had three songs on *Billboard*'s yearly retail sales chart: "Kaw-Liga" (1), "Your Cheatin' Heart" (2), "Take These Chains From My Heart" (9).
April 1954	Lillie signed a movie deal with MGM. MGM agreed not to mention the divorce from Audrey or the marriage to Billie Jean. The idea was shelved when Lillie died the next year.
21 September 1954	Hank's tombstone was unveiled in Montgomery after a celebration attended by some sixty thousand people. The event was sponsored by the Alcazar Temple of the Shrine.
1 December 1954	Fred Rose died.
1954	Billie Jean married Johnny ("Battle of New Orleans" and "North to Alaska") Horton. Horton died in an auto wreck on 5 November 1960.
26 February 1955	Lillie Skipper Williams died in her sleep. She is buried to Hank's immediate left.
1961	Hank Williams, Jimmie Rodgers, and Fred Rose became the first members of the Country Music Hall of Fame.
19 March 1963	Irene Williams, then administratrix of Hank's estate, sold renewal rights to his music to Acuff-Rose for $25,000. Hank Jr. and Audrey protested in a law suit that began in September 1967. Circuit Judge Richard Emmet of Montgomery upheld the original contract in a decision rendered 30 January 1968.
27 August 1963	Jim Denny died.
16 October 1963	Frank Walker died.
4 November 1964	The movie, *Your Cheatin' Heart,* premiered at the Paramount Theatre in Montgomery.
1967	Jerry Rivers published the first edition of his *Hank Williams: From Life to Legend.* The second edition came out ca. 1981.
1 August 1969	Irene Williams was arrested for smuggling $7 million worth of cocaine across the border at Laredo. She was sentenced to seven years and served time in the federal penitentiary in Alderson, West Virginia.
October 1969	Billie Jean sued MGM over *Your Cheatin' Heart.*

23 October 1970	Elonzo Huble Williams, Hank's father, died.
1970	Roger M. Williams published the first edition of *Sing A Sad Song: The Life of Hank Williams.*
March 1972	Billie Jean sued MGM, CBS, and Storer Broadcasting over *Your Cheatin' Heart.* The jury agreed that she was the legal widow and that she had been libeled. But it awarded her no damages.
4 May 1972	Billie Jean sued MGM again. She lost the suit.
12 December 1972	Hank Williams III born to Hank Jr. and his wife, Gwendolyn Sue Yeargin.
1972	Thurston Moore published a collection of articles on Hank, *Hank Williams The Legend.*
1973	Roger M. Williams published a paperback edition of *Sing A Sad Song: The Life of Hank Williams.*
19 October 1974	The unveiling of the Butler County Historical Association marker of Hank's birthplace.
22 October 1975	U.S. District Judge L. Clure Morton ruled in Nashville that Billie Jean Berlin had been Hank's wife at the time of his death and that she was to share in the copyright renewals.
October 1975	Jim Owen started his one-man show, "Hank."
4 November 1975	Audrey Williams died. She is buried near Hank in the Oakwood Cemetery Annex.
1978	Robert L. Krishef published his *Hank Williams,* a biography for children.
30 October 1979	Premier of Sneezy Waters's "Hank Williams: The Show He Never Gave," at the American Theatre in St. Louis.
1979	Jay Caress published his *Hank Williams: Country Music's Tragic King.*
12 April 1980	TV special, "A Tribute To Hank Williams: The Man and His Music," hosted by Hank Jr., aired in Nashville.
1981	Chet Flippo published his *Your Cheatin' Heart.*
	Roger Williams published the second edition of *Sing A Sad Song: The Life of Hank Williams.*
	Roger Williams published *Hank Williams,* a booklet for the *Time/Life* Country and Western Classics series. Notes on the music are by Charles K. Wolfe and Bob Pinson. The booklet accompanies a three-record set of Hank's music.

DISCOGRAPHY

Hank Williams began a brilliant and lucrative recording career in Nashville on 11 December 1946 in Studio D of the Castle Recording Company. He cut four of his own songs for Sterling Records that day; the most famous one was "When God Comes And Gathers His Jewels." The Oklahoma Wranglers, known later as the Willis Brothers and identified on the Sterling records as the Country Boys, furnished the backup music. Sterling had Hank back for four more sides and another $82.50 on 13 February 1947.

That spring, Hank began recording for MGM, and he stayed with that company for the rest of his career. Backup men on the early MGM sessions included Tommy Jackson, Chubby Wise, Dale Potter, Don Davis, Jerry Byrd, Jack Shook, Zeb Turner, Ernie Newton, Fred Rose, Owen Bradley, Bill Drake, Louie Innis, and Brownie Reynolds. The most enduring version of the Drifting Cowboys evolved in 1949; that band recorded with Hank for the first time on 9 January 1950. From that point on, the Drifting Cowboys were his standard backup group, though they were supplemented by various studio musicians, especially rhythm guitarist Jack Shook. The basic group had Don Helms on steel guitar, Bob McNett on lead guitar, Jerry Rivers on fiddle, and Hillous Butrum on bass. In the summer of 1950, Sammy Pruett replaced McNett, and Howard (Cedric Rainwater) Watts replaced Butrum. Hank usually played an open, rhythm guitar. They did almost all of their recording with Nashville's Castle Recording Company which had studios at WSM and in the Tulane Hotel. They did two sessions in the Herzog Studios in Cincinnati (22 December 1948 and 30 August 1949).

After about thirty-five sessions and just over ninety commercial recordings, Hank cut his last song, "Take These Chains From My Heart." That session fell on 23 September 1952. Hank was dead a few months later, and MGM was without one of its best properties. A fine songwriter and performer who should have had another forty years, one who would be only sixty years old now, was gone.

MGM proved resourceful in handling the Williams catalog. Hank had cut any number of demonstration records, some of them in Montgomery and others in Fred

Rose's attic studio. They were safe in the MGM vault. Obviously, these were not always finished products, but many of them were quite good. Besides, they were by Hank Williams and would sell. Some sixty-five of these "Nonsession" cuts have been issued, about two-thirds of them with overdubbed backup music supporting Hank and his guitar. No doubt, their steady appearance on the market fueled the rumor that Hank Williams was not dead after all.

MGM had additional resources. The company received cuts from the Armed Forces Radio Transcriptions of The Grand Ole Opry. And they took cuts from the eight sixteen-inch 33s that Hank had done for the LeBlanc Corporation in October 1949. MGM, of course, collected various records into sets. It issued 78 cuts as 45s; then the 45s went onto 33 LPs. The modern record buyer might like to note that Hank had long been dead before his first twelve-inch 33 LP hit the market.

MGM executive Jim Vienneau, the nephew of Frank Walker, gave things another turn when he started elaborate overdubbings of Hank's work. He was not dealing with the standard small band music that had gone behind many of the nonsession recordings. Vienneau brought orchestras to Hank; he put multiple strings behind him or superimposed Hank Jr.'s voice on that of his father's. Thanks to modern technology we can now hear something that never happened—Hank and Hank Jr. singing "My Son Calls Another Man Daddy." Vienneau's process is not very simple because the original cuts had gone directly into acetate discs, not onto the multiple tapes of today's recording studio. With the tapes, one can simply withdraw a voice or an instrument and substitute another. With the discs, the various voices and instruments were inseparable and permanent because they had all been recorded at the same moment. Overdubbing them means drowning out particular sounds, superimposing new sounds on the old recordings, keeping an orchestra in sync with a record that is being played over a studio sound system. Most serious Hank Williams fans consider such overdubbing a desecration. But such is the modern world's contribution.

The first major discography of Hank Williams was done by Jerry Rivers for his *Hank Williams: From Life To Legend.* Rivers cites each record and the songs on it. And he ends with a list of records in tribute to Hank. Almost the same discography appears at the end of the Ballantine edition of Roger M. Williams's *Sing a Sad Song: The Life Of Hank Williams;* at the end of Jay Caress's *Hank Williams: Country Music's Tragic King;* and at the end of Al Bock's *I Saw The Light: The Gospel Life Of Hank Williams.* In his second edition of *From Life To Legend,* Rivers corrects a few errors and adds a discography of the recordings made by the Drifting Cowboys since they reorganized in 1977.

The best discography, however, comes from Bob Pinson of the Country Music Foundation Library and Media Center. It appears at the end of the second edition of Roger M. Williams's *Sing A Sad Song.* Pinson works with individual songs, identifying the place and date of the recording of each song as well the records on which that song appears. Thus we might learn that "Calling You" was recorded in Nashville on 11 December 1946 and that the song appears on Sterling 201, MGM 11628, MGM K11628, MGM X4110, MGM X1648, MGM E243, MGM E3331, MGM 3E2, and MGM SE4576. Pinson also gives composer credits for most songs. His information is plentiful and meticulous, virtually a complete Hank Williams recording history for the careful reader. The Pinson discography should set a standard for country music scholarship.

The discography that follows is obviously indebted to both Rivers and Pinson; and except for a few minor additions, it supersedes their work in no way. But it does attempt to clarify and heighten the kind of information about Hank's recording career that might be of interest to the general reader as well as to the scholar and collector, and it lists those few composers whose names were left off of the original recordings. It identifies each record, the songs on them, the dates of the recordings of the individual songs, and the composers of the songs. Additionally, it offers some background information for each section of the discography. A quick glance through it can reveal just how many of his own songs Hank was recording and just when he was recording. A slightly more careful look will reveal the resourcefulness of a recording industry that developed a recording career lasting less than six years into the tremendous discography of Hank Williams. This is not a testimony just to MGMs commercial spirit but to the demand for more Hank Williams as well.

NOTE: "ns" indicates a nonsession recording, one not made in a formal studio; "od" indicates an overdubbed recording; "HW" indicates Hank Williams; "PD" indicates public domain.

THE FOUR STERLING RECORDS (All 78 RPM)

Date Recorded	Album	Composer
	S-201	
12/11/46	Calling You	HW
12/11/46	Never Again [Will I Knock On Your Door]	HW
	S-204	
12/11/46	Wealth Won't Save Your Soul	HW
12/11/46	When God Comes And Gathers His Jewels	HW
	S-208	
2/13/47	I Don't Care [If Tomorrow Never Comes]	HW
2/13/47	My Love For You [Has Turned To Hate]	HW
	S-210	
2/13/47	Honky Tonkin'	HW
2/13/47	Pan American	HW

The following are MGM singles. In most cases they were released as 78s and as 45s. (The letter "K" before the number indicates "45"; otherwise, the record is a "78.")

	10033 K10033	
4/21/47	Move It On Over	HW
4/21/47	[Last Night] I Heard You Crying in Your Sleep	HW
	10073 K10073	
8/4/47	Fly Trouble	Wilds-Biggs-Rose
8/4/47	On The Banks Of The Old Ponchartrain	HW-Vincent

10124
K10124

| 11/6/47 | Rootie Tootie | Rose |
| 11/7/47 | My Sweet Love Ain't Around | HW |

10171
K10171

| 11/6/47 | Honky Tonkin' | HW |
| 11/7/47 | I'll Be A Bachelor 'Til I Die | HW |

10212
K10212

| 11/7/47 | The Blues Come Around | HW |
| 11/6/47 | I'm A Long Gone Daddy | HW |

10226
K10226

| 2/13/47 | Pan American | HW |
| 2/13/47 | I Don't Care [If Tomorrow Never Comes] | HW |

10271

| 4/21/47 | I Saw the Light | HW |
| 4/21/47 | Six More Miles [To The Graveyard] | HW |

10328
K10328

| 11/6/47 | I Can't Get You Off My Mind | HW |
| 11/7/47 | Mansion On The Hill | HW-Rose |

10352
K10352

| 12/22/48 | Lovesick Blues | Mills-Friend |
| 12/11/46 | Never Again [Will I Knock On Your Door] | HW |

10401
K10401

| 3/20/49 | I've Just Told Mama Goodbye | Sweet-Kinsey |
| 3/20/49 | Wedding Bells | C. Boone |

10434
K10434

| 3/1/49 | Dear Brother (with Audrey Williams) | HW |
| 12/22/48 | Lost On The River (with Audrey Williams) | HW |

10461
K10461

| 3/1-2/49 | Mind Your Own Business | HW |
| 12/22/48 | There'll Be No Teardrops Tonight | HW |

10506
K10506

| 3/1/49 | Lost Highway | Payne |
| 3/1-2/49 | You're Gonna Change [Or I'm Gonna Leave] | HW |

10560
K10560

8/30/49	I'm So Lonesome I Could Cry	HW
8/30/49	My Bucket's Got a Hole In It	C. Williams

10609
K10609

8/30/49	I Just Don't Like This Kind Of Livin'	HW
3/1/49	May You Never Be Alone	HW

10630
K10630

1/10/50	Beyond The Sunset	Brock-Rowswell
1/10/50	The Funeral	Rose

10645
K10645

1/9/50	My Son Calls Another Man Daddy	HW
1/9/50	Long Gone Lonesome Blues	HW

10696
K10696

1/9/50	Why Don't You Love Me	HW
8/30/49	A House Without Love	HW

10718
K10718

1/10/50	Everything's Okay (Luke the Drifter)	HW
1/10/50	Too Many Parties and Too Many Pals (Luke the Drifter)	Rose-Dixon-Henderson

10760
K10760

1/9/50	Why Should We Try Anymore	HW
6/14/50	They'll Never Take Her Love From Me	L. Payne

10806
K10806

8/31/50	Help Me Understand (Luke the Drifter)	HW
8/31/50	No, No, Joe (Luke the Drifter)	Rose

10813
K10813

12/22/48	I Heard My Mother Praying For Me	A. Williams
3/1/49	Jesus Remembered Me	HW

10832
K10832

8/31/50	Nobody's Lonesome for Me	HW
8/31/50	Moanin' The Blues	HW

10904
K10904

| 12/21/50 | Cold, Cold Heart | HW |
| 12/21/50 | Dear John | Ritter-Gass |

10932
K10932

| 12/21/50 | Just Waitin' (Luke the Drifter) | HW-Gazzaway |
| 12/21/50 | Men With Broken Hearts (Luke the Drifter) | HW |

10961
K10961

| 3/16/51 | I Can't Help It [If I'm Still in Love with You] | HW |
| 3/16/51 | Howlin' At The Moon | HW |

11000
K11000

| 3/16/51 | Hey, Good Lookin' | HW |
| 3/16/51 | My Heart Would Know | HW |

11017
K11017

| 6/1/51 | I Dreamed About Mama Last Night (Luke the Drifter) | Rose |
| 6/1/51 | I've Been Down That Road Before (Luke the Drifter) | HW |

11054
K11054

| 7/25/51 | Lonesome Whistle | HW-Davis |
| 7/25/51 | Crazy Heart | Rose-Murray |

11100
K11100

| 7/25/51 | I'd Still Want You | HW |
| 8/10/51 | Baby, We're Really In Love | HW |

11120
K11120

| 6/1/51 | Ramblin' Man (Luke the Drifter) | HW |
| 6/1/51 | Pictures From Life's Other Side (Luke the Drifter) | HW |

11160
K11160

| 12/11/51 | I'm Sorry For You, My Friend | HW |
| 12/11/51 | Honky Tonk Blues | HW |

11202
K11202

| 12/11/51 | Let's Turn Back the Years | HW |
| 8/10/51 | Half As Much | C. Williams |

11283
K11283

| 6/13/52 | Jambalaya [on the Bayou] | HW |
| 6/13/52 | Window Shopping | Joseph |

11309
K11309

7/11/52	Why Don't You Make Up Your Mind	
	(Luke the Drifter)	HW
7/11/52	Be Careful Of Stones that You Throw	
	(Luke the Drifter)	Dodd

11318
K11318

| 6/13/52 | Settin' The Woods On Fire | Nelson-Rose |
| 7/11/52 | You Win Again | HW |

11366
K11366

| 6/13/52 | I'll Never Get Out Of This World Alive | HW-Rose |
| 9/23/52 | I Could Never Be Ashamed of You | HW |

11416
K11416

| 9/23/52 | Kaw-Liga | HW-Rose |
| 9/23/52 | Your Cheatin' Heart | HW |

11479
K11479

| 9/23/52 | Take These Chains From My Heart | Heath-Rose |
| 6/1/51 | Ramblin' Man | HW |

11533
K11533

| 2/13/47 | My Love For You [Has Turned To Hate] | HW |
| 7/11/52 | I Won't Be Home No More | HW |

11574
K11574

| ns/od | Weary Blues From Waitin' | HW |
| ns/od | I Can't Escape From You | HW |

11628
K11628

| 12/11/46 | Calling You | HW |
| 12/11/46 | When God Comes And Gathers His Jewels | HW |

11675
K11675

| ns/od | You Better Keep It On Your Mind | HW-V. McAlpin |
| ns/od | Low Down Blues | HW |

11707
K11707

| ns/od | How Can You Refuse Him Now | HW |
| ns/od | A House of Gold | HW |

11768
K11768

ns/od	I Ain't Got Nothin' But Time	HW
8/4/47	I'm Satisfied With You	Rose

11861
K11861

ns/od	The Angel Of Death	HW
ns/od	[I'm Gonna] Sing, Sing, Sing	HW

11928
K11928

ns	Faded Love And Winter Roses	Rose
ns	Please Don't Let Me Love You	Jones

11975
K11975

ns/od	Message to My Mother	HW
ns/od	Mother Is Gone	HW

12029
K12029

ns/od	A Teardrop On A Rose	HW
ns	Alone and Forsaken	HW

12077
K12077

ns	The First Fall Of Snow	Rose
ns	Someday You'll Call My Name	Branch-Hill

12127
K12127

ns	The Battle of Armageddon	Acuff-McLeod
ns	Thank God	Rose

12185
K12185

ns/od	California Zephyr	HW
ns	Thy Burdens Are Greater Than Mine	Stewart-King

12244
K12244

ns	I Wish I Had A Nickel	Sutton-Barnhart
ns	There's No Room In My Heart [for the Blues]	Rose-Turner

12332
K12332

ns	Blue Love [In My Heart]	Jenkins
ns	Singing Waterfall	HW

12394
K12394

3/23/51	The Pale Horse And His Rider	
	(with Audrey Williams)	Bailes-Staggs

| 3/23/51 | A Home in Heaven (with Audrey Williams) | HW |

12438
K12438

ns	Ready To Go Home	HW
ns/od	We're Getting Closer To The	
	Grave Each Day	HW

12484
K12484

| ns | Leave Me Alone With The Blues | Pope |
| ns | With Tears In My Eyes | Howard |

12535
K12535

| ns | The Waltz Of The Wind | Rose |
| ns | No One Will Ever Know | Rose-Foree |

K12611

| 3/16/51 | I Can't Help It [If I'm Still In Love With You] | HW |
| 1/9/50 | Why Don't You Love Me | HW |

K12635

| 8/30/49 | My Bucket's Got A Hole In It | C. Williams |
| ns/od | We Live In Two Different Worlds | Rose |

K12727

| 12/21/50 | Just Waitin' (Luke the Drifter) | HW-Gazzaway |
| ns/od | Roly Poly | Rose |

K13359

| 3/23/51 | The Pale Horse And His Rider | Bailes-Staggs |
| 12/21/50 | Cold, Cold Heart | HW |

K13305

| 12/22/48 | Lovesick Blues | Mills-Friend |
| 9/23/52 | Your Cheatin' Heart | HW |

13489*

| 7/11/52 | You Win Again | HW |
| 8/30/49 | I'm So Lonesome I Could Cry | HW |

*The original cuts were given new backup music on this record.

13630*

| 12/22/48 | There'll Be No Teardrops Tonight | HW |
| 6/14/50 | They'll Never Take Her Love From Me | L. Payne |

*The original cuts were given new backup music on this record.

The following KGC Records are all 45s:

KGC-107

| 12/22/48 | Lovesick Blues | Mills-Friend |
| 9/23/52 | Your Cheatin' Heart | HW |

KGC-108

| 1/9/50 | Why Don't You Love Me | HW |
| 3/16/51 | Hey, Good Lookin' | HW |

KGC-109

| 12/11/51 | Honky Tonk Blues | HW |
| 8/10/51 | Half As Much | C. Williams |

KGC-110

| 6/13/52 | Jambalaya [On The Bayou] | HW |
| 6/13/52 | I'll Never Get Out Of This World Alive | HW-Rose |

KGC-lll

| 6/1/51 | Ramblin' Man | HW |
| 9/23/52 | Kaw-Liga | HW-Rose |

KGC-112

| 8/31/50 | Moanin' The Blues | HW |
| 7/11/52 | You Win Again | HW |

KGC-113

| 12/21/50 | Cold, Cold Heart | HW |
| 8/30/49 | I'm So Lonesome I Could Cry | HW |

KGC-127

| 8/30/49 | My Bucket's Got A Hole In It | C. Williams |
| ns/od | We Live In Two Different Worlds | Rose |

KGC-128

| 3/16/51 | I Can't Help It [If I'm Still In Love With You] | HW |
| ns/od | A House Of Gold | HW |

KGC-134

| 1/9/50 | Long Gone Lonesome Blues | HW |
| 1/9/50 | My Son Calls Another Man Daddy | HW |

KGC-142

| ns/od | Roly Poly | Rose |
| 12/21/50 | Just Waitin' | HW-Gazzaway |

The following are albums, both 78 and 45 ("K" continues to indicate "45"). Each album has a designation, and each record within the album has a separate designation because the records were sold separately and as a group. Thus album 107 (which is also K107) is made up of 30453 (K30453), 30454 (K30454), 30455 (K30455), 30456 (K30456).

Album 107 (K107) includes the following:

30453
K30453

| 3/1/49 | Lost Highway | Payne |
| 3/20/49 | I've Just Told Mama Goodbye | Sweet-Kinsey |

	30454	
	K30454	
4/21/47	I Saw The Light	HW
4/21/47	Six More Miles [To The Graveyard]	HW

	30455	
	K30455	
11/7/47	Mansion On The Hill	HW-Rose
12/11/46	Wealth Won't Save Your Soul	HW

	30456	
	K30456	
8/30/49	A House Without Love	HW
3/20/49	Wedding Bells	C. Boone

Album 168 (K168) includes the following:

	30636	
	K30636	
12/22/48	Lovesick Blues	Mills-Friend
8/31/50	Moanin' The Blues	HW

	30637	
	K30637	
11/7/47	The Blues Come Around	HW
8/30/49	I'm So Lonesome I Could Cry	HW

	30638	
	K30638	
11/6/47	I'm A Long Gone Daddy	HW
11/7/47	My Sweet Love Ain't Around	HW

	30639	
	K30639	
1/9/50	Long Gone Lonesome Blues	HW
12/11/51	Honky Tonk Blues	HW

Album 202 (K202) includes the following:

	30751	
	K30751	
12/21/50	Cold, Cold Heart	HW
9/23/52	Your Cheatin' Heart	HW

	30752	
	K30752	
6/13/52	Settin' The Woods On Fire	Nelson-Rose
9/23/52	Kaw-Liga	HW-Rose

	30753	
	K30753	
7/11/52	You Win Again	HW
9/23/52	I Could Never Be Ashamed Of You	HW

	30754	
	K30754	
3/16/51	Hey, Good Lookin'	HW
8/10/51	Half As Much	C. Williams

Album 203 (K203) includes the following:

	30755	
	K30755	
7/11/52	Be Careful Of Stones That You Throw	
	(Luke the Drifter)	Dodd
6/1/51	Pictures From Life's Other Side	
	(Luke the Drifter)	HW

	30756	
	K30756	
6/1/51	I Dreamed About Mama Last Night	
	(Luke the Drifter)	Rose
12/21/50	Men With Broken Hearts	
	(Luke the Drifter)	HW

	30757	
	K30757	
1/10/50	The Funeral (Luke the Drifter)	Rose
8/31/50	Help Me Understand (Luke the Drifter)	HW

	30758	
	K30758	
1/10/50	Too Many Parties And Too Many Pals	
	(Luke the Drifter)	Rose-Dixon-Henderson
1/10/50	Beyond The Sunset	
	(Luke the Drifter)	Brock-Rowswell

The following are 45 RPM extended play recordings. Each record carried four songs. The first part of this section of the discography includes five two-records sets. The individual records in the sets are numbered separately.

Album X168 includes the following:

	X4041	
8/31/50	Moanin' The Blues	HW
8/30/49	I'm So Lonesome I Could Cry	HW
11/7/47	My Sweet Love Ain't Around	HW
12/11/51	Honky Tonk Blues	HW

	X4042	
1/9/50	Long Gone Lonesome Blues	HW
12/22/48	Lovesick Blues	Mills-Friend
11/7/47	The Blues Come Around	HW
11/6/47	I'm A Long Gone Daddy	HW

Album X202 includes the following:

X4102

9/23/52	Your Cheatin' Heart	HW
7/11/52	You Win Again	HW
6/13/52	Settin' The Woods On Fire	Nelson-Rose
3/16/51	Hey, Good Lookin'	HW

X4103

12/21/50	Cold, Cold Heart	HW
9/23/52	I Could Never Be Ashamed Of You	HW
9/23/52	Kaw-Liga	HW-Rose
8/10/51	Half As Much	C. Williams

Album X242 includes the following:

X4109

6/13/52	Jambalaya [On The Bayou]	HW
7/11/52	I Won't Be Home No More	HW
12/11/51	Honky Tonk Blues	HW
6/13/52	I'll Never Get Out Of This World Alive	HW-Rose

X4108

11/6/47	Honky Tonkin'	HW
3/16/51	Howlin' At The Moon	HW
8/30/49	My Bucket's Got A Hole In It	C. Williams
8/10/51	Baby, We're Really In Love	HW

Album X243 includes the following:

X4110

3/1/49	Dear Brother	HW
12/11/46	Wealth Won't Save Your Soul	HW
4/21/47	I Saw The Light	HW
12/11/46	Calling You	HW

X4111

3/1/49	Jesus Remembered Me	HW
ns/od	A House Of Gold	HW
ns/od	How Can You Refuse Him Now	HW
12/11/46	When God Comes And Gathers His Jewels	HW

Album X291 includes the following:

X4222

6/1/51	Ramblin' Man	HW
1/9/50	My Son Calls Another Man Daddy	HW
ns/od	I Can't Escape From You	HW
8/31/50	Nobody's Lonesome For Me	HW

X4223

7/25/51	Lonesome Whistle	HW-Davis
8/30/49	I Just Don't Like This Kind of Livin'	HW
9/23/52	Take These Chains From My Heart	Heath-Rose
1/9/50	Why Don't You Love Me	HW

The balance of this section of the discography is given to individual 45 extended play records. Each of the records in the five sets above reappears under a new number here (for example, X4041 of set X168 will appear below as X1216, and X4042 of set X168 will appear below as X1217). These records often form a sequence, not a set where two or three records have to be bought together but a series of recordings that suggest a set. The records X1216 and X1217, just mentioned, are basically blues songs. MGM added an individual record, X1215, which it identified as "Moanin' the Blues," thus creating a three-record sequence (X1215, X1216, and X1217).

X1014

CRAZY HEART

7/25/51	Crazy Heart	Rose-Murray
8/10/51	Baby, We're Really In Love	HW
3/16/51	My Heart Would Know	HW
3/16/51	I Can't Help It [If I'm Still In Love With You]	HW

X1047

LUKE THE DRIFTER

6/1/51	Pictures From Life's Other Side	HW
8/31/50	Help Me Understand	HW
12/21/50	Men With Broken Hearts	HW
1/10/50	Too Many Parties And Too Many Pals	Rose-Dixon-Henderson

X1076

MOVE IT ON OVER

4/21/47	Move It On Over	HW
8/4/47	Fly Trouble	Wilds-Biggs-Rose
6/13/52	Window Shopping	Joseph
2/13/47	Pan American	HW

X1082

THERE'LL BE NO TEARDROPS TONIGHT

12/22/48	There'll Be No Teardrops Tonight	HW
3/1-2/49	You're Gonna Change [Or I'm Gonna Leave]	HW
8/31/50	Nobody's Lonesome For Me	HW
3/1-2/49	Mind Your Own Business	HW

X1135

RAMBLIN' MAN
(X4222 in set X291)

6/1/51	Ramblin' Man	HW

1/9/50	My Son Calls Another Man Daddy	HW
ns/od	I Can't Escape From You	HW
8/31/50	Nobody's Lonesome For Me	HW

X1136*

RAMBLIN' MAN

(X4223 in set X291)

7/25/51	Lonesome Whistle	HW-Davis
8/30/49	I Just Don't Like This Kind Of Livin'	HW
9/23/52	Take These Chains From My Heart	Heath-Rose
1/9/50	Why Don't You Love Me	HW

*X1650, listed below, is "Ramblin' Man Vol. III." So X1135 and X1136 might be considered volumes I and II of "Ramblin' Man."

X1165*

LUKE THE DRIFTER

7/11/52	Why Don't You Make Up Your Mind	HW
12/21/50	Just Waitin'	HW-Gazzaway
6/1/51	I've Been Down That Road Before	HW
1/10/50	Everything's Okay	HW

*X1643 and X1644 are listed below as "Luke the Drifter," volumes II and III, respectively; X1165, then, might be called volume I in the "Luke the Drifter" series.

X1215

MOANIN' THE BLUES

ns/od	Low Down Blues	HW
ns	Someday You'll Call My Name	Branch-Hill
ns	Alone And Forsaken	HW
ns/od	Weary Blues From Waitin'	HW

X1216

MOANIN' THE BLUES

(X4041 in set X168)

8/31/50	Moanin' The Blues	HW
8/30/49	I'm So Lonesome I Could Cry	HW
11/7/47	My Sweet Ain't Around	HW
12/11/51	Honky Tonk Blues	HW

X1217

MOANIN' THE BLUES

(X4042 in set X168)

1/9/50	Long Gone Lonesome Blues	HW
12/22/48	Lovesick Blues	Mills-Friend
11/7/47	The Blues Come Around	HW
11/6/47	I'm A Long Gone Daddy	HW

X1218*

I SAW THE LIGHT

ns/od	[I'm Gonna] Sing, Sing, Sing	HW
ns/od	Message To My Mother	HW
ns	Thank God	Rose
ns/od	The Angel Of Death	HW

*X1648 and X1649, listed below, are volumes II and III of the "I Saw The Light" sequence. So X1218 might be considered volume I.

X1317

HONKY TONKIN'

(X4109 in set X242)

6/13/52	Jambalaya [On The Bayou]	HW
7/11/52	I Won't Be Home No More	HW
12/11/51	Honky Tonk Blues	HW
6/13/52	I'll Never Get Out Of This World Alive	HW-Rose

X1318

HONKY TONKIN'

(X4108 in set X242)

11/6/47	Honky Tonkin'	HW
3/16/51	Howlin' At The Moon	HW
8/30/49	My Bucket's Got A Hole In It	C. Williams
8/10/51	Baby, We're Really In Love	HW

X1319

HONKY TONKIN'

3/1-2/49	Mind Your Own Business	HW
11/6/47	Rootie Tootie	Rose
ns/od	I Ain't Got Nothin' But Time	HW
ns/od	You Better Keep It On Your Mind	HW-McAlpin

X1491

SING ME A BLUE SONG, VOL. I

3/20/49	Wedding Bells	C. Boone
3/1/49	May You Never Be Alone	HW
3/1/49	Lost Highway	Payne
1/9/50	Why Should We Try Anymore	HW

X1492

SING ME A BLUE SONG, VOL. II

4/21/47	[Last Night] I Heard You Crying In Your Sleep	HW
ns	Blue Love [In My Heart]	Jenkins
11/7/47	Mansion On The Hill	HW-Rose
6/14/50	They'll Never Take Her Love From Me	Payne

X1493

SING ME A BLUE SONG, VOL. III

3/20/49	I've Just Told Mama Goodbye	Sweet-Kinsey
8/30/49	A House Without Love	HW

X1554

| 4/21/47 | Six More Miles [To The Graveyard] | HW |
| ns | Singing Waterfall | HW |

THE IMMORTAL HANK WILLIAMS, VOL. I

ns	There's No Room In My Heart [For The Blues]	Rose-Turner
ns	The Waltz Of The Wind	Rose
2/13/47	Pan American	HW
ns	With Tears In My Eyes	Howard

X1555

THE IMMORTAL HANK WILLIAMS, VOL. II

ns	I Wish I Had a Nickel	Sutton-Barnhart
8/4/47	Fly Trouble	Wilds-Biggs-Rose
ns	Please Don't Let Me Love You	Jones
8/4/47	I'm Satisfied With You	Rose

X1556

THE IMMORTAL HANK WILLIAMS, VOL. III

ns	No One Will Ever Know	Rose-Foree
ns	Faded Love And Winter Roses	Rose
ns	The First Fall Of Snow	Rose
ns/od	California Zephyr	HW

X1612

MEMORIAL ALBUM

(X4102 in set X202)

9/23/52	Your Cheatin' Heart	HW
7/11/52	You Win Again	HW
6/13/52	Settin' The Woods On Fire	Nelson-Rose
3/16/51	Hey, Good Lookin'	HW

X1613

MEMORIAL ALBUM

(X4103 in set X202)

12/21/50	Cold, Cold Heart	HW
9/23/52	I Could Never Be Ashamed Of You	HW
9/23/52	Kaw-Liga	HW-Rose
8/10/51	Half As Much	C. Williams

X1636

MEMORIAL ALBUM

7/25/51	Crazy Heart	Rose-Murray
4/21/47	Move It On Over	HW
3/16/51	My Heart Would Know	HW
12/11/51	I'm Sorry For You My Friend	HW

X1637

THE UNFORGETTABLE HANK WILLIAMS, VOL. I

| 11/6/47 | I Can't Get You Off My Mind | HW |

2/13/47	I Don't Care [If Tomorrow	
	Never Comes]	HW
12/21/50	Dear John	Ritter-Gass
2/13/47	My Love For You [Has Turned	
	To Hate]	HW

X1638
THE UNFORGETTABLE HANK WILLIAMS, VOL. II

8/4/47	On The Banks Of The Old Ponchartrain	HW-Vincent
ns/od	We Live In Two Different Worlds	Rose
11/7/47	I'll Be A Bachelor 'Til I Die	HW
12/11/51	Let's Turn Back The Years	HW

X1639
THE UNFORGETTABLE HANK WILLIAMS, VOL. III

7/25/51	I'd Still Want You	HW
12/11/46	Never Again [Will I Knock On Your Door]	HW
ns	Blue Love [In My Heart]	Jenkins
ns	Leave Me Alone With The Blues	Pope

X1643
LUKE THE DRIFTER, VOL. II
(X1047)

6/1/51	Pictures From Life's Other Side	HW
12/21/50	Men With Broken Hearts	HW
8/31/50	Help Me Understand	HW
1/10/50	Too Many Parties And Too Many Pals	Rose-Dixon-Henderson

X1644*
LUKE THE DRIFTER, VOL. III

7/11/52	Be Careful Of Stones That You Throw	Dodd
6/1/51	I Dreamed About Mama Last Night	Rose
1/10/50	The Funeral	Rose
1/10/50	Beyond The Sunset	Brock-Rowswell

*Volume I of this series is 1165 listed above.

X1648
I SAW THE LIGHT, VOL. II
(X4110 in set X243)

4/21/47	I Saw The Light	HW
12/11/46	Calling You	HW
3/1/49	Dear Brother	HW
12/11/46	Wealth Won't Save Your Soul	HW

X1649*
I SAW THE LIGHT, VOL. III
(X4111 in set X243)

| 3/1/49 | Jesus Remembered Me | HW |

ns/od	A House Of Gold	HW
ns/od	How Can You Refuse Him Now	HW
12/11/46	When God Comes And Gathers His Jewels	HW

*Volume I of "I Saw The Light" is X1218.

X1650*
RAMBLIN' MAN, VOL. III

3/16/51	I Can't Help It [If I'm Still In Love With You]	HW
12/22/48	There'll Be No Teardrops Tonight	HW
3/16/51	My Heart Would Know	HW
3/1-2/49	You're Gonna Change [Or I'm Gonna Leave]	HW

*Volumes I and II of "Ramblin' Man" are X1135 and X1136 listed above.

X1698
THE LONESOME SOUND OF
HANK WILLIAMS, VOL. I

ns/od	It Just Doesn't Matter Now	Tubb
ns/od	First Year Blues	Tubb
ns/od	Cool Water	Nolan
ns/od	Dixie Cannonball	Autry-Foley

X1699
THE LONESOME SOUND OF
HANK WILLIAMS, VOL. II

ns/od	I'm Free At Last	Tubb
ns/od	Roly Poly	Rose
ns/od	The Old Home	Earls
ns/od	Rock My Cradle [Once Again]	Bond-Folger

X1700
THE LONESOME SOUND OF
HANK WILLIAMS, VOL. III

ns/od	Sundown And Sorrow	Frank-King
ns/od	Rockin' Chair Money	Glosson-Carlisle
ns/od	Tennessee Border	Work
ns/od	Swing Wide Your Gate Of Love	Thompson

Hank recorded six ten-inch 33⅓ RPM albums. Each one included eight songs. They are as follows:

E107
HANK WILLIAMS SINGS

8/30/49	A House Without Love	HW
3/20/49	Wedding Bells	C. Boone
11/7/47	Mansion On The Hill	HW-Rose
12/11/46	Wealth Won't Save Your Soul	HW
4/21/47	I Saw The Light	HW
4/21/47	Six More Miles [To The Graveyard]	HW
3/1/49	Lost Highway	Payne
3/20/49	I've Just Told Mama Goodbye	Sweet-Kinsey

E168
MOANIN' THE BLUES

8/31/50	Moanin' The Blues	HW
8/30/49	I'm So Lonesome I Could Cry	HW
11/7/47	My Sweet Love Ain't Around	HW
12/11/51	Honky Tonk Blues	HW
12/22/48	Lovesick Blues	Mills-Friend
11/7/47	The Blues Come Around	HW
1/9/50	Long Gone Lonesome Blues	HW
11/6/47	I'm A Long Gone Daddy	HW

E202
MEMORIAL ALBUM

9/23/52	Your Cheatin' Heart	HW
7/11/52	You Win Again	HW
12/21/50	Cold, Cold Heart	HW
9/23/52	I Could Never Be Ashamed of You	HW
6/13/52	Settin' The Woods On Fire	Nelson-Rose
3/16/51	Hey, Good Lookin'	HW
9/23/52	Kaw-Liga	HW-Rose
8/10/51	Half As Much	C. Williams

E203
LUKE THE DRIFTER

6/1/51	Pictures From Life's Other Side	HW
12/21/50	Men With Broken Hearts	HW
8/31/50	Help Me Understand	HW
1/10/50	Too Many Parties And Too Many Pals	Rose-Dixon-Henderson
7/11/52	Be Careful Of Stones That You Throw	Dodd
6/1/51	I Dreamed About Mama Last Night	Rose
1/10/50	The Funeral	Rose
1/10/50	Beyond The Sunset	Brock-Rowswell

E242
HONKY TONKIN'

6/13/52	Jambalaya [On The Bayou]	HW
7/11/52	I Won't Be Home No More	HW
12/11/51	Honky Tonk Blues	HW
1/13/52	I'll Never Get Out Of This World Alive	HW-Rose
11/6/47	Honky Tonkin'	HW
3/16/51	Howlin' At The Moon	HW
8/30/49	My Bucket's Got A Hole In It	C. Williams
8/10/51	Baby, We're Really In Love	HW

E243
I SAW THE LIGHT

4/21/47	I Saw The Light	HW
12/11/46	Calling You	HW
3/1/49	Dear Brother (with Audrey Williams)	HW
12/11/46	Wealth Won't Save Your Soul	HW
ns/od	How Can You Refuse Him Now	HW
12/11/46	When God Comes And Gathers His Jewels	HW

| 3/1/49 | Jesus Remembered Me | HW |
| ns/od | A House Of Gold | HW |

The following are 12-inch, 33⅓ RPM records ("S" indicates "stereo"):

E3219
RAMBLIN' MAN

6/1/51	Ramblin' Man	HW
7/25/51	Lonesome Whistle	HW-Davis
1/9/50	My Son Calls Another Man Daddy	HW
8/30/49	I Just Don't Like This Kind Of Livin'	HW
ns/od	I Can't Escape From You	HW
8/31/50	Nobody's Lonesome For Me	HW
9/23/52	Take These Chains From My Heart	Heath-Rose
1/9/50	Why Don't You Love Me	HW
3/16/51	I Can't Help It [If I'm Still In Love With You]	HW
12/22/48	There'll Be No Teardrops Tonight	HW
3/1-2/49	You're Gonna Change [Or I'm Gonna Leave]	HW
3/16/51	My Heart Would Know	HW

E3267
HANK WILLIAMS AS
LUKE THE DRIFTER

6/1/51	Pictures From Life's Other Side	HW
8/31/50	Help Me Understand	HW
7/11/52	Be Careful Of Stones That You Throw	Dodd
1/10/50	The Funeral	Rose
7/11/52	Why Don't You Make Up Your Mind	HW
12/21/50	Just Waitin'	HW-Gazzaway
12/21/50	Men With Broken Hearts	HW
1/10/50	Too Many Parties And Too Many Pals	Rose-Dixon-Henderson
6/1/50	I Dreamed About Mama Last Night	Rose
1/10/50	Beyond The Sunset	Brock-Rowswell
6/1/51	I've Been Down That Road Before	HW
1/10/50	Everything's Okay	HW

E3272
MEMORIAL ALBUM

9/23/52	Your Cheatin' Heart	HW
7/11/52	You Win Again	HW
12/21/50	Cold, Cold Heart	HW
9/23/52	I Could Never Be Ashamed Of You	HW
7/25/51	Crazy Heart	Rose-Murray
3/16/51	My Heart Would Know	HW
6/13/52	Settin' The Woods On Fire	Nelson-Rose
3/16/51	Hey, Good Lookin'	HW
9/23/52	Kaw-Liga	HW-Rose
8/10/51	Half As Much	C. Williams
4/21/47	Move It On Over	HW
12/11/51	I'm Sorry For You My Friend	HW

E3330

MOANIN' THE BLUES

ns/od	Low Down Blues	HW
ns	Someday You'll Call My Name	Branch-Hill
ns	Alone And Forsaken	HW
ns/od	Weary Blues From Waitin'	HW
8/31/50	Moanin' The Blues	HW
8/30/49	I'm So Lonesome I Could Cry	HW
11/7/47	My Sweet Love Ain't Around	HW
12/11/51	Honky Tonk Blues	HW
12/22/48	Lovesick Blues	Mills-Friend
11/6/47	I'm A Long Gone Daddy	HW
1/9/50	Long Gone Lonesome Blues	HW
11/7/47	The Blues Come Around	HW

E3331

I SAW THE LIGHT

4/21/47	I Saw The Light	HW
12/11/46	Calling You	HW
3/1/49	Dear Brother	HW
12/11/46	Wealth Won't Save Your Soul	HW
ns/od	How Can You Refuse Him Now	HW
12/11/46	When God Comes And Gathers His Jewels	HW
3/1/49	Jesus Remembered Me	HW-Audrey Williams
ns/od	A House of Gold	HW
ns/od	[I'm Gonna] Sing, Sing, Sing	HW
ns/od	Message To My Mother	HW
ns	Thank God	Rose
ns/od	The Angel Of Death	HW

E3412

HONKY-TONKIN'

6/13/52	Jambalaya [On The Bayou]	HW
7/11/52	I Won't Be Home No More	HW
12/11/51	Honky Tonk Blues	HW
6/13/52	I'll Never Get Out Of This World Alive	HW-Rose
11/6/47	Honky Tonkin'	HW
3/16/51	Howlin' At The Moon	HW
8/30/49	My Bucket's Got A Hole In It	C. Williams
8/10/51	Baby, We're Really In Love	HW
3/1-2/49	Mind Your Own Business	HW
11/6/47	Rootie Tootie	Rose
ns/od	I Ain't Got Nothin' But Time	HW
ns/od	You Better Keep It On Your Mind	HW-V. McAlpin

E3560

SING ME A BLUE SONG

3/20/49	Wedding Bells	C. Boone
3/1/49	May You Never Be Alone	HW
3/1/49	Lost Highway	Payne
1/9/50	Why Should We Try Anymore	HW

4/21/47	[Last Night] I Heard You Crying In Your Sleep	HW
ns	Blue Love	Jenkins
11/7/47	Mansion On The Hill	HW-Rose
6/14/50	They'll Never Take Her Love From Me	Payne
3/20/49	I've Just Told Mama Goodbye	Sweet-Kinsey
8/30/49	A House Without Love	HW
4/21/47	Six More Miles [To The Graveyard]	HW
ns	Singing Waterfall	HW

E3605*

THE IMMORTAL HANK WILLIAMS

ns	There's No Room In My Heart [For The Blues]	Rose-Turner
ns	The Waltz Of The Wind	Rose
2/13/47	Pan American	HW
ns	With Tears In My Eyes	Howard
ns	I Wish I Had A Nickel	Sutton-Barnhart
8/4/47	Fly Trouble	Wilds-Biggs-Rose
ns	Please Don't Let Me Love You	Jones
8/4/47	I'm Satisfied With You	Rose
ns	No One Will Ever Know	Rose-Foree
ns	Faded Love And Winter Roses	Rose
ns/od	The First Fall Of Snow	Rose
ns/od	California Zephyr	HW

*This record was released again as E3928 FIRST, LAST, AND ALWAYS.

E3733
SE3733
THE UNFORGETTABLE HANK WILLIAMS

11/6/47	I Can't Get You Off My Mind	HW
2/13/47	I Don't Care [If Tomorrow Never Comes]	HW
12/21/50	Dear John	T. Ritter-Gass
2/13/47	My Love For You [Has Turned To Hate]	HW
8/4/47	On The Banks Of The Old Ponchartrain	HW-Vincent
ns/od	We Live In Two Different Worlds	HW
11/7/47	I'll Be A Bachelor 'Til I Die	HW
12/11/51	Let's Turn Back The Years	HW
7/25/51	I'd Still Want You	HW
12/11/46	Never Again [Will I Knock On Your Door]	HW
ns	Blue Love [In My Heart]	Jenkins
ns	Leave Me Alone With The Blues	Pope

E3803
SE3803
THE LONESOME SOUND OF HANK WILLIAMS

ns/od	It Just Doesn't Matter Now	Tubb
ns/od	First Year Blues	Tubb
ns/od	Cool Water	Nolan
ns/od	Dixie Cannonball	Autry-Foley
ns/od	I'm Free At Last	Tubb
ns/od	Roly Poly	Rose

ns/od	The Old Home	Earls
ns/od	Rock My Cradle [Once Again]	Bond-Folger
ns/od	Sundown And Sorrow	Frank-King
ns/od	Rockin' Chair Money	Glosson-Carlisle
ns/od	Tennessee Border	Work
ns/od	Swing Wide Your Gate Of Love	Thompson

E3850
SE3850

WAIT FOR THE LIGHT TO SHINE

ns/od	Wait For The Light To Shine	HW-C. Monroe
ns/od	Jesus Is Calling	HW
ns	Ready To Go Home	HW
ns/od	Last Night I Dreamed of Heaven	HW
ns/od	When The Book Of Life Is Read	HW
ns/od	Devil's Train	Carlisle-Foree
ns	Thy Burdens Are Greater Than Mine	Stewart-King
ns/od	Are You Building A Temple In Heaven?	HW
10/49	The Prodigal	Eudy
ns/od	Are You Walkin' And Talkin' With The Lord	HW
ns	The Battle Of Armageddon	Acuff-McLeod
ns/od	Going Home	HW

E3918
SE3918

GREATEST HITS

12/21/50	Cold, Cold Heart	HW
6/13/52	Jambalaya [On The Bayou]	HW
7/11/52	You Win Again	HW
9/23/52	Kaw-Liga	HW-Rose
9/23/52	Your Cheatin' Heart	HW
3/16/51	Hey, Good Lookin'	HW
8/10/51	Half As Much	C. Williams
9/23/52	Take These Chains From My Heart	Heath-Rose
12/22/48	There'll Be No Teardrops Tonight	HW
6/13/52	Settin' The Woods On Fire	Nelson-Rose
11/6/47	Honky Tonkin'	HW
3/16/51	I Can't Help It [If I'm Still In Love With You]	HW
1/9/50	Why Don't You Love Me	HW
8/30/49	I'm So Lonesome I Could Cry	HW

E3923
SE3923

HANK WILLIAMS LIVES AGAIN

9/23/52	Your Cheatin' Heart	HW
7/11/52	You Win Again	HW
12/21/50	Cold, Cold Heart	HW
9/23/52	I Could Never Be Ashamed Of You	HW
7/25/51	Crazy Heart	Rose-Murray
3/16/51	My Heart Would Know	HW
6/13/52	Settin' The Woods On Fire	Nelson-Rose
3/16/51	Hey, Good Lookin'	HW

9/23/52	Kaw-Liga	HW-Rose
8/10/51	Half As Much	C. Williams
4/21/47	Move It On Over	HW
12/11/51	I'm Sorry For You, My Friend	HW

E3924
SE3924

SING ME A BLUE SONG

3/20/49	Wedding Bells	C. Boone
3/1/49	May You Never Be Alone	HW
3/1/49	Lost Highway	Payne
1/9/50	Why Should We Try Anymore	HW
4/21/47	[Last Night] I Heard You Crying In Your Sleep	HW
ns	Blue Love [In My Heart]	Jenkins
11/7/47	Mansion On The Hill	HW-Rose
6/14/50	They'll Never Take Her Love From Me	Payne
3/20/49	I've Just Told Mama Goodbye	Sweet-Kinsey
8/30/49	A House Without Love	HW
4/21/47	Six More Miles [To The Graveyard]	HW
ns	Singing Waterfall	HW

E3926
SE3926

WANDERIN' AROUND

6/1/51	Ramblin' Man	HW
1/9/50	My Son Calls Another Man Daddy	HW
ns/od	I Can't Escape From You	HW
8/31/50	Nobody's Lonesome For Me	HW
3/16/51	I Can't Help It [If I'm Still In Love With You]	HW
12/22/48	There'll Be No Teardrops Tonight	HW
8/30/49	I Just Don't Like This Kind Of Living	HW
7/25/51	Lonesome Whistle	HW-Davis
9/23/52	Take These Chains From My Heart	Heath-Rose
1/9/50	Why Don't You Love Me	HW
3/16/51	My Heart Would Know	HW
3/1-2/49	You're Gonna Change [Or I'm Gonna Leave]	HW

E3926
SE3926

I'M BLUE INSIDE

ns/od	Low Down Blues	HW
ns	Someday You'll Call My Name	Branch-Hill
ns	Alone And Forsaken	HW
ns/od	Weary Blues From Waitin'	HW
12/22/48	Lovesick Blues	Mills-Friend
11/7/47	The Blues Come Around	HW
11/6/47	I'm A Long Gone Daddy	HW
1/9/50	Long Gone Lonesome Blues	HW
8/31/50	Moanin' The Blues	HW
8/30/49	I'm So Lonesome I Could Cry	HW
11/7/47	My Sweet Love Ain't Around	HW
12/11/51	Honky Tonk Blues	HW

E3927
LUKE THE DRIFTER

1/10/50	Too Many Parties And Too Many Pals	Rose-Dixon-Henderson
1/10/50	Beyond The Sunset	Brock-Rowswell
1/10/50	The Funeral	Rose
1/10/50	Everything's Okay	HW
8/31/50	Help Me Understand	HW
12/21/50	Just Waitin'	HW-Gazzaway
12/21/50	Men With Broken Hearts	HW
6/1/51	Pictures From Life's Other Side	HW
6/1/51	I've Been Down That Road Before	HW
6/1/51	I Dreamed About Mama Last Night	Rose
7/11/52	Be Careful Of Stones That You Throw	Dodd
7/11/52	Why Don't You Make Up Your Mind	HW

E3928*
SE3928
FIRST, LAST AND ALWAYS

ns	There's No Room In My Heart For The Blues	Rose-Turner
ns	The Waltz Of The Wind	Rose
2/13/47	Pan American	HW
ns	With Tears In My Eyes	Howard
ns	I Wish I Had A Nickel	Sutton-Barnhart
8/4/47	Fly Trouble	Wilds-Biggs-Rose
ns	Please Don't Let Me Love You	Jones
8/4/47	I'm Satisfied With You	Rose
ns	No One Will Ever Know	Rose-Foree
ns	Faded Love And Winter Roses	Rose
ns	First Fall Of Snow	Rose
ns/od	California Zephyr	HW

*These same titles appear on E3605 THE IMMORTAL HANK WILLIAMS.

E3955
SE3955
THE SPIRIT OF HANK WILLIAMS

6/13/52	Window Shopping	Joseph
ns/od	Wearin' Out Your Walkin' Shoes	HW
ns/od	A Teardrop On A Rose	HW
12/22/48	Lost On The River	HW
ns/od	Jesus Died For Me	HW-Audrey Williams
3/23/51	A Home In Heaven	HW
ns/od	Fool About You	HW
3/23/51	The Pale Horse And His Rider	Bailes-Staggs
ns/od	If You'll Be A Baby [To Me]	HW
ns/od	Mother Is Gone	HW
3/1/49	Dear Brother	HW
ns/od	When You're Tired Of Breaking Other Hearts	HW-Curly Williams

E3999*
ON STAGE

10/49	I'm A Long Gone Daddy	HW

10/49	Rovin' Cowboy	Knowland
10/49	I'm Telling You	Hughes-Lewis
10/49	Bill Cheatam	PD
10/49	When God Comes And Gathers His Jewels	HW
11/7/47	The Blues Come Around	HW
10/49	I Wanna Live and Love Always	PD
10/49	Wedding Bells	Boone
10/49	Lovesick Blues	Mills-Friend
10/49	I'll Have A New Body	PD
10/49	Where The Soul Of Man Never Dies	Raney
10/49	Joe Clark	PD

*Most of these were recorded for the Hadacol shows, in Nashville in October 1949 on 16-inch 33⅓ records. MGM later put them on 12-inch records.

E4040
SE4040

7/25/51	Crazy Heart	Rose-Murray
4/21/47	Move It On Over	HW
12/11/51	Honky Tonk Blues	HW
11/7/47	I'll Be A Bachelor 'Til I Die	HW
11/7/47	My Sweet Love Ain't Around	HW
6/14/50	They'll Never Take Her Love From Me	Payne
11/7/47	Mansion On The Hill	Rose-Williams
6/13/52	Window Shopping	Joseph
8/31/50	Nobody's Lonesome For Me	HW
12/11/51	I'm Sorry For You, My Friend	HW
8/30/49	I Just Don't Like This Kind Of Livin'	HW
6/1/51	Ramblin' Man	HW
3/16/51	Howlin' At The Moon	HW
8/10/51	Baby, We're Really In Love	HW

E4109*
ON STAGE—HANK WILLIAMS

10/49	Happy Rovin' Cowboy	Knowland
10/49	You're Gonna Change [Or I'm Gonna Leave]	HW
6/13/52	Settin' The Woods On Fire	Nelson-Rose
10/49	There's A Bluebird On Your Windowsill	Clarke
4/21/47	I Saw The Light	HW
10/49	Happy Rovin' Cowboy	Knowland
10/49	Tramp On The Street	Cole
12/22/48	Lovesick Blues	Mills-Friend
8/31/50	Help Me Understand	HW
11/7/47	The Blues Come Around	HW
10/49	Fingers On Fire	Smith
10/49	Fire On The Mountain	PD

*A continuation of E3999, partially from the Hadacol session of October 1949.

E4138*
BEYOND THE SUNSET (LUKE THE DRIFTER)

1/10/50	Beyond The Sunset	Brock-Rowswell
6/1/51	Pictures From Life's Other Side	HW
12/21/50	Men With Broken Hearts	HW

8/31/50	Help Me Understand	HW
1/10/50	Too Many Parties And Too Many Pals	Rose-Dixon-Henderson
7/11/52	Why Don't You Make Up Your Mind	HW
6/1/51	I've Been Down That Road Before	HW
7/11/52	Be Careful Of Stones That You Throw	Dodd
6/1/51	I Dreamed About Mama Last Night	Rose
1/10/50	The Funeral	HW
12/21/50	Just Waitin'	HW-Gazzaway
1/10/50	Everything's Okay	HW

*These same titles appear on E4380 and SE4380, "Movin' On—Luke the Drifter."

E4140
GREATEST HITS, VOL. III

1/9/50	Long Gone Lonesome Blues	HW
12/11/51	Let's Turn Back The Years	HW
11/6/47	Rootie Tootie	Rose
3/1-2/49	Mind Your Own Business	HW
3/16/51	My Heart Would Know	HW
7/11/52	I Won't Be Home No More	HW
8/4/47	On The Banks Of The Old Ponchartrain	HW-Vincent
3/1/49	May You Never Be Alone	HW
3/1/49	Lost Highway	Payne
3/20/49	I've Just Told Mama Goodbye	Sweet-Kinsey
6/13/52	I'll Never Get Out Of This World Alive	HW-Rose
11/7/47	The Blues Come Around	HW
11/6/47	I'm A Long Gone Daddy	HW
3/1-2/49	You're Gonna Change [Or I'm Gonna Leave]	HW

E4168
VERY BEST

9/23/52	Your Cheatin' Heart	HW
10/49	Lovesick Blues	Mills-Friend
12/21/50	Cold, Cold Heart	HW
3/16/51	Hey, Good Lookin'	HW
9/23/52	Kaw-Liga	HW-Rose
6/1/51	Ramblin' Man	HW
6/13/52	Jambalaya [On The Bayou]	HW
8/10/51	Half As Much	C. Williams
1/9/50	Why Don't You Love Me	HW
10/49	Wedding Bells	Boone
8/30/49	I'm So Lonesome I Could Cry	HW
11/6/47	Honky Tonkin'	HW

E4227
SE4227
VERY BEST VOL. II

3/16/51	My Heart Would Know	HW
3/1/49	Lost Highway	Payne
3/16/51	Howlin' At The Moon	HW
3/1-2/49	Mind Your Own Business	HW

11/7/47	Mansion On The Hill	HW-Rose
7/11/52	You Win Again	HW
6/13/52	Settin' The Woods On Fire	Nelson-Rose
6/13/52	Window Shopping	Joseph
12/11/51	Honky Tonk Blues	HW
3/1/49	May You Never Be Alone	HW
6/14/50	They'll Never Take Her Love From Me	Payne
8/10/51	Half As Much	C. Williams

E4254

SE4254

LOST HIGHWAY

3/1/49	Lost Highway	Payne
7/11/52	Be Careful Of Stones That You Throw	Dodd
6/13/52	Jambalaya [On The Bayou]	HW
6/1/51	Ramblin' Man	HW
8/30/49	My Bucket's Got A Hole In It	C. Williams
3/20/49	I've Just Told Mama Goodbye	Sweet-Kinsey
1/9/50	Long Gone Lonesome Blues	HW
4/21/47	Six More Miles [To The Graveyard]	HW
ns	Thy Burdens Are Greater Than Mine	Stewart-King
9/23/52	Kaw-Liga	HW-Rose
6/1/51	Pictures From Life's Other Side	HW
ns/od	Cool Water	Nolan

E4267-4

HANK WILLIAMS STORY (4 RECORDS)

4/21/47	Move It On Over	HW
4/21/47	[Last Night] I Heard You Crying In Your Sleep	HW
11/6/47	Rootie Tootie	Rose
11/6/47	I'm A Long Gone Daddy	HW
11/6/47	Honky Tonkin'	HW
11/7/47	My Sweet Love Ain't Around	HW
11/7/47	The Blues Come Around	HW
11/7/47	Mansion On The Hill	HW-Rose
12/22/48	There'll Be No Teardrops Tonight	HW
3/1/49	Lost Highway	Payne
3/1/49	May You Never Be Alone	HW
3/1-2/49	Mind Your Own Business	HW
3/1-2/49	You're Gonna Change [Or I'm Gonna Leave]	HW
3/20/49	I've Just Told Mama Goodbye	Sweet-Kinsey
8/30/49	I'm So Lonesome I Could Cry	HW
8/30/49	A House Without Love	HW
8/30/49	My Bucket's Got A Hole In It	C. Williams
3/20/49	Wedding Bells	Boone
12/22/48	Lovesick Blues	Mills-Friend
1/9/50	Long Gone Lonesome Blues	HW
1/9/50	Why Don't You Love Me	HW
1/9/50	Why Should We Try Anymore	HW
1/9/50	My Son Calls Another Man Daddy	HW
8/31/50	Nobody's Lonesome For Me	HW

8/31/50	Moanin' The Blues	HW
12/21/50	Cold, Cold Heart	HW
3/16/51	I Can't Help It [If I'm Still In Love With You]	HW
3/16/51	Howlin' At The Moon	HW
3/16/51	Hey, Good Lookin'	HW
3/16/51	My Heart Would Know	HW
6/1/51	Ramblin' Man	HW
7/25/51	Lonesome Whistle	HW-Davis
8/10/51	Half As Much	C. Williams
8/10/51	Baby, We're Really In Love	HW
12/11/51	I'm Sorry For You, My Friend	HW
12/11/51	Honky Tonk Blues	HW
6/13/52	Jambalaya [On The Bayou]	HW
6/13/52	Settin' The Woods On Fire	Nelson-Rose
6/13/52	I'll Never Get Out Of This World Alive	HW-Rose
7/11/52	You Win Again	HW
7/11/52	I Won't Be Home No More	HW
9/23/52	I Could Never Be Ashamed Of You	HW
9/23/52	Your Cheatin' Heart	HW
9/23/52	Kaw-Liga	HW-Rose
9/23/52	Take These Chains From My Heart	Heath-Rose

E4276*
SE4276

HANK WILLIAMS, SR., AND HANK WILLIAMS, JR., FATHER AND SON

12/22/48	Lovesick Blues	Mills-Friend
12/11/51	Honky Tonk Blues	HW
1/9/50	Why Don't You Love Me	HW
3/20/49	Wedding Bells	Boone
7/11/52	I Won't Be Home No More	HW
4/21/47	Move It On Over	HW
3/1-2/49	Mind Your Own Business	HW
3/1/49	Lost Highway	Payne
7/25/51	Lonesome Whistle	HW-Davis
3/1/49	May You Never Be Alone	HW
7/25/51	Crazy Heart	Rose-Murray

*All of these are overdubbed; dates are of the original recording, not of the overdubbing.

E4300
SE4300

HANK WILLIAMS SINGS "KAW-LIGA" AND OTHER HUMOROUS SONGS

3/16/51	Howlin' At The Moon	HW
12/21/50	Just Waitin'	HW-Gazzaway
12/11/51	Honky Tonk Blues	HW
3/1-2/49	Mind Your Own Business	HW
6/13/52	I'll Never Get Out Of This World Alive	HW-Rose
8/31/50	Nobody's Lonesome For Me	HW
4/21/47	Move It On Over	HW
1/10/50	Everything's Okay	HW
8/4/47	Fly Trouble	Wilds-Biggs-Rose
6/1/51	I've Been Down That Road Before	HW

| 7/11/52 | Please Make Up Your Mind | HW |
| 9/23/52 | Kaw-Liga | HW-Rose |

E4377*
SE4377

THE LEGEND LIVES ANEW—HANK WILLIAMS WITH STRINGS

9/23/52	Kaw-Liga	HW-Rose
8/30/49	A House Without Love	HW
12/11/51	I'm Sorry For You My Friend	HW
12/22/48	Lovesick Blues	Mills-Friend
12/11/51	Let's Turn Back The Years	HW
12/21/50	Men With Broken Hearts	HW
8/30/49	I'm So Lonesome I Could Cry	HW
3/20/49	Wedding Bells	Boone
6/1/51	Pictures From Life's Other Side	HW
6/14/50	They'll Never Take Her Love From Me	Payne
7/11/52	You Win Again	HW
2/13/47	I Don't Care [If Tomorrow Never Comes]	HW

*All of these are overdubbed; dates are of the original recording, not of the overdubbing.

E4378*
SE4378

HANK WILLIAMS, HANK WILLIAMS, JR., AGAIN

11/7/47	My Sweet Love Ain't Around	HW
11/7/47	I'll Be A Bachelor 'Til I Die	HW
6/13/52	Window Shopping	Joseph
8/30/49	My Bucket's Got A Hole In It	C. Williams
3/16/51	I Can't Help It [If I'm Still In Love With You]	HW
3/16/51	Howlin' At The Moon	HW
1/9/50	My Son Calls Another Man Daddy	HW
8/31/50	Moanin' The Blues	HW
9/23/52	Kaw-Liga	HW-Rose
8/10/51	Baby We're Really In Love	HW
1/9/50	Why Should We Try Anymore	HW
6/13/52	I'll Never Get Out Of This World Alive	HW-Rose

*All of these are overdubbed; dates are of the original recording, not of the overdubbing.

E4380*
SE4380

MOVIN' ON—LUKE THE DRIFTER

6/1/51	Pictures From Life's Other side	HW
8/31/50	Help Me Understand	HW
7/11/52	Please Make Up Your Mind	HW
7/11/52	Be Careful Of Stones That You Throw	Dodd
1/10/50	The Funeral	Rose
12/21/50	Just Waitin'	HW-Gazzaway
12/21/50	Men With Broken Hearts	HW
1/10/50	Too Many Parties And Too Many Pals	Rose-Dixon-Henderson
6/1/51	I've Been Down That Road Before	HW
6/1/51	I Dreamed About Mama Last Night	Rose

| 1/10/50 | Beyond The Sunset | Brock-Rowswell |
| 1/10/50 | Everything's Okay | HW |

*These same titles appear on E4138, "Beyond The Sunset" (Luke the Drifter).

E4429*
SE4429

MORE HANK WILLIAMS AND STRINGS

12/21/50	Dear John	Ritter-Gass
9/23/52	Your Cheatin' Heart	HW
1/9/50	Long Gone Lonesome Blues	HW
7/25/51	Lonesome Whistle	HW-Davis
6/13/52	Jambalaya [On The Bayou]	HW
6/1/51	Ramblin' Man	HW
3/16/51	Howlin' At The Moon	HW
12/22/48	There'll Be No Teardrops Tonight	HW
6/13/52	Settin' The Woods On Fire	Nelson-Rose
8/10/51	Half As Much	C. Williams
12/21/50	Someday You'll Call My Name	Branch-Hill

*All of these are overdubbed; dates are of the original recording, not of the overdubbing.

E4481*
SE4481

7/11/52	I Won't Be Home No More	HW
3/1/49	Lost Highway	Payne
3/1-2/49	Mind Your Own Business	HW
3/16/51	My Heart Would Know	HW
8/31/50	Nobody's Lonesome For Me	HW
3/1/49	May You Never Be Alone	HW
11/7/47	Mansion On The Hill	HW-Rose
4/21/47	Move It On Over	HW
12/11/51	Honky Tonk Blues	HW
8/30/49	I Just Don't Like This Kind Of Livin'	HW
8/10/51	Baby, We're Really In Love	HW

*All of these are overdubbed; dates are of the original recording, not of the overdubbing.

E4529*
SE4529

HANK WILLIAMS AND STRINGS—VOL. III

6/13/52	Window Shopping	Joseph
8/30/49	My Bucket's Got A Hole In It	C. Williams
12/21/50	Just Waitin'	HW-Gazzaway
4/21/50	[Last Night] I Heard You Crying In Your Sleep	HW
1/9/50	Why Should We Try Anymore	HW
7/11/52	Be Careful Of Stones That You Throw	Dodd
6/13/52	I'll Never Get Out Of This World Alive	HW-Rose
8/31/50	Moanin' The Blues	HW
11/7/47	My Sweet Love Ain't Around	HW

1/9/50	Why Don't You Love Me	HW
7/25/51	Crazy Heart	Rose-Murray

*All of these are overdubbed; dates are of the original recording, not of the overdubbing.

SE240-2*
24 KARAT HANK WILLIAMS

9/23/52	Your Cheatin' Heart	HW
7/25/51	Lonesome Whistle	HW
6/13/52	I'll Never Get Out Of This World Alive	HW-Rose
12/22/48	Lovesick Blues	Mills-Friend
3/1/49	Lost Highway	Payne
9/23/52	Kaw-Liga	HW-Rose
12/21/50	Cold, Cold Heart	HW
11/7/47	Mansion On The Hill	HW-Rose
7/11/52	You Win Again	HW
8/30/49	My Bucket's Got A Hole In It	C. Williams
7/25/51	Crazy Heart	Murray-Rose
6/1/51	Ramblin' Man	HW
8/10/51	Half As Much	HW
6/13/52	Window Shopping	Joseph
12/22/48	There'll Be No Teardrops Tonight	HW
8/30/49	I'm So Lonesome I Could Cry	HW
3/16/51	Howlin' At The Moon	HW
2/13/47	I Don't Care [If Tomorrow Never Comes]	HW
6/13/52	Jambalaya [On The Bayou]	HW
8/30/49	A House Without Love	HW
7/11/52	I Won't Be Home No More	HW
1/9/50	Long Gone Lonesome Blues	HW
12/11/51	Honky Tonk Blues	HW
6/13/52	Settin' The Woods On Fire	Rose-Nelson

*All of these are overdubbed; dates are of the original recording, not of the overdubbing.

E4576
SE4576
IN THE BEGINNING

12/11/46	Calling You	HW
11/6/47	Honky Tonkin'	HW
2/13/47	I Don't Care [If Tomorrow Never Comes]	HW
12/11/46	Never Again [Will I Knock On Your Door]	HW
2/13/47	Pan American*	HW
12/11/46	Wealth Won't Save Your Soul	HW
12/11/46	When God Comes And Gathers His Jewels	HW
4/21/47	Move It On Over	HW
4/21/47	[Last Night] I Heard You Crying In Your Sleep	HW
8/4/47	On The Banks Of The Old Ponchartrain	HW-Vincent

*Only "Pan American" is not overdubbed. A second SE4576 was issued without any overdubbing.

SE4651
THE ESSENTIAL HANK WILLIAMS

8/30/49	My Bucket's Got A Hole In It	C. Williams
12/11/51	Honky Tonk Blues	HW
3/1/49	May You Never Be Alone	HW
12/22/48	Lovesick Blues	Mills-Friend
9/23/52	Kaw-Liga	HW-Rose
8/30/49	I'm So Lonesome I Could Cry	HW
4/21/47	Move It On Over	HW
6/1/51	Ramblin' Man	HW
11/6/47	Honky Tonkin'	HW
1/9/50	Long Gone Lonesome Blues	HW
3/16/51	Howlin' At The Moon	HW

SE4680
LIFE TO LEGEND—HANK WILLIAMS

4/21/47	Move It On Over	HW
11/7/47	Mansion On The Hill	HW-Rose
12/22/48	Lovesick Blues	Mills-Friend
12/21/50	Cold, Cold Heart	HW
3/16/51	Hey, Good Lookin'	HW
3/16/51	I Can't Help It [If I'm Still In Love With You]	HW
6/13/52	Jambalaya [On The Bayou]	HW
8/10/51	Half As Much	C.Williams
9/23/52	Your Cheatin' Heart	HW
9/23/52	Kaw-Liga	HW-Rose

SE4755-2
24 OF HANK WILLIAMS'
GREATEST HITS

9/23/52	Your Cheatin' Heart	HW
4/21/47	Move It On Over	HW
8/30/49	I'm So Lonesome I Could Cry	HW
12/11/51	Honky Tonk Blues	HW
3/16/51	My Heart Would Know	HW
9/23/52	Kaw-Liga	HW-Rose
12/21/50	Cold, Cold Heart	HW
11/6/47	Honky Tonkin'	HW
3/1-2/49	Mind Your Own Business	HW
3/20/49	Wedding Bells	C. Boone
6/13/52	Jambalaya [On The Bayou]	HW
3/16/51	Hey, Good Lookin'	HW
6/13/52	Window Shopping	HW
6/13/52	Settin' The Woods On Fire	Nelson-Rose
8/10/51	Half As Much	C. Williams
7/11/52	You Win Again	HW
3/1/49	May You Never Be Alone	HW
8/10/51	Baby, We're Really In Love	HW
12/22/48	Lovesick Blues	Mills-Friend
6/1/51	Ramblin' Man	HW
12/22/48	There'll Be No Teardrops Tonight	HW

3/16/51	I Can't Help It [If I'm Still In Love With You]	HW
1/9/50	Why Don't You Love Me	HW
9/23/52	Take These Chains From My Heart	Heath-Rose

Note: The last six of these are overdubbed; dates are of the original recordings.

2SES4865

HANK WILLIAMS/HANK WILLIAMS, JR.—
THE LEGEND OF HANK WILLIAMS IN SONG AND STORY

4/21/47	Move It On Over	HW
8/30/49	I'm So Lonesome I Could Cry	HW
1/9/50	Long Gone Lonesome Blues	HW
12/21/50	Cold, Cold Heart	HW
6/13/52	I'll Never Get Out Of This World Alive	HW-Rose
9/23/52	Your Cheatin' Heart	HW
9/23/52	Kaw-Liga	HW-Rose
12/22/48	Lovesick Blues	Mills-Friend
4/21/47	I Saw The Light	HW
undated	Recitation Of Little Bocephus	HW
3/16/51	I Can't Help It [If I'm Still In Love With You]	HW
3/1/49	May You Never Be Alone	HW

M3F-4954

ARCHETYPES

4/21/47	Move It On Over	HW
11/6/47	Honky Tonkin'	HW
12/22/48	Lovesick Blues	Mills-Friend
3/1/49	May You Never Be Alone	HW
8/30/49	My Bucket's Got A Hole In It	C. Williams
8/30/49	I'm So Lonesome I Could Cry	HW
1/9/50	Long Gone Lonesome Blues	HW
3/16/51	Howlin' At The Moon	HW
6/1/51	Ramblin' Man	HW
12/11/51	Honky Tonk Blues	HW
9/23/52	Kaw-Liga	HW-Rose

M3HB4975*

HANK WILLIAMS/HANK WILLIAMS, JR.—
INSIGHTS INTO HANK WILLIAMS IN STORY AND SONG

8/30/49	My Bucket's Got A Hole In It	C. Williams
12/21/50	Men With Broken Hearts	HW
6/1/51	Pictures From Life's Other Side	HW
6/1/51	I Dreamed About Mama Last Night	Rose
6/13/52	Jambalaya [On The Bayou]	HW
1/9/50	Why Don't You Love Me	HW
8/31/50	Nobody's Lonesome For Me	HW
3/16/51	Hey, Good Lookin'	HW
8/10/51	Half As Much	C. Williams
3/20/40	Weddings Bells	C. Boone
12/22/48	There'll Be No Teardrops Tonight	HW

*Hank Williams, Jr., sings "I Just Didn't Have The Heart To Say Goodbye," "When He Sang," "[I'm Praying For The Day That] Peace Will Come," and "Standing In The Shadows."

M3G4991
A HOME IN HEAVEN

3/1/49	Jesus Remembered Me	HW
ns	Thank God	Rose
8/31/50	Help Me Understand	HW
ns/od	Jesus Is Calling	HW-C. Monroe
ns/od	When The Book Of Life Is Read	HW
3/23/51	A Home In Heaven	HW
1/10/50	Beyond The Sunset	Brock-Rowswell
10/49	Where The Soul Of Man Never Dies	Raney
ns/od	Jesus Died For Me	HW
ns/od	Going Home	HW

MG15019
LIVE AT THE GRAND OLE OPRY

11/12/49	You're Gonna Change [Or I'm Gonna Leave]	HW
2/18/50	I Just Don't Like This Kind Of Livin'	HW
2/18/50	Lovesick Blues	Mills-Friend
6/10/50	Long Gone Lonesome Blues	HW
6/10/50	Talk With Minnie Pearl	
8/12/50	Why Don't You Love Me	HW
8/12/50	They'll Never Take Her Love From Me	L. Payne
11/11/50	Moanin' The Blues	HW
11/11/50	Nobody's Lonesome For Me	HW
5/5/51	Cold, Cold Heart	HW
5/5/51	Dear John	Ritter-Gass
9/22/51	Hey, Good Lookin'	HW

MG25041
24 GREATEST HITS, VOL. 2

11/7/47	Mansion On The Hill	HW-Rose
3/1/49	Lost Highway	Payne
3/1-2/49	You're Gonna Change [Or I'm Gonna Leave]	HW
8/30/49	A House Without Love	HW
8/30/49	I Just Don't Like This Kind Of Livin'	HW
8/30/49	My Bucket's Got A Hole In It	C. Williams
1/9/50	Why Should We Try Anymore	HW
6/14/50	They'll Never Take Her Love From Me	Payne
12/21/50	Dear John	Ritter-Gass
3/16/51	Howlin' At The Moon	HW
7/25/51	I'd Still Want You	HW
7/25/51	Lonesome Whistle	HW-Davis
12/11/51	I'm Sorry For You, My Friend	HW
12/11/51	Let's Turn Back The Years	HW
6/13/52	I'll Never Get Out Of This World Alive	HW-Rose
7/11/52	I Won't Be Home No More	HW
9/23/52	I Could Never Be Ashamed Of You	HW

7/25/51	Crazy Heart	Rose-Murray
8/31/50	Moanin' The Blues	HW
4/21/47	I Saw The Light	HW
11/6/47	I'm A Long Gone Daddy	HW
8/31/50	Nobody's Lonesome For Me	HW
11/7/47	My Sweet Love Ain't Around	HW
6/10/50	Long Gone Lonesome Blues	HW

3E2

HANK WILLIAMS, VOL. I (3 LP BOXED SET)

12/11/46	Calling You	HW
12/11/46	When God Comes And Gathers His Jewels	HW
4/21/47	Move It On Over	HW
4/21/47	I Saw The Light	HW
11/6/47	Honky Tonkin'	HW
11/7/47	Mansion On The Hill	HW-Rose
12/22/48	There'll Be No Teardrops Tonight	HW
12/22/48	Lovesick Blues	Mills-Friend
3/1-2/49	Mind Your Own Business	HW
3/1-2/49	You're Gonna Change [Or I'm Gonna Leave]	HW
3/20/49	Wedding Bells	C. Boone
8/30/49	I'm So Lonesome I Could Cry	HW
8/30/49	My Bucket's Got A Hole In It	C. Williams
1/9/50	Long Gone Lonesome Blues	HW
1/9/50	Why Don't You Love Me	HW
8/31/50	Nobody's Lonesome For Me	HW
8/31/50	Moanin' The Blues	HW
12/21/50	Cold, Cold Heart	HW
3/16/51	Howlin' At The Moon	HW
3/16/51	Hey, Good Lookin'	HW
3/16/51	My Heart Would Know	HW
6/1/51	Ramblin' Man	HW
7/25/51	Lonesome Whistle	HW-Davis
8/10/51	Half As Much	C. Williams
12/11/51	Honky Tonk Blues	HW
6/13/52	Window Shopping	Joseph
6/13/52	Jambalaya [On The Bayou]	HW
6/13/52	Settin' The Woods On Fire	Nelson-Rose
6/13/52	I'll Never Get Out Of This World Alive	HW-Rose
7/11/52	You Win Again	HW
7/11/52	I Won't Be Home No More	HW
9/23/52	I Could Never Be Ashamed Of You	HW
9/23/52	Your Cheatin' Heart	HW
9/23/52	Kaw-Liga	HW-Rose
9/23/52	Take These Chains From My Heart	Heath-Rose
ns/od	How Can You Refuse Him Now	HW

3E4

HANK WILLIAMS, VOL. II (3 LP BOXED SET)

12/11/46	Never Again [Will I Knock On Your Door]	HW
2/13/47	My Love For You [Has Turned To Hate]	HW
8/4/47	Fly Trouble	Wilds-Biggs-Rose

11/6/47	Rootie Tootie	Rose
11/6/47	I Can't Get You Off Of My Mind	HW
11/6/47	I'm A Long Gone Daddy	HW
11/7/47	The Blues Come Around	HW
11/7/47	I'll Be A Bachelor 'Til I Die	HW
12/22/48	Lost On The River	HW
3/1/49	Dear Brother	HW
3/1/49	Lost Highway	Payne
3/1/49	May You Never Be Alone	HW
3/20/49	I've Just Told Mama Goodbye	Sweet-Kinsey
8/30/49	A House Without Love	HW
8/30/49	I Just Don't Like This Kind Of Livin'	HW
1/9/50	Why Should We Try Anymore	HW
1/9/50	My Son Calls Another Man Daddy	HW
6/14/50	They'll Never Take Her Love From Me	Payne
12/21/50	Dear John	Ritter-Gass
12/21/50	Just Waitin' (Luke the Drifter)	HW-Gazzaway
3/16/51	I Can't Help It [If I'm Still In Love With You]	HW
6/1/51	Pictures From Life's Other Side	HW
6/1/51	I've Been Down That Road Before	HW
6/1/51	I Dreamed About Mama Last Night	Rose
7/25/51	I'd Still Want You	HW
7/25/51	Crazy Heart	Rose-Murray
8/10/51	Baby, We're Really In Love	HW
12/11/51	I'm Sorry For You, My Friend	HW
12/11/51	Let's Turn Back The Years	HW
7/11/52	Be Careful Of Stones That You Throw	Dodd
7/11/52	Why Don't You Make Up Your Mind	HW
ns	Ready To Go Home	HW
ns/od	[I'm Gonna] Sing, Sing, Sing	HW
ns/od	Mother Is Gone	HW
ns/od	The Angel Of Death	HW

Nine cuts by Hank Williams became part of the sound track of *The Last Picture Show;* the album (MGM 1SE33ST) was issued in 12/71.

1/9/50	My Son Calls Another Man Daddy	HW
12/21/50	Cold, Cold Heart	HW
3/16/51	Half As Much	C. Williams
6/13/52	Jambalaya [On The Bayou]	HW
9/23/52	Kaw-Liga	HW-Rose
1/9/50	Why Don't You Love Me	HW
12/22/48	Lovesick Blues	Mills-Friend
3/16/51	I Can't Help It [If I'm Still In Love With You]	HW

The following records were issued by Metro, a subsidiary of MGM:

M509

MS509

HANK WILLIAMS

3/20/49	Wedding Bells	C. Boone
1/10/50	Too Many Parties And Too Many Pals	Rose-Dixon-Henderson

7/25/51	Lonesome Whistle	HW-Davis
ns	Alone And Forsaken	HW
11/7/47	I'll Be A Bachelor 'Til I Die	HW
1/10/50	Beyond The Sunset	Brock-Rowswell
ns/od	Rockin' Chair Money	Glosson-Carlisle
ns/od	Rock My Cradle [Once Again]	Bond-Folger
ns/od	Tennessee Border	Work
ns/od	I'm Free At Last	Tubb

M547
MS547

MR. AND MRS. HANK WILLIAMS

12/22/48	Lost On The River	HW
3/1/49	Dear Brother	HW
3/1/49	Jesus Remembered Me	HW
3/23/51	The Pale Horse And His Rider	Bailes-Staggs
3/23/51	A Home In Heaven	HW
6/1/51	I Dreamed About Mama Last Night	Rose

M602
MS602

IMMORTAL

12/11/46	Never Again [Will I Knock On Your Door]	HW
2/13/47	Pan American	HW
11/7/47	My Sweet Love Ain't Around	HW
2/13/47	I Don't Care If Tomorrow Never Comes	HW
10/49	Lovesick Blues	Mills-Friend
8/31/50	Nobody's Lonesome For Me	HW
3/16/51	Hey, Good Lookin'	HW
3/1/49	May You Never Be Alone	HW
ns/od	Sundown And Sorrow	Frank-King
ns/od	Last Night I Dreamed Of Heaven	HW

TLCW-01

HANK WILLIAMS

This is the first volume in the *Time/Life* "Country and Western Classics" series. (The booklet accompanying this three-record set includes notes by Charles K. Wolfe and Bob Pinson on each recording.)

12/11/46	When God Comes And Gathers His Jewels	HW
4/21/47	Move It On Over	HW
4/21/47	I Saw The Light	HW
4/21/47	Six More Miles [To The Graveyard]	HW
11/6/47	Honky Tonkin'	HW
11/7/47	My Sweet Love Ain't Around	HW
12/22/48	I Heard My Mother Praying For Me	Audrey Williams
12/22/48	Lovesick Blues	Friend-Mills
3/1/49	Lost Highway	Payne
3/1-2/49	Mind Your Own Business	HW
3/20/49	Wedding Bells	C. Boone
8/30/49	I'm So Lonesome I Could Cry	HW
8/30/49	My Bucket's Got A Hole In It	C. Williams

1/9/50	Long Gone Lonesome Blues	HW
1/9/50	Why Don't You Love Me	HW
1/9/50	Why Should We Try Anymore	HW
1/10/50	Beyond The Sunset	Brock-Rowswell
1/10/50	The Funeral	Arranged by HW
8/31/50	No, No, Joe	Rose
12/21/50	Cold, Cold Heart	HW
3/16/51	I Can't Help It	
	[If I'm Still In Love With You]	HW
3/16/51	Howlin' At The Moon	HW
3/16/51	Hey, Good Lookin'	HW
3/23/51	The Pale Horse And His Rider	Bailes-Staggs
6/1/51	Pictures From Life's Other Side	Arranged by HW
7/25/51	Lonesome Whistle	J. Davis-HW
8/10/51	Half As Much	Audrey Williams
8/10/51	Baby, We're Really In Love	HW
12/11/51	Honky Tonk Blues	HW
6/13/52	Jambalaya [On The Bayou]	HW
6/13/52	Settin' The Woods On Fire	Nelson-Rose
6/13/52	I'll Never Get Out Of This World Alive	HW-Rose
7/11/52	You Win Again	HW
7/11/52	Be Careful Of Stones That You Throw	B. Dodd
9/23/52	Your Cheatin' Heart	HW
9/23/52	Kaw-Liga	HW-Rose
9/23/52	Take These Chains From My Heart	Heath-Rose
ns	My Main Trial Is Yet To Come*	King-Frank
ns	The Log Train*	HW

*The first issue of these two songs.

INDEX

About the Author

GEORGE WILLIAM KOON is Associate Professor of English and Acting Head of the Department of English at Clemson University. His articles have appeared in *The South Carolina Review, Style, Tennis, Sandlapper, The Southern Review, American Poets since World War II, CLA Journal, Atlanta Weekly,* and *Studies in Popular Culture.*